Ludwig Hilberseimer

Metropolisarchitecture
and Selected Essays

Ludwig Hilberseimer

Metropolisarchitecture
and Selected Essays

To Noah,

Turn space into

time.

Ed. Richard Anderson

A Columbia University GSAPP Sourcebook
Craig Buckley, Series Editor

In the same series:
John McHale, *The Expendable Reader: Articles on Art, Architecture, Design, and Media* (1951–79), Ed. Alex Kitnick

GSAPP SOURCEBOOKS

The last decades have witnessed a rapid expansion of the field of architecture. If the contemporary panorama appears increasingly vast and accelerated, it is simultaneously populated by a number of openings, holes, and gaps. The Columbia University GSAPP Sourcebooks series addresses itself to overlooked writings on architecture and the city. Emphasizing the specificity and nuance of a single writer, each Sourcebook is guest edited and introduced by a different scholar, critic, or architect, and concentrates on assembling texts previously scattered in disparate sources and on translating works currently unavailable to English-speaking readers. While refusing to conform to a common ideological outlook or specific institutional agenda, the desire to put these writings back into circulation is nevertheless motivated by a sense of urgency and a commitment to discourse and debate.

This edition first published by GSAPP BOOKS 2012
© The Trustees of Columbia University in the City of New York.
Essays © the authors.
All images © their respective owners.

GSAPP BOOKS
An imprint of The Graduate School of Architecture, Planning, and
Preservation

Columbia University
1172 Amsterdam Ave., 409 Avery Hall, New York, NY 10027

Visit our website at www.arch.columbia.edu/publications

The editors would like to thank the Office of the Dean, Mark Wigley,
for supporting the Sourcebooks series.

GSAPP Sourcebooks Series 2
Editor: Richard Anderson
Series Editor: Craig Buckley
Graphic Design: Geoff Han
Translators: *Metropolisarchitecture* translated by Richard Anderson;
appendices translated by Julie Dawson
Copy Editor: Stephanie Salomon
Printed in Belgium by Die Keure

Library of Congress Cataloging-in-Publication Data
Hilberseimer, Ludwig.
  [Works. Selections. English]
  Metropolisarchitecture and selected essays / Ludwig Hilber-
seimer; ed. Richard Anderson.
      pages cm. —(Columbia University GSAPP sourcebooks; 2)
  Includes bibliographical references.
  ISBN 978-1-883584-75-7
1. Architecture, Modern—20th century. 2. City planning—
History—20th century. I. Anderson, Richard, 1980- editor of
compilation, translator. II. Aureli, Pier Vittorio, writer of added
commentary. III. Hilberseimer, Ludwig. Grossstadtarchitektur.
English. IV. Title.
  NA680.H4513 2012
  724'.6—dc23

Contents

Visual Documents

Afterword

Acknowledgments

During this book's long gestation period it bene-fited from the support of many institutions and individuals. The idea for the project was conceived at the Technical University in Berlin, where I had the opportunity to study under the auspices of a Fulbright Fellowship in 2002–03. The initial translation of *Großstadtarchitektur* was completed in the summer of 2005 in Rome, where I was able to work with the generous support of Patricia Anderson, who has provided extraordinary assis-tance in all of my metropolitan endeavors. A seminar led by Jean-Louis Cohen and Robert Lubar at New York University's Institute of Fine Arts deepened my understanding of the visual and architectural cultures of the twentieth-century metropolis. The Moscow Architecture Institute deserves special recognition here: the staff of the bookshop in the Institute's vestibule let me purchase a copy of Hilberseimer's book for next to nothing. This exemplar served as the mas-ter copy for the majority of the images reproduced in the present volume.

Research for this project was made possible by Columbia University's Department of Art History and Archaeology. I thank Barry Bergdoll and Vittoria Di Palma for their continued sup-port. Caleb Smith, Gabriel Rodriguez, and Emily Shaw of Columbia's Media Center for Art His-tory provided invaluable technical assistance throughout the production of the book. The staff of Columbia University's Avery Architectural and Fine Arts Library facilitated research and production for this project. I thank Carolyn Yerkes and Brooke Baldeschwiler of the Avery Classics Collection for responding to my requests with generosity and expedition.

Discussions with colleagues currently and formerly at Columbia have been invaluable. I thank in particular Albert Narath, who generously shared research he conducted at the Art Institute of Chicago. Insights gained from discussions with Albert, Cesare Birignani, and John Harwood contributed to a shared enthusiasm for the metropolis that propelled this project forward.

I thank Julie Dawson for her superb translations and for accommodating my editorial hand in rendering Hilberseimer's at-times cryptic texts into English. Craig Buckley deserves special thanks for initiating this series, steering this volume through its many stages, and providing insightful criticism on the introduction. I am grateful to Pier Vittorio Aureli, who generously agreed to contribute his trenchant afterword to this volume. Geoff Han's meticulous design has enhanced the book's intelligibility and visual appeal. I would also like to thank Columbia University's Graduate School of Architecture, Planning and Preservation for making the publication of this book possible.

As always, Tara Lynch's untiring support was indispensable to me and to this project.

Finally, I thank Greta, whose presence helps me see the metropolis with younger, fresher eyes and to whom this book is dedicated.

Translators' Notes

The challenge of translating Ludwig Hilberseimer's *Großstadtarchitektur* begins with the book's title. Hilberseimer's decision to connect its two terms — *Großstadt* (metropolis), and *Architektur* (architecture) — placed the book in a polemical relationship to a constellation of other German theories of the city. Prominent books he addressed include August Endell's *Die Schönheit der großen Stadt* (The Beauty of the Big City), 1908, and Karl Scheffler's *Die Architektur der Großstadt* (The Architecture of the Metropolis), 1913. Their titles suggest a mediated relationship between architecture and the city, implying that the terms belong to distinct orders of creation; Hilberseimer's is an argument for their immediate unity. To capture this immediacy, we have departed from the pattern established by the book's Spanish and Italian editions (*La arquitectura de la gran ciudad; L'architettura della grande città*), the titles of which may be translated as "The Architecture of the Big City." We have adopted the unfamiliar compound word "metropolisarchitecture" as our title. We hope the novelty of this articulation will at once defamiliarize its elements and convey the originality of Hilberseimer's conceptual categories.

In his early writing, much of which is synthesized in *Großstadtarchitektur*, Hilberseimer drew on the concept of *Gestaltung* in a variety of ways. A word notoriously rich in connotation, *Gestaltung*, as Detlef Mertins and Michael Jennings have described, was a polemical term in the early 1920s because it could describe (and thus unify) both artistic and industrial creation.[1] It is a nominalization of the verb *gestalten*, which encompasses a range of meanings: to shape, form, produce, construct, design, configure, and organize, among others. Notably, the term was used in the title of the avant-garde magazine *G: Material zur elementaren Gestaltung* (*G: Material for Elementary Form-Creation*), to which Hilberseimer contributed; and from 1926 the Bauhaus, where Hilberseimer would teach, was officially recognized as a Hochschule für Gestaltung (college of design). We have departed slightly from the translation of *Gestaltung* as "form-creation," which Mertins and Jennings have adopted in the scholarly edition of *G*. *Gestaltung* is rendered here predominantly as "design" or as "organization" when appropriate. We feel the creative, non-mimetic connotations of these English terms communicate the sense of Hilberseimer's discourse.

Hilberseimer's personal style is characterized by a staccato rhythm of short, declarative

[1]   See Detlef Mertins and Michael Jennings, "Introduction: The G-Group and the European Avant-Garde," in *G: An Avant-Garde Journal of Art, Architecture, Design, and Film, 1923–1926*, eds. Detlef Mertins and Michael Jennings, trans. Steven Lindberg and Margareta Ingrid Christian (Los Angeles: Getty Research Institute, 2010), 4–5.

phrases. At times his sentences are deliberately incomplete. We have resisted the urge to naturalize his style in English, and opted instead for approximations of his telegraphic cadence. And like most critics who write as much and as frequently as Hilberseimer did, his essays and books are marked by the repetition and refinement of key concepts and passages. We hope this presentation conveys the correspondence between Hilberseimer's idiosyncratic approach to writing and his architectural projects for the metropolis.

Richard Anderson
Julie Dawson

Introduction

Fig. 1 Ludwig Hilberseimer, Großstadtarchitektur, *Stuttgart: J. Hoffmann, 1927*

An End to Speculation

Introduction by Richard Anderson

It is impossible nowadays for any contractor to get along without speculative building, and on a large scale at that.[1]
—Karl Marx, *Capital*, Volume II

Ludwig Hilberseimer's *Großstadtarchitektur* (1927) offers one of the most cogent analyses undertaken between the two world wars of architecture's relationship to the city. In this work, Hilberseimer approached the metropolis as the fundamental condition for rational architecture and planning. While others found escape from the city in the utopian archipelago of suburban settlements, the *Siedlungen* that represent the finest achievements of the Weimar Republic's social housing policy, Hilberseimer, in both words and projects, confronted the dynamics of the metropolis directly. "The present form of the metropolis," he maintained, "owes its appearance primarily to the economic form of capitalist imperialism." He recognized that the principles that manage and regulate industrial operations and trade cartels failed to make the metropolis

---

[1] Karl Marx, *Capital*, trans. David Fernbach, 3 vols. (London: Penguin Books in association with New Left Review, 1978), 2: 312.

an object of organization. He described the reign of disorganization in capitalist cities: housing districts are built next to noisy, smoking factories; the concentration of the city center is reproduced in residential quarters; building codes are applied haphazardly; "the various forces that compose metropolises run rampant, working against each other instead of collaborating, so energy is lost rather than gained." Speculative development, which Marx had already identified as a driving force in the capitalist city, produces "a misuse and consumption of people without result."[2]

Although Hilberseimer's views were shared by many, his response to the city was unique. The chaos and lack of regulation in the metropolis aroused an anti-urban ideology among Germany's leading architects and planners: Bruno Taut's call for the "dissolution of cities" is emblematic of this position.[3] Despite its deficiencies, Hilberseimer asserted the necessity of the metropolis in a world defined by global economic interdependencies on the grounds that "the metropolis itself accelerates economic production processes by drawing economic control ever faster and more consciously to itself."[4] The rational organization of production and

[2] Ludwig Hilberseimer, *Großstadtarchitektur*, Die Baubücher, Bd. 3 (Stuttgart: J. Hoffmann, 1927), 1; 2; 2; see this volume, pp. 86; 89; 89.

[3] Bruno Taut, *Die Auflösung der Städte, oder, Die Erde, eine gute Wohnung oder auch: Der Weg zur alpinen Architektur* (Hagen: Folkwang-Verlag, 1920).

reproduction—of labor, leisure, and everyday life—required not an end to the metropolis but, in Hilberseimer's words:

> *an end to the metropolis that is based on the principle of speculation and whose very organism cannot free itself from the model of the city of the past despite all the modifications it has experienced—an end to the metropolis that has yet to discover its own laws.*[5]

With this, Hilberseimer advanced one of the principal theses contained in *Großstadtarchitektur*: the coordination of the relationships that govern the metropolis requires an end to speculation as a category of both economic and aesthetic activity.

The challenge that Hilberseimer presented in *Großstadtarchitektur*, however, has been interpreted largely through the images that the book contains. The gray, single-point perspective renderings of his *Hochhausstadt* (High-rise City), 1924, that figure prominently in the book's second chapter have evoked a variety of extreme reactions, most of them negative. Standard texts on the history of modern architecture use these

Figs. 17–18

[4] Hilberseimer, *Großstadtarchitektur*, 2; see this volume, p. 87.
[5] Ibid., 3; see this volume, p. 90. This statement first appeared in *G* 4: Ludwig Hilberseimer, "Amerikanische Architektur: Ausstellung in der Akademie der Bildenden Künste," *G* 4 (1926): 8.

images of "eerie, uniform blocks" to illustrate
the dangers of functionalism.[6] Richard Pommer,
one of the most astute commentators on Hilberseimer's work, counted these images "among the
standard illustrations of the horrors of modern
housing and city planning."[7] But Hilberseimer
himself offered the most damning assessment of
the High-rise City and its conceptual underpin-
ning. In 1963 he described the project as "more a
necropolis than a metropolis, a sterile landscape
of asphalt and cement; inhuman in every
respect."[8] What is more, Hilberseimer's retro-
spective commentary was part of his effort,
intentionally or unintentionally, to expunge the
radical propositions set forth in *Großstadtarchitektur* from his record. The exclusion of these
images from *Berliner Architektur der 20er Jahre*
(Berlin Architecture of the 1920s), 1967, the
final text in his long bibliography, marked the
culmination of an extended process that has
hitherto impeded research on Hilberseimer's
radical projects for the city.[9]

[6]   William J. R. Curtis, *Modern Architecture Since 1900*,
3rd ed. (London: Phaidon, 1996), 251.
[7]   Richard Pommer, "'More a Necropolis than a Metropolis': Ludwig Hilberseimer's Highrise City and Modern
City Planning," in *In the Shadow of Mies: Ludwig Hilberseimer: Architect, Educator, and Urban Planner*, eds.
Richard Pommer, David Spaeth, and Kevin Harrington
(Chicago: The Art Institute of Chicago, 1988), 17.
[8]   Ludwig Hilberseimer, *Entfaltung einer Planungsidee*
(Berlin: Ullstein, 1963), 22. Unless otherwise noted, all
translations are my own.

Großstadtarchitektur, however, offers much more than a commentary on the images of the High-rise City. The book's theoretical import has been recognized by a diverse group of scholars and architects: Giorgio Grassi, Manfredo Tafuri, Marco De Michelis, Christine Mengin, Juan José Lahuerta, K. Michael Hays, and most recently Pier Vittorio Aureli.[10] Their work has situated Hilberseimer's writing within the architectural culture of Weimar Germany and

[9] Ludwig Hilberseimer, *Berliner Architektur der 20er Jahre* (Mainz: Kupferberg, 1967).

[10] Giorgio Grassi, "Introduzione," in Ludwig Hilberseimer, *Un'idea di piano* (Padua: Marsilio, 1967), 7–22; Giorgio Grassi, "Architettura e formalismo," in Ludwig Hilberseimer, *Architettura a Berlino negli anni venti* (Milan: Franco Angeli, 1979), 7–29; Manfredo Tafuri, *Architecture and Utopia: Design and Capitalist Development* (Cambridge: The MIT Press, 1976); Manfredo Tafuri, "Sozialpolitik and the City in Weimar Germany," in *The Sphere and the Labyrinth: Avant-Gardes and Architecture from Piranesi to the 1970s* (Cambridge: The MIT Press, 1987), 197–233; Marco De Michelis, "Ritratto di un architetto come giovane artista," *Rassegna* 27 (1986): 6–25; Christine Mengin, "Modelle für eine moderne Großstadt: Ludwig Mies van der Rohe und Ludwig Hilberseimer," in *Moderne Architektur in Deutschland 1900 bis 1950: Expressionismus und Neue Sachlichkeit*, eds. Vittorio Magnago Lampugnani and Romana Schneider (Stuttgart: G. Hatje, 1994), 184–203; Juan José Lahuerta, *1927, la abstracción necesaria en el arte y la arquitectura europeos d'entreguerras* (Barcelona: Anthropos, 1989); K. Michael Hays, *Modernism and the Posthumanist Subject: The Architecture of Hannes Meyer and Ludwig Hilberseimer* (Cambridge: The MIT Press, 1992); Pier Vittorio Aureli, "Architecture for Barbarians: Ludwig Hilberseimer and

demonstrated its singularity. That much of
the critical work on Hilberseimer has been
undertaken in languages other than English corresponds in part to the availability of his texts in
translation. Large portions of *Großstadtarchitektur* appeared in Russian translation in 1932.[11]
The entire text appeared in Spanish in 1979, with
a second edition in 1999, and in Italian in 1981,
with a second edition in 1998.[12] The book's
first and final chapters appeared in English
translation in the journal *Australian Planner* in

the Rise of the Generic City," *AA files* 63 (2011): 3–18; see
also Markus Kilian, "Großstadtarchitektur und New
City: Eine planungsmethodische Untersuchung der
Stadtplanungsmodelle Ludwig Hilberseimers" (Dr.-Ing.
diss., Universität Karlsruhe, 2002); Francesco Bruno,
*Ludwig Hilberseimer: la costruzione di un'idea di città: il
periodo tedesco* (Milan: Libraccio, 2008).

[11] Significant portions of *Großstadtarchitektur* appeared
in David Arkin's anthology of contemporary architecture
of the capitalist West: David Arkin, ed., *Arkhitektura
sovremennogo zapada* (Moscow: IZOGIZ, 1932). The portion of Hilberseimer's chapter "Hallen und Theaterbauten"
(translated in this volume as "Halls and Theaters") that
had previously appeared as "Attrappenarchitektur" in
the journal *Qualität* in 1925 appeared as "Protiv maskiro-
vochnoi arkhitektury" ("Against Mask-like Architecture"),
115–117; most of Hilberseimer's chapter "Städtebau"
(translated in this volume as "Urban Planning") appeared
as "Problemy gradostroitel'stva" ("Problems of Urban
Planning"), 150–59. Both excerpts were translated from
German to Russian by Arkin.

[12] Ludwig Hilberseimer, *La arquitectura de la gran ciudad,*
trans. Pedro Madrigal Devesa (Barcelona: Gustavo Gili,
1979), 2nd ed., Gustavo Gili, 1999; Ludwig Hilberseimer,

1998.[13] This volume presents a first, and belated, translation of the complete text of *Großstadtarchitektur*, offering an opportunity to reconsider one of the most important contributions to urban and architectural thought of the 1920s.

Großstadtarchitektur was unlike contemporary books on architecture and urban planning. It was the third number in a series, the *Baubücher* (Building Books), published by Julius Hoffmann in Stuttgart. It followed Richard Neutra's exposition of American building practices, *Wie baut Amerika?* (How Does America Build?), 1927, and Hilberseimer's own panoramic view of international modernism, *Internationale neue Baukunst* (New International Building Art), also 1927, which was published on the opening of the Werkbund's Weissenhofsiedlung in Stuttgart.[14] While Neutra felt it necessary to plead with the reader to endure the abundance of technical detail that he hastily recorded during his practical work in the United States, *Internationale neue Baukunst* is primarily a picture book. *Großstadtarchitektur*, in contrast, was the result of extended theoretical

Groszstadt Architektur: L'architettura della grande città, trans. Bianca Spagnuolo Vigorita (Naples: CLEAN, 1981), 2nd ed., CLEAN, 1998.

[13] Ludwig Hilberseimer, "Groszstadtarchitektur," ed. Kim Halik, trans. Heinz Arndt, *Australian Planner* 35, no. 3 (1998): 147–57.

[14] Richard Neutra, *Wie baut Amerika?*, Die Baubücher, Bd. 1 (Stuttgart: J. Hoffmann, 1927); Ludwig Hilberseimer, *Internationale neue Baukunst*, Die Baubücher, Bd. 2 (Stuttgart: J. Hoffmann, 1927).

reflection. At the same time, it offers a broad cross section of modern architectural achievements in Europe and North America. It nevertheless has a more definite focus on urban architecture than such contemporary texts as Walter Curt Behrendt's *Der Sieg des neuen Baustils* (*The Victory of the New Building Style*) or Gustav Adolf Platz's *Die Baukunst der neuesten Zeit* (Building-Art of the Most Recent Era), both published in 1927.[15] Hilberseimer would have compared his book to Le Corbusier's *Urbanisme* (*The City of Tomorrow and its Planning*), 1925, the contents of which influenced significant elements of his own thinking.[16]

And yet *Großstadtarchitektur* is neither a manual on urban planning nor an outline of modern architecture's origins. Rather, it is a meditation on the relationship between the two terms of its compound title: "metropolis" and

[15] Walter Curt Behrendt, *Der Sieg des Neuen Baustils* (Stuttgart: Fr. Wedekind, 1927); Walter Curt Behrendt, *The Victory of the New Building Style*, ed. Detlef Mertins, trans. Harry Francis Mallgrave (Los Angeles: Getty Research Institute, 2000); Gustav Adolf Platz, *Die Baukunst der neuesten Zeit* (Berlin: Propyläen-Verlag in association with "Bauwelt," 1927).

[16] Le Corbusier, *Urbanisme*, Collection de "L'esprit nouveau" (Paris: Les Editions G. Cres & Co., 1925); Le Corbusier, *The City of Tomorrow and its Planning*, trans. Frederick Etchells (New York: Payson & Clarke, 1929). Hans Hildebrandt's translation of *Urbanisme* into German, *Städtebau*, was published in 1929 by the Deutsche Verlags-Anstalt in Stuttgart.

"architecture." It is as much an analysis of the conditions for architecture in the metropolis as it is a prescriptive theory of form. Written from a distinctly socialist perspective, Hilberseimer's text combines a critique of the social, techno-logical, and economic factors that have shaped the capitalist city with a Nietzschean "will to architecture." Coupling analysis with advocacy, Hilberseimer articulated a program for the lib-eration of architecture from the speculative regime of the capitalist marketplace and the sub-ordination of the city to the elementary laws of art. "Metropolisarchitecture" was the name he gave to the unity of part and whole that would be achieved when his propositions were fulfilled.

The present volume takes this unity for its title and assembles a range of texts and images that offers a definitive representation of Hilber-seimer's theory of the metropolis. Not a facsimile of *Großstadtarchitektur*, this volume presents a selection of the more than 200 images in the 1927 edition. Hilberseimer's argument informed this selection, and each of his own designs included in the first edition is illustrated. An image-based dossier of visual documents repro-duces select pages from *Großstadtarchitektur* and Hilberseimer's other writings. These documents facilitate a fuller understanding of the graphic dimension of Hilberseimer's theory of the metropolis. Two additional texts, "Der Wille zur Architektur" (The Will to Architecture, 1923) and "Vorschlag zur City-Bebauung" (Proposal for City-Center Development, 1930), are translated here for the first time and appear as appendices. These essays supplement *Großstadt-architektur* and reconstruct the genealogy of Hilberseimer's theory of the metropolis from its origins in the avant-gardes of the 1920s through its most concrete formalization at the end of the decade. But the texts and images presented here have not been compiled merely as documents for the archive of urban and architectural thought. For to read this book today—in the midst of an economic and urban crisis whose origins lie in the speculative housing market; surrounded by a variety of speculative theories of architecture, be they iconic, parametric, or affect-based—is to see that Hilberseimer's call for an end to speculation, in both its economic and aesthetic modes, has acquired a surplus value, one derived not from the patina of age but from the force of urgency.

Dionysian Origins

Ludwig Karl Hilberseimer was born on September 14, 1885, in Karlsruhe. The geometric rigor of the city's radial-concentric street system surely influenced him during his childhood and student years. He enrolled in the Grand Ducal Technical University in 1906 and would complete his architectural training in 1911.[17] Among his most

---

[17] For an excellent account of Hilberseimer's biography see De Michelis, "Ritratto di un architetto come giovane artista," 6–25.

significant professors were Friedrich Ostendorf and Reinhard Baumeister. Ostendorf is primarily remembered today for his polemical criticism of the work of Hermann Muthesius. Ostendorf believed that an arbitrary approach to form lurked behind both the picturesque asymmetry of Muthesius's country houses and his rhetoric of *Sachlichkeit* (objectivity). Although Hilberseimer made little reference to Ostendorf's influence, it is hard to imagine that his teacher's oft-repeated dictum failed to leave a mark on his thinking: "to design is to find the simplest form of appearance for a building program."[18] Baumeister's landmark treatise *Stadt-Erweiterungen* (City Extensions) of 1876 informed a generation of planners on the technical basis of urban expansion.[19] Like Baumeister, Hilberseimer would emphasize the paramount importance of housing and circulation in planning.

In 1911 Hilberseimer moved to Berlin, where he would live and work until he moved to the United States in 1938. During World War I he directed an institute of aeronautical research, and he flourished in the atmosphere of postwar Berlin. The city's intellectual and artistic culture allowed him to exercise his philosophical and

[18] Friedrich Ostendorf, *Sechs Bücher vom Bauen, enthaltend eine Theorie des architektonischen Entwerfens*, 3rd ed., (Berlin: W. Ernst & Sohn, 1918), 1: 3.
[19] Reinhard Baumeister, *Stadt-Erweiterungen in technischer baupolizeilicher und wirthschaftlicher Beziehung* (Berlin: Ernst & Korn, 1876).

literary talents in a variety of venues. During his time in Berlin he wrote for numerous journals, published several books, and secured his reputation as an authority on architecture and urban planning. Hilberseimer's professional stature was reflected in his membership in the Ring of modern architects, his invitation to build a house at the Weissenhofsiedlung in Stuttgart in 1927, and his appointment as a professor at Hannes Meyer's Bauhaus.[20] *Großstadtarchitektur* grew out of Hilberseimer's intensive engagement with the complex and varied intellectual currents that coursed through the metropolis. Written before he turned his attention exclusively to the decentralization of cities — the topic that would occupy

Figs. 46–47

[20] The nature of Hilberseimer's relationship to Hannes Meyer lacks precise definition despite K. Michael Hays's study of the two as representatives of a shared "post-humanist" position within the history of modern architecture. In a letter explaining his removal from the Bauhaus in Dessau, Meyer noted that his appointment of the "socialist architect L. Hilberseimer" was part of the pedagogical changes undertaken during his tenure as director. After Meyer moved to the USSR in 1930, Hilberseimer continued to teach at the Bauhaus, which was relocated to Berlin under Mies van der Rohe's leadership. Both Meyer and Hilberseimer were associated with the "Kollektiv für sozialistisches Bauen" (Collective for Socialist Building), which was organized by a group of young, left-leaning architects in Berlin in 1930. The Kollektiv sponsored the "Proletarian Building Exhibition" of 1931, during which Meyer lectured while traveling through Western Europe on leave from his responsibilities in the Soviet Union. Hilberseimer

him from the early 1930s through the rest of his career—the book represents a synthesis of his reflections on the metropolitan condition.[21]

In 1919, Hilberseimer worked closely with a group of intellectuals gathered around the magazine *Der Einzige* (The Singularity).[22] Edited by the literary historian Ernst Samuel (also known as Anselm Ruest) and the philosopher Salomo Friedländer, the publication was dedicated to Max Stirner's individualist legacy and to

participated in seminars on urban planning held by the Kollektiv at the Marxistische Arbeiterschule (Marxist Workers' School, MASCH) in Berlin in 1932. See Hays, *Modernism and the Posthumanist Subject*, 4–6; Hannes Meyer, "Mein Hinauswurf aus dem Bauhaus," in *Bauen und Gesellschaft: Schriften, Briefe, Projekte*, eds. Lena Meyer-Bergner and Klaus-Jürgen Winkler (Dresden: Verlag der Kunst, 1980), 69; Kollektiv für sozialistisches Bauen, "Jahresbericht für das Jahr 1931," 28 January 1932, Erwin Gräff Papers, Bauhaus Archive, Berlin.

[21] From about 1930, Hilberseimer developed an approach to decentralized settlement he called *Mischbebauung*, or mixed-height development, in which residential high-rises and single-story row houses would become the basic elements of the residential city. He would pursue this avenue of research in numerous projects and studies completed in the United States. See Ludwig Hilberseimer, "Flachbau und Stadtraum," *Zentralblatt für Bauverwaltung* 51, 23 December 1931, 773–78; Hilberseimer, *Entfaltung einer Planungsidee*, 24–26.

[22] There is very little work on this important journal and its editors. See Constantin Parvelescu, "After the Revolution: The Individualist Anarchist Journal *Der Einzige* and the Making of the Radical Left in the Early Post-World War I Germany" (Ph.D. diss., University of Minnesota, 2006).

the development of Nietzschean philosophical themes. The magazine's first issue contained Hilberseimer's essay "Schöpfung und Entwicklung" (Creation and Development)—his first attempt to articulate the value of "the primitive."[23] "Primitive artworks are the most pure," he wrote, "because they have not yet fallen to the civilizing urge for beauty." In his cultural genealogy, the Renaissance marked a critical turning point at which culture became primarily interested in the imitation and reproduction of ancient culture: "One wanted to appear just as others were." Hilberseimer identified the first signs of a way out of this reproductive culture in the early work of Nietzsche, particularly his *Die Geburt der Tragödie* (*The Birth of Tragedy*) of 1872: "Then the young Nietzsche discovered the polarity (Dionysian–Apollonian) of Greek art. The entirety of allegedly well-grounded Aesthetics collapsed." The world, Hilberseimer wrote, was shocked by the barbarism that Nietzsche revealed to be present in every aspect of Greek culture. "One finally recognized the high value of the primitive in contrast to the reproductive."[24]

Hilberseimer's concept of the primitive and its relationship to architecture acquired further definition throughout 1919. That year saw the

[23] Ludwig Hilberseimer, "Schöpfung und Entwicklung," *Der Einzige* 1, no. 1 (1919): 5–6. This essay was excerpted from a much longer text. The Art Institute of Chicago holds the manuscript in its entirety.
[24] Ibid., 5; 5; 6.

founding of the *Arbeitsrat für Kunst* (Work Council for Art) under the leadership of Walter
Gropius and Bruno Taut. The group's "Exhibition of Unknown Architects," which was held in
April, was a defining event in the advent of architectural Expressionism. Although Hilberseimer
signed the *Arbeitsrat*'s proclamation, his work,
along with Ludwig Mies van der Rohe's, was not
accepted by the show's jury. He later noted that it
was probably the "architectural clarity" of their
work that contradicted the "romantic nature of
the exhibition."[25] Hilberseimer responded with
an article in *Das Kunstblatt* (The Art Journal)
about Paul Scheerbart, the poetic inspiration for
Taut and many other Expressionists, and architecture.[26] Without identifying specific architects,
he charged the Expressionists with a "naturalistic misunderstanding of Cubist imagery" and
claimed that in their work a "lack of creative
power is replaced by a search for originality."
"An artwork," Hilberseimer wrote, "is a unity;
the unfolding and revelation of an idea; it is independent of the accidental."[27]

We find the primitive, productive architecture that Hilberseimer offered in response to
Expressionism in the first major publication of

---

[25] Hilberseimer, *Berliner Architektur der 20er Jahre*, 30.
Mies's unrealized Kröller-Müller Villa Project was also
rejected by the jury.
[26] Ludwig Hilberseimer, "Paul Scheerbart und die Architekten," *Das Kunstblatt* 3 (1919): 271–74.
[27] Ibid., 273.

Architektonische Entwürfe von L. Hilberseimer.

ARCHITEKT L. HILBERSEIMER.   ENTWURF ZU EINEM WARENHAUS.

Diese Kunst ist von einem Deutschen für Deutsche gemacht und so werden auch viele den Weg zu ihr finden.

Man wird erkennen, daß diese Harmonie, die Eurhythmie der Formgebung nicht errechnet, sondern erfühlt ist. Und das gibt Wärme. Ist schon das Gesetz allein an sich niemals häß-lich, so wird es erst schön, wenn es vom Menschen für den Menschen durchgeistigt ist, durch ein Temperament uns verdeutlicht wird, durch die künstlerische Form Sinn und Leben bekommt. Schönheit ist empfundene Gesetzmäßigkeit, die Empfindung vermittelt uns im Kunstwerk der Schöpfer. Der Kunst Zweck ist

ENTWURF ZU EINEM GESCHÄFTSHAUS.

Fig. 2 Ludwig Hilberseimer, early projects: above, *department store;* below, *office building; from* Deutsche Kunst und Dekoration, *1919*

his architectural designs in *Deutsche Kunst und*   Fig. 2
Dekoration (German Art and Decoration).[28] Published in June 1919, this series includes projects
for an urban theater, urban and suburban villas, a
train station, a covered market, an embassy, a
department store, and an office building. As
Marco De Michelis has pointed out, these projects bear the marks of Ostendorf's and Heinrich
Tessenow's influence, and they were probably executed before 1919.[29] They were nevertheless
embedded within Hilberseimer's discourse on the
primitive by the time of their publication. Under
the definite sway of Hilberseimer's conceptual
categories, the critic Max Wagenführ wrote:

> *Reconstruction means starting over from the
> beginning. The primitive also applies to art.
> Thus Hilberseimer returns to the basic forms*
> (Urformen): *rectangle; square and right
> angle; the triangle; the circle, semi-circle, and
> arc define surface—cube, pyramid, prism, and
> sphere form mass.*[30]

The primitive is thus productive, not reproductive, in its elemental, geometric rigor.

[28] Max Wagenführ, "Architektonische Entwürfe von L.
Hilberseimer," *Deutsche Kunst und Dekoration* 22, no. 6
(1919): 208–16.
[29] De Michelis, "Ritratto di un architetto come giovane
artista," 8–10.
[30] Wagenführ, "Architektonische Entwürfe von L. Hilberseimer," 211–12.

Hilberseimer would later identify an important source for his primitive geometries: "Cézanne spoke of the sphere, cone, and cylinder according to which one much formatively realize nature."[31] Hilberseimer also detected the primitive force of geometric forms in the Pre-Columbian monuments of Mesoamerica; his analysis of the "pure cubic elements" and "sustained effects" of simple linear arrangements at Palenque and Chichen Itza read like descriptions of his own architectural projects.[32]

Hilberseimer's engagement with the arts landed him a job as the art critic for *Sozialistische Monatshefte* (Socialist Monthly), a journal closely associated with the German Social Democratic Party. He occupied this post from 1920 until 1933, when the publication was banned. In this position he commented on topics including African Art, experimental film, contemporary architecture, and avant-garde artistic movements. His friendship with the Dadaist and filmmaker Hans Richter, whom he had met in 1912, brought him particularly close to Hannah Höch, Raoul Hausmann, and other Berlin Dadaists.[33] In his criticism, Hilberseimer was remarkably optimistic about Dada, a movement that made destructive irony a

[31] Ludwig Hilberseimer, "Cézanne," *Sozialistische Monatshefte* 28, nos. 1–2 (1922): 64.
[32] Ludwig Hilberseimer, "Mexikanische Baukunst," *Das Kunstblatt* 6 (1922): 163–71.
[33] Hans Richter, *Köpfe und Hinterköpfe* (Zurich: Der Arche, 1967), 75–76.

principle of artistic work. He warned that "the immediate future will demonstrate the essential seriousness that is concealed in the apparent flippancy of Dada." Significantly, his characterization of Dada's aims prefigured his interest in integrating the part and the whole—the room and the city—in the capitalist metropolis and revealed a new political charge to his formal aspirations: "Dada wants to free the ego from inoperative systems; let it merge with the cosmos; make it autonomously active; restore the total unity (*Alleinheit*) that has been crushed by bourgeois morality."[34]

The Metropolis

If Hilberseimer viewed Dada as an attempt to destroy the mechanisms that isolated the individual subject from the totality, the metropolis itself was among the most powerful "inoperative systems" that crushed "total unity." In 1903 the sociologist Georg Simmel had identified the specific psychological character of the big city in his essay "The Metropolis and Mental Life."[35] Metropolitan individuality was characterized above all by the "intensification

[34] Ludwig Hilberseimer, "Dadaismus," *Sozialistische Monatshefte* 26, nos. 25–26 (1920): 1120.
[35] Georg Simmel, "Die Großstädte und das Geistesleben," in *Die Großstadt: Vorträge und Aufsätze zur Städteausstellung*, ed. Th. Petermann (Dresden: V. Zahn & Jaensch, 1903), 185–206; see Georg Simmel, "The Metropolis and Mental Life," in *The Sociology of Georg Simmel* (New York: Free Press, 1950), 409–24.

of nervous stimulation" produced by rapidly changing images, discontinuous impressions, and the constant flow of people, goods, and money. The subjective response to these conditions was to develop a "protective organ" to guard against the forces that threaten to uproot the individual. This organ produced a blasé attitude toward the shocks of everyday life in the metropolis. This attitude freed the individual from the deleterious effects of the "intensification of consciousness," but it also manifested itself as extreme social alienation in the crowd, where "bodily proximity and narrowness of space make the mental distance only the more visible."[36] What is more, the blasé attitude toward the shocks of the metropolis, in Simmel's analysis, corresponds to a subjective internalization of the abstraction—the leveling of all difference—on which exchange value depends:

> The mood is the faithful subjective reflection of a completely internalized money economy.... All things float with equal specific gravity in the constantly moving stream of money. All things lie on the same level and differ from one another in the size of the area which they cover.[37]

---

[36] Simmel, "The Metropolis and Mental Life," 418.
[37] Ibid., 414. On this line of argumentation see in particular Tafuri, *Architecture and Utopia*, 84–89.

The problem taken up by both urban avant-gardes and metropolitan theorists was thus how to respond to the neutralization of both mental life and the world of objects in cities born of the "principle of speculation."

Hilberseimer's first response to this problem appeared in 1914 in a manuscript for a study titled "Die Architektur der Großstadt" (The Architecture of the Metropolis), which constitutes the theoretical kernel of *Großstadtarchitektur*.[38] His writing coincided with the high point of a period marked by intense urban thought. In 1908, August Endell identified the "beauty of the big city" in the ugly buildings and noise that "surrounds us in the total force of the

[38] Ludwig Hilberseimer, "Die Architektur der Großstadt," Ludwig Karl Hilberseimer Papers, Series 8/3, Box 1, 1914, The Art Institute of Chicago. As Richard Pommer has pointed out, Hilberseimer developed his manuscript in two later drafts, written between 1916 and 1918, in collaboration with his friend Udo Rusker. See Pommer, "'More a Necropolis than a Metropolis,'" 27. Although Hilberseimer called this work "Die Architektur der Großstadt," he did use the compound term *Großstadtarchitektur* in the first draft. The word was something of a neologism, but Hilberseimer was not the first to use it in this sense. Walter Curt Behrendt had used the term in passing in his monograph on Alfred Messel published by Bruno Cassirer in 1911. Joseph August Lux had used the term to greater effect in his monograph on Otto Wagner of 1914, stating that "Die neue Großstadtarchitektur beginnt ihre Zeitrechnung mit Otto Wagner...." (The new metropolisarchitecture starts its clock with Otto Wagner....); see Joseph August Lux, *Otto Wagner: Eine Monographie* (Munich: Delphin, 1914), 43.

present."[39] Others sought to regulate the metropolis with new forms of organization. The competition for the design of Greater Berlin of 1910 captured the attention of the German Reich and stimulated such innovative urban proposals as Rudolf Eberstadt and Bruno Möhring's plan for wedge-shaped "green lungs" that would connect Berlin to its hinterland. Hilberseimer wrote that "the task of the architect is to bring order and clarity to the chaos."[40]

Hilberseimer's text engaged with the most recent literature on architecture and urban planning. It was particularly indebted to Karl Scheffler's *Die Architektur der Großstadt* (The Architecture of the Metropolis) of 1913.[41] Scheffler explicitly identified the metropolis as the site where a new form of architecture would come into being. Employing a mode of analysis Hilberseimer would later apply in *Großstadtarchitektur*, Scheffler reduced the metropolis to its typological elements: the apartment building, the commercial building, and the suburban villa. The first of these three was most important for both Scheffler and Hilberseimer because the apartment building expressed the uniformity of the big city, and, in Scheffler's words, "the typical is the first prerequisite of a new style."[42] Hilberseimer turned to

[39] August Endell, *Die Schönheit der großen Stadt* (Stuttgart: Strecker & Schröder, 1908), 23.
[40] Hilberseimer, "Die Architektur der Großstadt."
[41] Karl Scheffler, *Die Architektur der Großstadt* (Berlin: Bruno Cassirer, 1913).

Walter Curt Behrendt's *Die einheitliche Blockfront als Raumelement im Stadtbau* (The Unified Block as a Spatial Element in City Building), 1911, for an analysis of the positive value of uniform blocks of apartment buildings for metropolitan form. The harsh criticism that Hilberseimer directed at Camillo Sitte's "artistic principles" of urban planning in this early text would be repeated in *Großstadtarchitektur*. Significantly, Hilberseimer discussed Otto Wagner's plans for an expanding metropolis in this early text; Wagner's project would not be included in Hilberseimer's later analysis of urban planning proposals.[43]

The economic basis of urban form was already among Hilberseimer's concerns in 1914: "today it is capital above all else that forces concentrated settlements."[44] Hilberseimer attributed the "lack of planning in the total organism" of the metropolis to the motors of urban development. In this he followed Scheffler's critique of the *Mietskaserne* (rental barrack), the derogatory designation for the towering, densely built apartment buildings that had radically transformed German cities since the building boom of the 1870s that followed German unification and the country's victory in the Franco-Prussian War.[45] "The multi-story

[42] Ibid., 33.
[43] Otto Wagner, *Die Großstadt: Eine Studie über diese* (Vienna: A. Schroll u. Komp., 1911).
[44] Hilberseimer, "Die Architektur der Großstadt."

dwelling," Scheffler wrote, "exists in its present form as the result of an immense entrepreneurial will but also as an effect of an irresponsible and unplanned speculative instinct."[46] Scheffler, in turn, based his analysis on the work of Rudolf Eberstadt, who, in addition to preparing such practical urban proposals as his entry to the 1910 competition for Greater Berlin and his project for the development of Berlin-Treptow, was a preeminent theorist and advocate for housing reform. His *Handbuch des Wohnungswesens und der Wohnungsfrage* (Handbook for Housing and the Housing Question), 1909, went through many editions and was widely read by students and practitioners.[47] Eberstadt analyzed the economics of housing and urban planning with perhaps more rigor than anyone else and emerged as a staunch opponent of speculation's role in the development of the metropolis. In 1907 he devoted an entire book to the subject, *Die Spekulation im neuzeitlichen Städtebau* (Speculation in Modern Urban Planning). He described the hegemony of speculation as follows:

Among the phenomena that characterize the most recent period of urban planning in Ger-

[45] On the development of the Berlin apartment building see Johann Friedrich Geist and Klaus Kürvers, *Das Berliner Mietshaus*, 3 vols. (Munich: Prestel, 1980).

[46] Scheffler, *Die Architektur der Großstadt*, 29.

[47] Rudolf Eberstadt, *Handbuch des Wohnungswesens und der Wohnungsfrage* (Jena: Gustav Fischer, 1909).

many one stands out with particular clarity: the development and ultimately complete reign of speculation in all spheres of housing. From the preparation and partitioning of building sites to the ownership of finished apartments, speculation determines the organization of urban planning and the traffic in land values. The parceling of building sites is a speculative affair. Construction, housing form, and housing production are determined by speculation. In its hands lie land and building ownership; it has mortgages and land registries at its disposal.[48]

Speculation, Eberstadt wrote, was nothing other than "opportunistic acquisition of the lowest, least valuable kind." He admitted that the solution to the problem of speculation would not be easily found. Sweeping reforms in planning regulation and housing finance were needed, and his call for a radical reform of the metropolis prefigures the arguments made by Hilberseimer after World War I. Eberstadt: "Every isolated intervention that leaves the foundations unchanged must in this case be understood as an evil."[49]

Hilberseimer's first published response to the metropolis appeared in 1923 in *Sozialistische Monatshefte*. His essay "Vom städtebaulichen Problem der Großstadt" (On the Urban-

---

[48] Rudolf Eberstadt, *Die Spekulation im neuzeitlichen Städtebau* (Jena: Gustav Fischer, 1907), 1.
[49] Ibid., 2; 208.

Planning Problem of the Metropolis) contains much of the text of the first chapter of *Groß-stadtarchitektur*. Hilberseimer described the design of the environment as one of the principal tasks of humanity and distinguished between the metropolis and the city of the past: the metropolis is "the natural and necessary consequence of the industrialization of the world."[50] But there are crucial differences between the position Hilberseimer articulated here and the arguments he presented in his later book; the most important concerns decentralization. In his 1923 text, Hilberseimer identified one of the most important sources for his thinking: the architect, planner, and polymath Martin Mächler. Mächler's activities were wide-ranging: he developed a plan for a new north-south axis for Berlin in 1908 that would become an idée fixe for a generation of planners that included Albert Speer; he advised Lenin on the importance of energy networks in Zurich in 1917; and he developed the theory of the *Weltstadt* (World-City) and the *Großsiedlung* (Great-Settlement) that Hilberseimer would expand.[51] Also a contributor to *Sozialistische Monatshefte*, Mächler articulated his theory of the metropolis in a

[50] Ludwig Hilberseimer, "Vom städtebaulichen Problem der Großstadt," *Sozialistische Monatshefte* 29, no. 6 (1923): 352.
[51] On Mächler see Ilse Balg, ed., *Martin Mächler, Weltstadt Berlin*, Wannseer Hefte 13 (Berlin: Galerie Wannsee, 1986).

series of articles in 1921–22. Mächler wrote that "if urban planners and speculators had ... considered the settlement that they created as ... a cell in a total-state (*Gesamtstaat*); if they had learned to see it as an organic element in a large organism ... they would have seen how narrow, limited, and without insight or foresight their behavior was."[52] Hilberseimer made Mächler's analysis the basis of his response to the problem of the metropolis and called for a strict separation of places of work from places of dwelling. The city was to expand in the horizontal dimension. Invoking the work of Raymond Unwin, Erwin Gutkind, and Ernst May, Hilberseimer here advocated for the construction of "satellite cities," to use May's terminology.[53] His design for a *Wohnstadt* (Residential City) of 1923 follows the satellite-city principle and enforces a strict separation of functional zones.[54]

Figs. 25–27

[52] Martin Mächler, "Das Siedelungsproblem," *Sozialistische Monatshefte* 27, no. 4 (1921): 185.
[53] Raymond Unwin, *Town Planning in Practice: An Introduction to the Art of Designing Cities and Suburbs* (London: T. F. Unwin, 1909); first German edition, 1910; Erwin Gutkind, *Vom städtebaulichen Problem der Einheitsgemeinde Berlin* (Berlin: Hans Robert Engelmann, 1922); Ernst May, "Stadterweiterung mittels Trabanten," *Der Städtebau* 19, nos. 5–6 (1922): 51–55.
[54] Although Hilberseimer included a diagram for a system of satellite cities in several publications, this decentralized model of urban development would not appear in *Großstadtarchitektur*. See Ludwig Hilberseimer, "Stadt- und Wohnungsbau," *Soziale Bauwirtschaft* 5, no. 14 (1925): 185–88.

Hilberseimer described how this form of growth would radically alter the very concept of the city:

> *At present our concept of the city is based on an ideology that is tied to the past. Although walls and towers have long since fallen, they haunt our memories even today. Urban structures, such as those that are designed to provide space for nine million people in Tokyo and as many as thirty-five million in New York, are based on premises entirely different from those we are accustomed to. They will thus produce an entirely new type of city that dispenses with spatial cohesion—the concept that we have until now used to imagine the city. Their enormous expansion necessarily forces decentralization. The traffic question will become the Alpha and Omega of the entire urban organism.*[55]

Thus, in 1923, Hilberseimer considered disaggregation to be the most appropriate response to the problem of the metropolis. Spatial cohesion, which had been intensified by the speculative development of German cities since the late nineteenth century, gave way to the principle of spatial dispersal. Following Mächler, Hilberseimer envisioned this new form of expansion constituting new regional patterns, eventually encompassing an economically unified Euro-

[55] Hilberseimer, "Vom städtebaulichen Problem der Großstadt," 357; compare to this volume, p. 133

pean continent. For the time being, Hilberseimer's response to speculation was articulated in the horizontal dimension; by the end of 1924 he would turn to a vertical solution.

Aesthetic Speculation

Speculation is not only a mode of economic activity; it is also a category of artistic practice. Reviewing the development of the arts in France since the beginning of World War I, Hilberseimer noted that "the epoch of speculation is not yet past."[56] He referred to the persistent desire for verisimilitude among French artists and accused them of cultivating a decorative sensibility. To this speculative trend Hilberseimer opposed the work of the Parisian avant-garde. "Picasso, Braque, Gris, Metzinger, Leger are attempting to reach the absolute in painting; seeking to replace the naturalistic illusion of the perspectival mechanism with an architectonic rhythm of the image (*Bildrhythmus*)."[57] Hilberseimer would later describe the architectonic of the visual arts as preparatory work for architectural and urban design.

[56] Ludwig Hilberseimer, "Von der Kunst des jungen Frankreichs," *Sozialistische Monatshefte* 26, no. 11 (1920): 673. Paul Westheim would later link the rampant monetary inflation of the early years of the Weimar Republic to the practice of "art-speculation." See Paul Westheim, "Die tote Kunst der Gegenwart," *Das Kunstblatt* 8 (1924): 141–49.

[57] Hilberseimer, "Von der Kunst des jungen Frankreichs," 673.

The importance of Hilberseimer's sustained engagement with Constructivism cannot be underestimated. Born in the Soviet Union, Constructivism spread rapidly throughout Eastern and Western Europe as artists sought to transform practice from the production of images to the design of objects.[58] Berlin was the epicenter of International Constructivism, which was distinct from its Soviet counterpart in both its goals and political commitments. Hilberseimer described the development of Constructivism in an article of 1922. He viewed the movement as a response to the exhaustion of the recent experiments of Kazimir Malevich and Aleksandr Rodchenko, whose monochromatic paintings of 1919 had pushed Suprematism to its final consequences. After this, a new decisive phase had been reached:

> *Either one clung to abstraction and lost oneself in individualistic speculations. Or one began to renounce composition and turn to construction: to the construction of new objects.*[59]

Hilberseimer referred to a series of debates that took place in Moscow's Institute of Artistic Culture (INKhUK) in the winter of 1921 at

[58]   Christina Lodder, *Russian Constructivism* (New Haven: Yale University Press, 1983).
[59]   Ludwig Hilberseimer, "Konstruktivismus," *Sozialistische Monatshefte* 28, nos. 19–20 (1922): 831.

which sharp distinctions were made between composition and construction: the former came to be seen as a remnant of illusionistic art, the latter as a mode of artistic practice that might transform everyday life.[60] Recalling his earlier essay "Schöpfung und Entwicklung," he defined Constructivism as an attempt to break with the illusionism of Renaissance art and initiate a "creative design of the world." "The laws of artistic formation," he wrote, "should also be applied to space as an object and no longer to the pictorial illusion of space." Significantly, Hilberseimer identified the most successful attempt at Constructivist creation in Viking Eggeling's abstract films, what Hilberseimer called his *Bewegungskunst* (Movement-Art). In such a work as Eggeling's *Diagonal-Symphonie* (Diagonal Symphony) of 1921, "the final remains of illusionism have been eliminated, and a truly new object has been created and formed with the utmost precision."[61] The values Hilberseimer associated with the primitive thus reappear in his reading of Constructivism and experimental cinema.

In his 1922 essay on Constructivism, Hilberseimer identified a number of international publications that supported the movement: the

---

[60] On these debates see Maria Gough, *The Artist as Producer: Russian Constructivism in Revolution* (Berkeley: University of California Press, 2005).

[61] Hilberseimer, "Konstruktivismus," 832.

Netherlands had *De Stijl*; France, *L'esprit nouveau*; Hungary, *Ma*; and Russia, *Veshch'/Objet/Gegenstand*. "Germany," he noted parenthetically, "does not possess such a publication." Despite the fact that the trilingual journal *Veshch'* was published in Berlin by Il'ia Ehrenburg and El Lissitzky, he was right. But this would change the following year with the publication of the first issue of *G: Material zur elementaren Gestaltung* (*G: Material for Elementary Form-Creation*), which would appear at irregular intervals until 1926.[62] Hilberseimer was deeply involved with the journal and its contributors from the beginning, and some of the essays he contributed to *G* would feature in *Großstadtarchitektur*. The so-called G-Group consisted of prominent members of the European avant-garde. It included Richter, the journal's chief editor, El Lissitzky, László Moholy-Nagy, Mies van der Rohe, Theo van Doesburg, Tristan Tzara, Hans Arp, and Kurt Schwitters, among others. As Detlef Mertins has described, the journal's commitment to "elementare Gestaltung," which may be translated as "elementary design" or "elementary form-creation," grew out of a cultural position that can be traced back to Gotthold Ephraim Lessing's *Laocoön* of 1766. Like Lessing, the

[62] See the recent translation of the journal by Steven Lindberg and Margareta Ingrid Christian: Detlef Mertins and Michael Jennings, eds., *G: An Avant-Garde Journal of Art, Architecture, Design, and Film, 1923–1926* (Los Angeles: Getty Research Institute, 2010); hereafter referred to as *G: An Avant-Garde Journal*.

G-Group sought to uncover the structural logic of each respective mode of artistic expression; the group sought to reduce art to its elements in order to shape them anew.[63]

While the G-Group was committed to exploring the intrinsic laws of art, it was equally opposed to aesthetic speculation in all its forms. Van Doesburg established this conjunction of values in two essays from 1923. In "On Elemental Form-Creation," which was published in the first issue of *G*, van Doesburg distinguished between decorative and monumental approaches to expression. He associated the decorative approach with personal taste and intuition—qualities that failed to meet the modern demand for precision. Elsewhere he wrote that "the speculative method, a childish disease, has arrested the healthy development of construction according to universal and objective laws."[64] In *G* he wrote that without "precise distinction (sculpture from painting, painting from architecture, etc.) it is impossible to create order from chaos and to become acquainted with elemental means of form-creation."[65] For van Doesburg

[63] Detlef Mertins, "Architecture, Worldview, and World Image in *G*," in *G: An Avant-Garde Journal*, 77.
[64] Theo van Doesburg and Cornelius van Eesteren, "Toward a Collective Construction [1923]," in *The Tradition of Constructivism*, ed. Steven Bann (New York: Viking Press, 1974), 118.
[65] Theo van Doesburg, "On Elemental Form-Creation [1923]," in *G: An Avant-Garde Journal*, 101–02.

the "speculative method" corresponds to a mode of practice that is based on caprice and subjective individuality—qualities diametrically opposed to the G-Group's commitment to economy, order, regularity, and collectivity.

Certain members of the G-Group understood aesthetic speculation and speculative building to be fundamentally linked. Mies made this clear in the first two issues of *G*. He juxtaposed his project for a concrete office building with a powerful statement of purpose in *G*'s debut issue: "We reject: every aesthetic speculation; every doctrine; and every formalism... create the form from the nature of the task with the means of our time. That is our task."[66] In the following issue Mies articulated aesthetic and economic modes of speculation in his statement titled "Building": "Our task is precisely to liberate building activity from the aesthetic speculation of developers and to make it once again the only thing it should be, namely, BUILDING."[67] The alleged contradiction between aesthetic speculation and elemental design was made forcefully apparent in 1924 in an unsigned, two-page spread that was published between Mies's article "Industrial Building" and Hilberseimer's article "Construction and Form" in the

Fig. 55

[66] Ludwig Mies van der Rohe, "'We reject...' [1923]," in *G: An Avant-Garde Journal*, 103.
[67] Ludwig Mies van der Rohe, "Building [1923]," in *G: An Avant-Garde Journal*, 105.

Die Bauunternehmer werden sich entscheiden müssen, ob sie wirklich rationell bauen wollen oder ob die in Europa noch immer vorherrschende ästhetische Spekulation (in welchem Gewande auch immer) ihre Produktion bestimmen.

Die Organisation der Baubetriebe, das Prinzip, in dem sie aufgebaut sind, entscheidet auch letzthin über die Art ihrer Entwicklung. Großzügige Arbeit läßt sich nur da erreichen, wo der Betrieb großzügig ist. Eine Industrialisierung des Bauens selbst ist seiner Natur nach gebunden an einen industriellen Betrieb.

La réorganisation fondamentale de nos habitations est urgente.

The fondamental reorganisation of the housing problem is urgent,

Дома и жилища должны неотменно быть заменены новейшими и современными методами касающимися этого вопроса.

In den nächsten Heften werden wir Projekte der Firma Sommerfeld veröffentlichen und besprechen, die auf rationelles und ökonomisches Bauen hinzielen.

Fig. 3 Page from G 3, 1924; top paragraph: *"Building contractors will have to decide whether they really want to build rationally or whether the aesthetic speculation that is still dominant in Europe (in whatever guise that may be) will determine their production."*

third issue of *G*. At left, bold red text states: "We consider a fundamental change to our form of housing necessary." At right, a photograph of a neo-baroque urban villa is crossed out by a large *Fig. 3* red "X." The text above the photograph reads: "Building contractors will have to decide whether they really want to build rationally or whether the aesthetic speculation that is still dominant in Europe (in whatever guise that may be) will determine their production."[68] The editorial lauds the "rational and economical building practices" of Adolf Sommerfeld's firm, which was responsible for several large settlements in Berlin.[69] This spread places aesthetic speculation in opposition to rationality—individualist caprice is identified with the arbitrary (and profit-driven) inflation of architectural values, while building appears as a self-evident activity that is governed by immanent laws. Aesthetic speculation thus forms the antithesis to elemental design because it distorts both the economy of form and the economy of the building industry. This position buttressed Hilberseimer's call for "the end to the metropolis based on the principle of speculation ... the metropolis ... that has not found its own laws," which first appeared in

[68] "'We consider a fundamental change...' [1924]," in *G: An Avant-Garde Journal*, 124–25.
[69] On the Sommerfeld firm's rationalization of building production see Celina Kress, *Adolf Sommerfeld/ Andrew Sommerfield: Bauen für Berlin 1910–1970* (Berlin: Lukas, 2011).

the fourth issue of *G* in 1926 in a review of an exhibition of American architecture that was on view at Berlin's Academy of Fine Arts.[70]

Hilberseimer's interest in American architecture proved to be of vital importance to both his relationship to Constructivism and his approach to the metropolis. Late in life he recalled that his 1920 essay "Amerikanische Architektur" (American Architecture), which he wrote with his friend and collaborator Udo Rusker, attracted the attention of the Hungarian critic Ernő (Ernst) Kállai, who invited Hilberseimer into a circle of young Hungarian artists and architects.[71] Kállai was deeply invested in the cause of Constructivism, and it was through him that Hilberseimer was introduced to László Péri. Péri's arrival on the Berlin art scene was marked by the publication of a portfolio of reductive, geometrical linoleum prints by Herwarth Walden's Der Sturm gallery in 1922. The critic Alfréd Kemény praised the spatial qualities of Péri's black, white, and gray images for their "economy of minimal forms; spatial tension produced by the extreme opposition of minimal forms; massive strength; [and] sharp, objective determinacy without any possible association with nature."[72] These words could

[70] Hilberseimer, "Amerikanische Architektur: Ausstellung in der Akademie der Bildenden Künste," 4–8.
[71] Hilberseimer, *Berliner Architektur der 20er Jahre*, 39; Ludwig Hilberseimer and Udo Rusker, "Amerikanische Architektur," *Kunst und Künstler* 18, no. 12 (1920): 537–39.

apply to many contemporary projects Hilberseimer executed, and it is no accident that he was
impressed by an exhibition of Péri's work at the
Sturm gallery in early 1923. Hilberseimer was
particularly interested in Péri's space-constructions—painted canvases that defied the planarity
and rectangular shape of traditional paintings.
He wrote that "Péri's elementary architectonic
explodes the narrow concept of the picture,
forms space, and turns his pictures into functional spatial parts." "Thus," Hilberseimer
continued, "his constructions become elementary spatial figures of vital intensity." Most
important, Hilberseimer wrote that "in Péri's
spatial constructions the latent will to architecture of the new artistic movements is manifest in
elementary fashion."[73]

The Nietzschean qualities that Hilberseimer found in Péri's work would form the basis
for Hilberseimer's essay "Der Wille zur Architektur" (The Will to Architecture), which
was published in *Das Kunstblatt* in 1923.[74] Influenced by the immanent logic demonstrated by

[72] Alfréd Kemény, "Die konstruktive Kunst und Péris
Raumkonstruktionen [1922]," in *Wechselwirkungen:
Ungarische Avantgarde in der Weimarer Republik*, ed.
Hubertus Gassner (Marburg: Jonas, 1986), 246.
[73] Ludwig Hilberseimer, "Peri," *Sozialistische Monatshefte*
29, no. 4 (1923): 257.
[74] Ludwig Hilberseimer, "Der Wille zur Architektur,"
Das Kunstblatt 7 (1923): 133–40; see this volume, pp. 282–
89. "Der Wille zur Architektur" develops themes
Hilberseimer had introduced in his important essay

Constructivist artifacts and van Doesburg's lecture "Der Wille zum Stil" (The Will to Style), this essay presents Hilberseimer's view of the relationship between artistic experiment and the laws of architectural form.[75] He recapitulated his criticism of the "subjective speculation" of Expressionism and praised the valuable work of the Constructivists:

> *Their provisional, as yet non-utilitarian constructions reveal the unmistakable will to possess reality. The world itself became the material of their design; every object was drawn into their domain. From the construction of painting, the Constructivists transitioned to the construction of objects, to architecture in the most all-encompassing sense of the word. The Constructivists most lucidly recognized the*

"Anmerkungen zur neuen Kunst" (Observations on the New Art) of 1923. "Anmerkungen zur neuen Kunst" would be republished in German in 1928, and it exists in two English translations. See Ludwig Hilberseimer, "Anmerkungen zur neuen Kunst," in *Sammlung Gabrielson* (Gothenburg, 1923), unpaginated; "Anmerkungen zur neuen Kunst," *Kunst der Zeit* 3, nos. 1–3 (1928): 52–57; "Observations on the New Art," trans. Howard Dearstyne, *College Art Journal* 18, no. 4 (1959): 349–51; "[Observations on the New Art]," in Manfredo Tafuri, *The Sphere and the Labyrinth*, 336–38.

[75] Theo van Doesburg, "Der Wille zum Stil [1922]," in *De Stijl: Schriften und Manifeste zu einem theoretischen Konzept ästhetischer Umweltgestaltung*, ed. Hagen Bächler and Herbert Letsch (Leipzig: Gustav Kiepenhauer Verlag, 1984), 163–79.

*new aim, putting their entire creative power at
its disposal.*[76]

While he acknowledged that the work of the
Constructivists represented only experiments, he
asserted that their work had revealed immanent
laws of material and form. "These newly discovered laws of form," he stated, "will achieve an
all-encompassing influence on modern architecture." The task was to articulate such laws at the
scale of the metropolis, where "the most heterogeneous material masses require a law of form
applicable for every element in equal measure."[77]

Hilberseimer presented his first major
statement of the architectural laws of the
metropolis in 1924. In fall of that year the Sturm
gallery mounted an exhibition of Hilberseimer's
and Péri's architectural work, and Herwarth
Walden invited Hilberseimer to publish an
accompanying essay in the September issue of
Der Sturm (The Storm). His essay "Großstadtarchitektur" (Metropolisarchitecture) constitutes
much of the final chapter of *Großstadtarchitektur* and offers a critical gloss on the
work featured in the exhibition.[78] Although we
do not have an exhibition checklist, it appears
that Hilberseimer presented drawings for his

[76] Hilberseimer, "Der Wille zur Architektur," 134; see
this volume, p. 284.
[77] Ibid., 134; 135; see this volume, pp. 285; 286.
[78] Ludwig Hilberseimer, "Großstadtarchitektur," *Der
Sturm* 15, no. 4 (1924): 177–89.

Residential City, a series of row houses, and perhaps his design for the Chicago Tribune competition; Péri presented designs for an apartment building with communal services, a row-house district, and a monument to Lenin in the form of a hammer and sickle. Reviewing the show in *Die Rote Fahne* (The Red Banner), the organ of the German Communist Party, Alfréd Kemény emphasized the political nature Hilberseimer's and Péri's work:

Figs. 25–27, 40–41, 4

> *With the severe structure of their blocks of houses, Hilberseimer and Péri fight not only* formally *against the lack of structure in metropolitan architecture; they at the same time lead an* ideological fight *against the anarchic production processes of capitalism, whose corresponding expression is found in the current, chaotic form of the metropolis.*[79]

Kemény's assertion of the anti-capitalist content of the work presented at the Sturm gallery may have contributed to the sympathetic review Hilberseimer's and Péri's work received from the Russian architect Grigorii Barkhin after their designs were exhibited in Moscow in late 1924.[80]

---

[79] Alfréd Kemény, "Neue Versuche in der Architektur-Ausstellung von Hilberseimer und Péri im 'Sturm' [1924]," in *Wechselwirkungen*, ed. Hubertus Gassner (Marburg: Jonas, 1986), 249.

[80] G. Barkhin, "Arkhitektura na vystavke nemetskikh khudozhnikov v Moskve," *Stroitel'naia promyshlennost'* 2, no. 11 (1924): 736–38.

"Großstadtarchitektur" lacks the sharp political edge that Kémeny identified in Hilberseimer's work. Instead, it supports Hilberseimer's assertion that "metropolisarchitecture is a new type of architecture with its own forms and laws." Although Hilberseimer comments on space, style, color, and material in this essay, his statements concerning mass, unity, and organization carry the most weight in his attempt to reduce architecture to its basic elements.[81] Painting served as a model of elementarization. He wrote that every discipline needs a clear understanding of its means and argued that painting was "the first to call attention to the basic forms of all art: geometric and cubic elements that resist any further objectification."[82] Recalling Wagenführ's comments on the "primitivism" of his early work, Hilberseimer

[81] Hilberseimer's discussion of style and will (*Wollen*) in this essay is related to the interest he expressed in Alois Riegl's concept of *Kunstwollen*, or artistic volition. Already in his 1914 draft for "Die Architektur der Großstadt," Hilberseimer had opposed Riegl's concept of art to the allegedly "materialistic" theory of Gottfried Semper. In his creative misreading of Semper's thoughts on style, Hilberseimer adopted a position framed by Riegl himself and propagated by such leaders of the modern movement as Peter Behrens and Walter Gropius. On Riegl's reception of Semper, see Harry Francis Mallgrave, *Gottfried Semper: Architect of the Nineteenth Century* (New Haven: Yale University Press, 1996), 355–82.

[82] Hilberseimer, "Großstadtarchitektur," 180; compare to this volume, p. 268.

enumerated the "basic elements of every architecture": cube and sphere, prism and cylinder, pyramid and cone. He defined architecture's fundamental task as follows:

> *The problem of architecture, apart from the practicality of materials and their appropriate use, is the spatial design of masses, which encompasses the organization, visualization, realization, and formation of a vision.*[83]

Hilberseimer was certainly aware of Le Corbusier's definition of architecture as "the masterful, correct, and magnificent play of volumes brought together in light," but he carefully avoided any reference to the Franco-Swiss architect's influential ideas.[84] Instead, Hilberseimer invoked Auguste Rodin's writing on architecture. In his *Les cathédrales de France* (*The Cathedrals of France*), 1914, Rodin had written that "in order to use light and shadow according to their essential properties and intentions, the architect has only certain geometrical combinations at his disposal."[85] Hilberseimer shared

[83] Ibid., 180; compare to this volume, p. 268.
[84] Le Corbusier, *Toward an Architecture*, ed. Jean-Louis Cohen, trans. John Goodman (Los Angeles: Getty Research Institute, 2007), 102. Hans Hildebrandt's translation of this book into German, *Kommende Baukunst*, was published in 1926 in Stuttgart by the Deutsche Verlags-Anstalt, but Hilberseimer evidently worked with the original French edition. He later recalled the privilege of

Rodin's wonder at the powerful effects achieved with reduced means and called for the architect to limit his work to the use of "fundamental architectural elements": body, surface, color, window and door openings, balconies, loggias, and chimneys. "Working with these elements he will arrive at an architecture which emerges from its own principles," he wrote.[86]

For Hilberseimer the emergence of an architecture proper to the metropolis depends on the application of these principles across multiple scales:

> *Metropolisarchitecture is considerably dependent on solving two factors: the individual cell of the room and the collective urban organism. The solution will be determined by the manner in which the room is manifested as an element of buildings linked together in one street block, thus becoming a designing factor of the city structure, which is the actual objective of architecture. Inversely, the constructive design of the urban plan will gain considerable influ-*

having received a copy of *Vers une architecture* from a friend immediately after World War I. See Hilberseimer, *Berliner Architektur der 20er Jahre*, 20.

[85] Auguste Rodin, *Les cathédrales de France* (Paris: Armand Colin, 1914); cited from the German edition of 1917: *Die Kathedralen Frankreichs* (Leipzig: K. Wolff, 1917), 4. An English translation of this book was published in 1981.

[86] Hilberseimer, "Großstadtarchitektur," 182; compare to this volume, p. 269.

ence on the formation of the room and the building as such.[87]

The relationship between cell and organism, part and whole, is thus the central problem of metropolisarchitecture. Although many architects had called for an organic architecture by the time Hilberseimer wrote these lines, Hilberseimer had very specific sources in mind. His language of urban cells and organisms was derived from his close reading of Martin Mächler's writing on the city. Hilberseimer's interest in articulating small and large scales in an unbroken continuum was first expressed in an analysis of the experimental films of his friends and colleagues Viking Eggeling and Hans Richter:

> *The works of Eggeling and Richter demonstrate a clear path. The principles according to which they are ordered are the constructive principles of our own nature, a creative synthesis—a great condensation and seamless integration from the smallest to the largest, from the largest to the smallest.*[88]

Thus the principle of unity according to which Hilberseimer sought to shape the metropolis appeared in exemplary form in avant-garde cinema, suggesting

[87] Ibid., 182; compare to this volume, p. 270.
[88] Ludwig Hilberseimer, "Bewegungskunst," *Sozialistische Monatshefte* 27, no. 10 (1921): 468.

that Hilberseimer's interest in integration across scales was coupled with an interest in conceptual integration across disciplines. In this way the laws of art might have an impact on the laws of architecture in the metropolis.

In Hilberseimer's theory, the individual building is no longer a basic element of architecture. Instead, buildings are either aggregations of rooms or units of larger urban blocks. The task of metropolisarchitecture is thus not the design of singular monuments; it is the shaping of "an often monstrous and heterogeneous mass of material." As Manfredo Tafuri long ago recognized, Hilberseimer's theory rejects the unique architectural object as a possible basis for practice: "Hilberseimer did not offer 'models' for designing, but rather established, at the most abstract and therefore most general level possible, the coordinates and dimensions of design itself."[89] For Hilberseimer it was not the formal model but the law of form that mattered; he displaced architectural design from an aesthetic of speculation to one based on the architect's "organizational ability." Hilberseimer summarized this position by recalling his own philosophical roots:

To form great masses by suppressing rampant multiplicity according to a general law is Nietzsche's definition of style: the general case,

[89]   Tafuri, *Architecture and Utopia*, 106.

the law is respected and emphasized; the exception, however, is put aside, nuance is swept away; measure becomes master, chaos is forced to become form: logical, unambiguous, mathematics, law.[90]

The Vertical Dimension

In October 1924, soon after the exhibition of his work in the Sturm gallery, Hilberseimer embarked on a tour of Western Europe. He traveled to the Netherlands where he visited Amsterdam, Utrecht, Rotterdam, and The Hague and met Gerrit Rietveld, Jan Wils, J. J. P. Oud, and others. Hilberseimer then traveled to Paris, and with the help of a letter of introduction from Paul Westheim, the editor of *Das Kunstblatt*, met Le Corbusier.[91] Hilberseimer was already familiar with Le Corbusier's work, but the meeting of the two in Paris seems to have been decisive for

[90] Hilberseimer, "Großstadtarchitektur," 188–89; compare to this volume, pp. 279–80. Fritz Neumeyer has located the source of Hilberseimer's statement in one of Nietzsche's posthumously published fragments of 1888: Fritz Neumeyer, "Nietzsche and Modern Architecture," in *Nietzsche and "An Architecture of our Minds,"* ed. Alexandre Kostka and Irving Wohlfarth (Los Angeles: Getty Research Institute, 1999), 303; Friedrich Wilhelm Nietzsche, *Sämtliche Werke: Kritische Studienausgabe*, eds. Giorgio Colli and Mazzino Montinari, 15 vols. (Munich: Deutscher Taschenbuch Verlag and de Gruyter, 1980), 13: 246. Hilberseimer would use this paraphrase of Nietzsche's thoughts on style in many texts, including the final lines of *Großstadtarchitektur*.
[91] Mengin, "Modelle für eine moderne Großstadt," 203.

Figs.
17–19

Figs.
14–16

Hilberseimer's urban thinking. After his return to Berlin, Hilberseimer developed his schema for a High-rise City, which represented both a departure from his earlier interest in the decentralized programs of Ernst May and a response to Le Corbusier's Ville Contemporaine for three million inhabitants (1922). First published in his pamphlet *Großstadtbauten* (Metropolis buildings) of 1925, the High-rise City lent Hilberseimer's conceptual program visual form and presented a synthesis of his critique of the capitalist metropolis.[92]

Hilberseimer's response to Le Corbusier notwithstanding, the High-rise City also represents a condensation of German thought on the tall building and urban density. Already in 1899, the industrialist, politician, and writer Walter Rathenau had recommended the introduction of the "City principle" into German urban planning to accommodate the fact that Berlin was transforming from "Athens on the Spree" to "Chicago on the Spree."[93] Rathenau used the English word "City," shorthand for the City of London, to distinguish the central business district from the rest of the *Stadt*, or city. And as Rathenau's identification of Berlin with Chicago suggests, the City also referred to what Americans might call downtown or the city center. Following

[92] Ludwig Hilberseimer, *Großstadtbauten* (Hannover: Aposs-Verlag, 1925).
[93] Walther Rathenau, "Die schönste Stadt der Welt," *Die Zukunft* 26, no. 1 (1899): 36–48.

Rathenau's recommendations on urban form, Karl Scheffler offered a program for an ideal metropolis based on the City principle in his 1913 book *Die Architektur der Großstadt*:

> *In the center is a logically formed City, a commercial city, which constitutes the core of the metropolitan form and accommodates nothing but the forms that serve commerce and the historically valuable parts of the old city. At many essential points in this City, if not entirely, tall buildings will predominate, primarily office buildings composed of many equally valuable stories.*[94]

The City was imagined as a zone of increased vertical dimensions that was to be devoted entirely to commerce. As Scheffler made his recommendations, the tall building became a topic of popular interest. The daily newspaper *Berliner Morgenpost* (Berlin Morning Post) published a pamphlet on *Berlins dritte Dimension* (Berlin's Third Dimension) in 1912, which featured an affirmative contribution from Peter Behrens and a cover illustrating a city of towers by the artist Kurt Szafranski. In 1913 the architect-artist K. Paul Andrae initiated his series of views of Berlin as a city of skyscrapers, some of which would be featured in the "Exhibition of Unknown Architects" in 1919.

[94] Scheffler, *Die Architektur der Großstadt*, 14.

Hilberseimer's first serious consideration of the tall building appeared in the essay "Amerikanische Architektur" of 1920. In the firm grip of *Amerikanismus*—a particular mix of enthusiasm and apprehension for all things American that spread throughout Europe between the wars—Hilberseimer focused on the new formal problems presented by the skyscraper.[95] He praised John Root's Monadnock Building in Chicago for having demonstrated and interpreted anew the "cubic-rhythmic" basis of architecture. For Hilberseimer, Root's "reinterpretation of the window" was a major achievement. In the Monadnock Building the window lacks formal accentuation; it appears, in Hilberseimer's words, as a "positive function" that represents an "element in a pattern that is stretched around the entire building."[96] In Hilberseimer's interpretation, this simple, repetitive articulation based on the alternation of surface and aperture represented a "new unifying architectural moment." While Hilberseimer criticized many later skyscraper designs for their typical "Palladian misunderstandings à la Parisienne," he celebrated the strong "vertical-cubic" masses of Ernest Graham's Equitable Building in New York. Hilberseimer refined his thinking on the

Fig. 58

[95] On *Amerikanismus* see Jean-Louis Cohen, *Scenes of the World to Come: European Architecture and the American Challenge, 1893–1960* (Paris: Flammarion, 1995).
[96] Hilberseimer and Rusker, "Amerikanische Architektur," 541.

tall building two years later in *Das Kunstblatt*. His essay "Das Hochhaus" (The High-rise) of 1922 reiterated many of the points he had already made and expressed his wonder at the tall buildings of American cities:

Fig. 10

> *In New York's high mountain ranges of houses, the material ethos of our time found its most powerful expression. Like everything authentic that seeks formation* (Gestaltung), *materialism found its form here. While in Europe this hypertrophy remained limited, the uninhibited drive for speculation with the high-rises of American metropolises has produced something almost fantastical. Only in the East are there urban forms of similar, uninhibited fantasy.*[97]

Hilberseimer noted that the high-rises of New York appear as mountains because the tall building in America had generally been treated as a row house, which "despite the masquerade of styles relinquishes any individual effect." The situation in Germany was different, he claimed, where high-rises were being planned as the dominant features of individual streets and squares.

Hilberseimer was writing in the midst of Germany's *Hochhausfieber* (High-rise fever).[98] Prewar enthusiasm for the building type grew

[97] Ludwig Hilberseimer, "Das Hochhaus," *Das Kunstblatt* 6 (1922): 525.

into a variety of speculative proposals, the most widely publicized of which was the competition, announced in 1921, for a high-rise on a triangular site next to the Friedrichstrasse station in Berlin. With more than 140 projects submitted, the competition offered a panorama of German interpretations of the tall building. Reviewing the competition, Hilberseimer identified Hans Poelzig's brick-clad, tri-corner project and the Luckhardt brothers' horizontally articulated high-rise as the best of the competition. Echoing his critique of the extravagances of Expressionism, he noted that most architects had turned the event into an opportunity to "lose oneself in romanticism." Hilberseimer described Hans Scharoun's project as "more original than resolved."[99] While he failed to mention Mies's submission to the competition, in *Großstadtarchitektur* Hilberseimer offered an affirmative review of Mies's projects for tall buildings, calling his high-rise in iron and glass an attempt to "design the object from the very essence of the new task."[100] Hilberseimer's praise for Mies's project could describe his own approach to high-rise design, the first examples of which date from 1922–23. His project for the competition

Fig. 60

[98] Dietrich Neumann, *Die Wolkenkratzer kommen!: Deutsche Hochhäuser der Zwanziger Jahre: Debatten, Projekte, Bauten* (Wiesbaden: Vieweg, 1995).

[99] Ludwig Hilberseimer, "Architektur," *Das Kunstblatt* 6 (1922): 132.

[100] Hilberseimer, *Großstadtarchitektur*, 68.

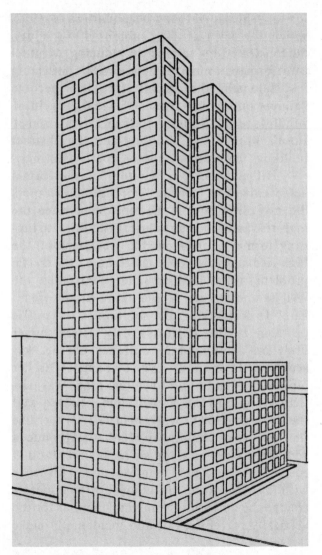

Fig. 4 Ludwig Hilberseimer, Tribune Tower project, 1922

Fig. 4

for the Chicago Tribune headquarters of 1922, which was never actually submitted to the jury, demonstrated his interest in reducing architectural form to its most elemental state, confirming his statement that architecture had become "almost pure construction."[101] Its tight grid of windows recalls both the minimal articulation of Root's Monadnock Building and the abstract buildings featured in George Grosz's paintings.

Hilberseimer's celebration of the formal achievements of certain American skyscrapers did not blind him to the tension between the high-rise and urban structure. In addition to limiting formal expression, the treatment of the high-rise as a row house exacerbated the traffic problem, which Hilberseimer considered the "Alpha and Omega of the entire urban organism." In formulating his solution to the traffic problem in the High-rise City, Hilberseimer drew on contemporary critiques of the skyscraper. Raymond Unwin's paper "Higher building in relation to town planning" was particularly important. Unwin demonstrated that the concentration of workers in a skyscraper like the Woolworth Building in Manhattan produced

Fig. 56

congested sidewalks and sluggish circulation at rush hours. He argued that "you do not dispense with transportation by going up; you merely change the horizontally moving omnibus for the vertically travelling lift, and incidentally make

---

[101] Hilberseimer, "Das Hochhaus," 526.

walking for even short journeys far more difficult."[102] Unwin's conclusion that nothing was to
be gained from crowding was echoed by Werner
Hegemann in his book *Amerikanische Architektur
und Stadtbaukunst* (American Architecture and
Urban Building-Art) of 1925.[103] A résumé of the
international urban planning exhibition held in
Gothenburg in 1923, Hegemann's book celebrated neo-Renaissance and other traditionalist
trends then active in the United States. It also
presented preliminary studies by the Regional
Plan Association of New York. Harvey Wiley
Corbett's proposal for the superimposition of
multiple types of circulation was extensively
illustrated. Corbett had explored the vertical
stacking of transportation already in 1913, when
his provocative image of a city of elevated sidewalks was featured in *Scientific American*.[104] In
1924 he published a proposal for "different levels   *Fig. 5*
for foot, wheel, and rail" that was illustrated in a
series of drawings by Hugh Ferriss.[105] These
images featured prominently in both Hege-   *Figs.*
mann's book and *Großstadtarchitektur*. Corbett's   *11–12*

[102] Raymond Unwin, "Higher building in relation to town
planning," *RIBA Journal* 31, no. 5 (1924): 126.
[103] Werner Hegemann, *Amerikanische Architektur und
Stadtbaukunst: Ein Überblick über den heutigen Stand der
amerikanischen Baukunst in ihrer Beziehung zum Städtebau*
(Berlin: E. Wasmuth, 1925).
[104] Henry Harrison Suplee, "The Elevated Sidewalk,"
Scientific American 69, no. 4 (1913): 67.
[105] Harvey Wiley Corbett, "Different Levels for Foot,
Wheel, and Rail," *American City* 31, no. 7 (1924): 2–6.

Fig. 5 Harvey Wiley Corbett, Future New York, 1913; from Scientific American, *26 July 1913*

proposal for the submersion of rail traffic below grade and the elevation of pedestrian traffic above the street undoubtedly appeared to Hilberseimer as an exemplary solution to the circulation problems created by the high-rise.

Hilberseimer's critique of Le Corbusier's Ville Contemporaine echoed Unwin's and Corbett's critique of the skyscraper. He maintained that Le Corbusier's plan, for all its geometric elegance, was based on a faulty circulation pattern. Specifically, Hilberseimer questioned the arithmetic that allowed Le Corbusier to claim that he had increased the density of his city center and preserved 95 percent of the area as green space by concentrating workplaces in sixty-story skyscrapers. Through a calculation of the space required for the movement of pedestrians and automobiles, Hilberseimer determined that the demands of circulation would reduce the amount of green space available to each person in the central city to a minimal two to three square meters. This reduction effectively neutralized the value of open space in Le Corbusier's city center. "Furthermore," Hilberseimer wrote, "the vertical traffic will become downright catastrophic in these enormous sixty-story commercial buildings during rush-hour periods or in an emergency situation because, in eradicating the horizontal congestion of streets by imposing great spaciousness, Le Corbusier did nothing other than shift this horizontal congestion into a vertical congestion of

*Figs.
14–16*

high-rises."[106] Although he appreciated the strict order of Le Corbusier's geometric system, Hilberseimer understood it as only a relative solution to the traffic problem. An absolute solution would have to render traffic superfluous.

Despite Le Corbusier's emphatic application of the skyscraper, Hilberseimer viewed the Ville Contemporaine as an essentially horizontal urban form. Hilberseimer's High-rise City, on the other hand, depends on the superimposition of functional zones. It is, in his words, "two cities stacked vertically, as it were."[107] Hilberseimer's plan for a city of one million inhabitants is based on a series of long, slender slabs. In each block, five lower stories serve commercial functions; fifteen upper stories contain residences. As in Corbett's proposal for New York, elevated footpaths link residential zones; automobile traffic travels on grade; and rail traffic is submerged below ground. Because city dwellers are to live above their places of work, horizontal circulation within the city is reduced to a minimum. Although Hilberseimer's High-rise City has often been criticized for its lack of green space, he considered access to the natural world to be among the advantages offered by concentration: "in contrast to today's urban fragmentation, which results in hours of travel in

Figs. 17–19

---

[106] Hilberseimer, *Großstadtarchitektur*, 16; see this volume, p. 121.
[107] Ibid., 17; see this volume, p.123.

order to reach the countryside, the spatial concentration of this city enables one to reach the countryside quickly with the help of a corresponding well-developed rail system."[108] The High-rise City thus appears as a dense, organized, city center that integrates spaces of habitation and spaces of labor through vertical concentration—a site of metropolitan intensity situated within a broader regional landscape.

Hilberseimer's High-rise City was one of several projects for the reform of the metropolis produced in the early 1920s. The proposal could be compared to Richard Neutra's Rush City or Farkas Molnár's so-called KURI City.[109] Hilberseimer's contemporaries most often considered the High-rise City in relation to Le Corbusier's Ville Contemporaine. Hugo Häring offered a trenchant critique of each of their proposals in his essay "Zwei Städte" (Two Cities) of 1926.

---

[108] Ibid., 20; see this volume, p. 131.

[109] On Neutra's Rush City see Thomas S. Hines, *Richard Neutra and the Search for Modern Architecture: A Biography and History* (Berkeley: University of California Press, 1994); on Molnár's KURI City see Renate Banik-Schweitzer, "Urban Visions, Plans, and Projects, 1890–1937," in *Shaping the Great City: Modern Architecture in Central Europe 1890–1937*, ed. Eve Blau and Monika Platzer (Munich: Prestel, 1999), 58–72. Hilberseimer's High-rise City should also be compared to his relatively undocumented project for a *Wohlfahrtsstadt* (Welfare City), which sought to synthesize the seemingly countervailing tendencies of concentration and decentralization and was exhibited as a large model in Suttgart in 1928.

Häring saw the basic problem of urban planning as the creation of a "non-geometric concept of planning" that could accommodate human individuality. He opposed the subordination of human development to the "principles of organization of a mechanistic world" and noted that "man is entirely banished from Hilberseimer's city; in Le Corbusier's city he is only a guest, passing through."[110] Despite Hilberseimer's intentions, the Czech critic Karel Teige wrote in his essay "K sociologii architektury" (Toward a Sociology of Architecture) that Hilberseimer's city was based on the fundamentally Corbusian principles of maximum centralization.[111] Hilberseimer's High-rise City, and *Großstadtarchitektur* as a whole, found perhaps its strongest and most sustained resonance in the Soviet Union. In 1928, as the USSR was preparing for a wave of urbanization foreseen by the First Five-year Plan, Hilberseimer's High-rise City became the center of a debate in the pages of *Stroitel'stvo Moskvy* (Construction of Moscow). One commentator compared the project to Le Corbusier's ideas, which Soviet architects knew well, and praised it as a "rational attempt at solving the most pressing questions posed by the contemporary science of urban planning."[112]

---

[110] Hugo Häring, "Zwei Städte," *Die Form* 1, no. 8 (1926): 172–73.

[111] Karel Teige, "K sociologii architektury," *ReD* 3, nos. 6–7 (1930): 191.

In response, another critic anticipated Hilberseimer's later description of the High-rise City as a necropolis: "What is the vertical city? It is a cemetery! A row of houses shaped like gravestones enclosed by a green fence."[113] In 1932 significant portions of *Großstadtarchitektur* appeared in Russian translation in David Arkin's anthology of recent architecture of Europe and America *Arkhitektura sovremennogo zapada* (Architecture of the Contemporary West).[114] And the High-rise City would be featured, albeit with critical commentary, in Aleksei Shchusev and L. E. Zagorskii's *Arkhitekturnaia organizatsiia goroda* (Architectural Organization of the City) of 1934.[115]

Hilberseimer offered a final proposal for the vertical organization of the city in his "Vorschlag zur City-Bebauung" (Proposal for City-Center Development), 1929–30.[116] Created in response the Berlin City Council's decision to

Figs. 78–86

[112] Vit. L-v, "Vertikal'nyi gorod," *Stroitel'stvo Moskvy* 5, no. 7 (1928): 21–23.

[113] Iu. G., "Otvet na stat'iu Vit. L-va 'Vertikal'nyi gorod'," *Stroitel'stvo Moskvy* 5, no. 12 (1928): 18.

[114] See note 11, p. 22.

[115] A. V. Shchusev and L. E. Zagorskii, *Arkhitekturnaia organizatsiia goroda* (Moscow: Gosstroiizdat, 1934).

[116] The project was first published in *Das Kunstblatt* and subsequently expanded in *Die Form*. The essay published in *Die Form* was reprinted in *Moderne Bauformen* and is included in this volume: Ludwig Hilberseimer, "Vorschlag zur City-Bebauung," *Das Kunstblatt* 13 (1929): 93–95; "Vorschlag zur City-Bebauung," *Die Form* 5, nos.

institute new guidelines for high-rise construction in the city center, Hilberseimer's proposal represents a further development of
the High-rise City.[117] The project retains the superimposition transportation networks but removes
dwellings from the city center. This was to be a city
of work; specifically, *Kopfarbeit*, intellectual work
of the kind Siegfried Kracauer documented in his
study of the "intellectually homeless" salaried
masses of Germany's new class of white-collar
workers.[118] Underground parking garages and
subway platforms connect directly to the lower
floors of long, narrow blocks. The first two floors
of each block contain spaces for commerce: vast

23–24 (1930): 608–11; "Vorschlag zur City-Bebauung,"
Moderne Bauformen 30, no. 3 (1931): 55–59; see this volume, pp. 290–305.

[117] Hilberseimer's project was one of several responses to
this policy change that the Berliner City-Ausschuss (Berlin City Committee) had promoted since its founding in
1926. The Committee was a nongovernmental interest
group of Berlin-based businessmen. It was chaired by
Alexander Flinsch and received intellectual direction
from Martin Mächler. Hilberseimer's proposal can be
compared to Hugo Häring's studies for Berlin's city center. See Balg, ed., *Martin Mächler*, 169–172; Matthias
Schirren and Sylvia Claus, eds., *Hugo Häring: Architekt
des neuen Bauens 1882–1958* (Ostfildern-Ruit: Hatje
Cantz, 2001), 184–85.

[118] On Hilberseimer's city and the problem of intellectual
labor see Aureli, "Architecture for Barbarians," 6. On
Germany's white-collar workers see Siegfried Kracauer,
Die Angestellten (Frankfurt: Societäts-Verlag, 1930); Sieg-
fried Kracauer, *The Salaried Masses*, trans. Quintin Hoare
(London: Verso, 1998).

halls, storage spaces, sales floors, and so on. Above, two narrow, six-story slabs rise from the broad base. Separated by a courtyard that runs the length of the block, the slabs are devoted exclusively to office space. Their interiors are entirely open, constituting generic surfaces that can be reconfigured at will. Hilberseimer presented his proposal in refined plans and sections and a striking axonometric line drawing, which has been interpreted as an image in which "all dissonances and disjunctions are absorbed, all differences canceled."[119] Hilberseimer also presented his proposal in an iconic photomontage demonstrating the implementation of his plan on a multi-block site in a rectangle bordered by Unter den Linden and the Gendarmenmarkt in the center of historical Berlin.

The tension between the axonometric purity and the photographic concreteness that Hilberseimer deployed in his proposal corresponds to the tension that animates the relationship between the general and the particular in Hilberseimer's theory of the metropolis. If his Proposal for City-Center Development sought to address the questions raised by the city of intellectual work, Hilberseimer approached these questions from two extremes:

These very important and incisive questions require detailed clarification, which can only be

---

[119] Hays, *Modernism and the Posthumanist Subject*, 182.

accomplished through theoretical preparatory work, because the chaos of the contemporary metropolis can only be confronted with experiments in theoretical demonstration.[120]

The aim of experiment is "to develop, in the purely abstract, the basic principles of urban planning from contemporary requirements."[121] Abstraction from the particular is thus preparatory work toward the identification and coordination of the disparate relationships that constitute the metropolis.

This method—confrontation through abstraction—was already present in the High-rise City, and it might characterize Hilberseimer's fundamental approach to the metropolis. Both Hilberseimer's writing and projects can be seen as theoretical demonstrations that, despite the chaos engendered by "the principle of speculation," the metropolis, like the Constructivist object and the abstract film, possesses immanent laws of organization. In this way, Hilberseimer's projects for the metropolis were abstractions designed to reveal the elementary logic of architecture and urban form—theoretical experiments intended, in Hilberseimer's words, to enable the metropolis to "discover its own laws." Once discovered,

---

[120] Hilberseimer, "Vorschlag zur City-Bebauung," *Das Kunstblatt*, 93; compare to this volume, p. 112.
[121] Ibid., 94; compare to this volume, p. 112.

Hilberseimer thought, the basic elements of the metropolis could then be reassembled as a complex, ordered unity. Measure would then rule, chaos could become form, and logic would reign. Although Hilberseimer regularly insisted that his projects had no prospect of realization, he nevertheless maintained that "seemingly utopian hypotheses indicate the real path that necessity will force us to follow sooner or later."[122] The question today is whether we are too early or too late to see Hilberseimer's hypotheses tested by the force of necessity.

[122] Ibid., 94.

Metropolisarchitecture

The Metropolis

Design
of the
environment

The design of the environment is one of humanity's primary tasks. State and city planning constitute essential elements of this design. States and cities are mutually dependent and always interrelated. Metropolises, and world cities in particular, are the energy centers of both states and the world these states produce; they are intersections of the flow of human activity, economics, and spirit. The city, and above all the metropolis, therefore cannot be considered an independent organism existing for itself alone. The city grows with and is connected to the people who produce it; the all-encompassing economic system connects it to the entire civilized world. This world constitutes a collective organism. Comprehending the laws of this organism is a crucial preliminary task of planned design. The constructive method must follow an investigative analysis—a systematic investigation and evaluation of the fundamental and the essential.

Community
formation

Human societies produce organizational forms that correspond to their respective productive capacities: the loosely defined tribal area is replaced by the more firmly articulated village at the level of agrarian production. The firmly organized city emerges at the level of artisan production. At the final stage of industry, trade, and traffic—the highest stage of human social organization to date—the metropolis and world city appear.

The metropolis is a product of the economic development of the modern era. It is the natural and necessary result of global industrialization. Large cities of the past differ from modern metropolises primarily in their entirely disparate economic foundations. These cities of the past corresponded to the stage of material productive forces that determined the economic structure of the society that produced them. Therefore these historical cities cannot be compared to the modern metropolis and no portentous parallel can be drawn between them. According to Friedrich Engels, Roman imperial society reached the summit of simple commodity production but collapsed at the threshold of capitalist modes of production, while the modern metropolis presupposes the capitalist mode of production.[1]

Economic premises

The conspicuously large number of metropolises, in contrast to the relatively isolated larger cities of the past, is a further result of this modern economic organization. Indeed, there is a tendency to extend the metropolis across an entire country—across the entire civilized world. For the moment this trend operates in an overly exploitative fashion that corresponds to speculative private interests, which lack planned organization. Yet this tendency has the undeniable aim of productively integrating every

The large number of metropolises

[1] [Hilberseimer refers to the outline of the social and economic development of the Roman Empire that Engels provides in *The Origin of the Family, Private Property, and the State*, which was first published in 1884.]

person into the collective economic organism. It is important to recognize that the metropolis is not an enlargement of the antiquated urban model. The metropolis differentiates itself according to its characteristics, not only according to its size. A city becomes a metropolis only through the introduction of certain economic phenomena, primarily through the concentration of capital, people, and the industrial exploitation of both. With the disappearance of these factors, the metropolis will dissolve—a large population alone is not enough to make a large city a metropolis.

Today's metro-polis

Thus the present form of the metropolis owes its appearance primarily to the economic form of capitalist imperialism, which, for its part, developed in close collaboration with science and technologies of production. Its powers extend far beyond national economies and increasingly into the global economy. An excess of intensity and energy is achieved through extreme concentration and comprehensive organization. Since production for one's own needs is no longer sufficient, aggressive overproduction is encouraged; the focus is on stimulating needs rather than satisfying them. Thus the metropolis appears first and foremost as a creation of all-powerful capital; as a feature of its anonymity; as an urban form with its own economic, social, and collective psychic foundations that enable the simultaneous isolation and tightest amalgamation of its inhabitants. A rhythm of life amplified a thousand times displaces the local and the individual. Metropolises share a certain resemblance with one another; one finds an internationalism in their appearance. They do not relate to specific domains like royal capitals; that is, they represent neither the physiognomy nor the image of their state and nation.

Interna-
tionalism

By confusing metropolises with royal capitals, the seats of bureaucracy, many have branded metropolises parasites on the rest of their respective countries. They are seen only as consumers, not producers. Entirely misjudging its true essence, many have overlooked the fact that the metropolis itself accelerates economic production processes by drawing economic control ever faster and more consciously to itself. This acceleration has contributed greatly to the productive labor and intellectual achievements of the nation. Today's economic relationships simultaneously condition the metropolis and are, in turn, conditioned by the activity of the metropolis. Thus it is understandable that the metropolis is most strongly formed in nations that in recent generations have experienced the most intense industrial development: America, England, Germany, and Belgium. The Romance and Slavic nations have, as yet, very little of the required concentration of capital and highly reproductive proletariat.

With the fall of feudalism the bourgeoisie saw itself as the master of the world and assumed a place of power for which is was ill prepared.

Nineteenth-century forms of production brought unexpected development to nations that, without the organizational capacities required to manage such production, implemented entirely insufficient regulatory measures. With surprising abundance, a great number of forces clamored for and instigated the formation of metropolises, yet it was not possible to harness or organize these forces or to make their excesses useful to the general public or the collective population. Instead of thoughtfully and systematically addressing all public needs, one attempted merely to satisfy fleeting demands without consideration for general interests. Long-term responsibility was quite easily deferred. Everything was left to private initiative, whose essential point of view was to drive up land values and rental profits as high as possible. There was no general or directed aim, which would have been necessary to turn such a comprehensive social form as the metropolis into a functioning organism.

This is why the primary characteristic of metropolises is disorganization. The organizing spirit, as it is expressed in the management of great industrial and trade corporations, has been entirely disregarded in the planning and construction of metropolises. In the former the principle of the division of labor systematically organizes the entire company. In the latter everything is confused. Residential quarters are infiltrated by noisy, smoking factories or by traffic-producing

Disorganized city building

False growth

commercial buildings. The spatial exploitation required in the city center is thoughtlessly applied to residential districts as well.[2] Streets are schematically planned. Building codes are applied uniformly to all types of buildings without differentiating according to purpose or taking into consideration special characteristics. Metropolises lack any sort of organizing design. The more spontaneously and unexpectedly they developed, the more they are the products of mere happenstance. The various forces that compose metropolises run rampant, working against each other instead of collaborating, so energy is lost rather than gained. It is a misuse and consumption of people without result.

That the metropolis can be abused like everything else does not speak against the metropolis, but against the abuser. And the abuser is capitalism. Its ruthless exploitative orientation is concerned only with profit and profitability not with people. This is the basis of the destructive character of all of capitalism's enterprises, including the metropolis. Only in a socially ordered society, where production corresponds to the needs of people, not to the greed for profit of the privileged, can the metropolis become a purposeful organism, can it change from a destructive to a constructive entity. This

Abuse

---

[2]   [Hilberseimer uses the English word City in the original, which is rendered here as city center. He follows British usage of City as shorthand for a specialized business district. See this volume, pp. 64–65]

depends on the spirit that builds the city, which is today, however, of a very comfortable mechanistic variety.

A city born of the spirit of speculation will be always an artificial, never a necessary product. And everything artificial awaits an imminent downfall. According to Henry Ford the modern metropolis has been wasteful. It is bankrupt today and will tomorrow cease to exist because its lifespan is determined solely by its functionality and profitability.[3] When both fail, decline will set in.

The end of the metropolis?

So the end of the metropolis?

NO!

But an end to the metropolis that is based on the principle of speculation and whose very organism cannot free itself from the model of the city of the past despite all the modifications it has experienced—an end to the metropolis that has yet to discover its own laws.

[3] [Hilberseimer paraphrases Henry Ford's statement in *My Life and Work* (1922): "The modern city has been prodigal, it is to-day bankrupt, and to-morrow it will cease to be." Ford's book was translated into German in 1923. In German, "the modern city" is rendered as "Die moderne Großstadt" (the modern metropolis), bringing Ford's statement semantically closer to Hilberseimer's concerns. See Henry Ford with Samuel Crowther, *My Life and Work* (Garden City: Garden City Publishing Co., 1922), 193; *Mein Leben und Werk* (Leipzig: Paul List, 1923), 225.]

Urban Planning

The task of the urban planner extends far beyond the present. It is he who will determine, in broad strokes, the city and the urban life of the future. Therefore the basis of all urban construction must be a comprehensive plan, which, with thought and care, takes into account the various needs of a future community; considers the geographic and topographic location of the city; and does not leave the city's national, economic, and productive importance out of consideration. The definition of the means of transportation—train and canal routes, main streets, elevated and underground trains—is of primary importance. These are the arteries of the entire organism. Of similar importance is the division of the city into residential, commercial, and industrial quarters according to the conditions and qualities of the territory and in consideration of the corresponding needs. Likewise the building of parks, green spaces, and bodies of water throughout the urban organism is of great importance. In order to eliminate land speculation, which has had devastating effects on our cities, in the future such a plan must be preceded by a comprehensive expropriation of the land so that the city can develop spatially unhindered. The claims of private property must necessarily concede to the claims of the general public in the construction of a city. Urban planning is not a private concern but a public matter.

The task

Compre-
hensive
plan

Transpor-
tation

Func-
tional
division

Two
urban
types

Over the centuries two urban types have emerged, which seem, from a philosophical perspective, to be diametrically opposed, but in practice have influenced one another greatly: the naturally developing city and the artificial, geometric city.

The
natural
city

The naturally developed city is not the creation of a single will, but the product of a long evolution. Like the city of the Middle Ages, it is the work of many generations. It was organized either radially around a center—with a cloister, a cathedral, or a castle as the focal point—or it was organized along a river or military road with an extended center, so that the streets radiate out like fingers. The advantages of the natural city are found in its complete adaptation to the terrain. The physiognomy of its streets depends on the individual house, whose narrowness can

Camillo
Sitte

adapt to any form. Depressed by the desolation of today's cities, Camillo Sitte was the first to attempt to identify the causes of this bleakness and to propose remedies.[4] He took the medieval city as a model and made an artificial system the principle of this form of development. He mistakenly sought models in the past and tried to pose the problem of urban planning in purely formal terms, divorced from technical and hygienic factors. This urban system has nothing to offer the present. It is the result of slow

[4] [See Camillo Sitte, *Der Städtebau nach seinen künstlerischen Grundsätzen* (Vienna: Karl Gaeser, 1889).]

organic evolution. On the other hand, contemporary urban development, particularly in its scope, requires extensive foresight. Its specifications guide development down certain paths, so that the plan, which in the past was a result, becomes today a necessary precondition. These demands correspond in large measure to the geometrically partitioned urban system. It is a typical product of colonization. Even the peoples of antiquity used such a system for founding cities. It proved itself to be very suitable when it was important to quickly and crudely delimit urban terrain that was to be rapidly developed.

The geometric city

Yet despite the various forms this urban system acquired from the Renaissance through the Baroque, it has nevertheless been applied to the modern metropolis as primitively as it was to those old colonial cities, though the scope is indeed far greater. As a result of its schematic application, this urban system has been greatly discredited. Due to convenience, thoughtlessness, and lack of imagination, it has been senselessly applied without consideration for the terrain, the relationship to the sun, and without proper perspective or architectonic sense.

Schematic application

It has been much disputed as to which of these systems is superior. It is unnecessary to try to reach a general decision on this matter. Practical requirements and artistic sensibility alone are decisive. More important than any system is the organism that is to be designed. For creative people, systems are only a means toward design, never ends unto themselves. The widespread opinion that any unevenness of terrain prevents geometric planning is unfounded. The Baroque has shown that even on uneven terrain a completely organized and geometric layout can be achieved, as in the city of Bath built on the hills of Avon to the east of Bristol. Or to name a more recent example, Canberra, the new Australian capital which is being built according to the plans of the American architect Walter Burley Griffin. It is a consistently executed geometric design laid out on a hilly terrain dotted with lakes.

For the time being, American metropolises most purely embody the metropolitan type. Americans created straight streets for objective reasons: in addition to the clarity attained, which eases the flow of traffic, a rectilinear network of streets has the advantage of producing rectangular city blocks. New York has already had a district designed according to these principles for 100 years: Manhattan, today's business center. The layout of Philadelphia, whose center is based on a plan by William Penn, is founded on similar principles. In Washington the rectilinear network of streets is overlaid by a system of diagonal streets in order to ease traffic. Of particular note is the plan of the projected city Prince Rupert in British Columbia by Brett and Hall of Boston. The city is laid out on two plateaus that are divided by a deep stone ravine. The residential quarter extends along the inclination of a hill, with streets that are adapted to the

(Margin notes:)

Bath and Canberra

Fig. 6

American metropolises

Fig. 7

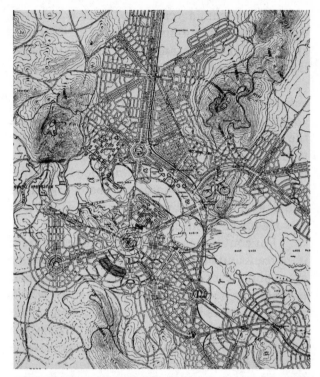

Fig. 6 Walter Burley Griffin, Plan for Canberra, Australia, 1911

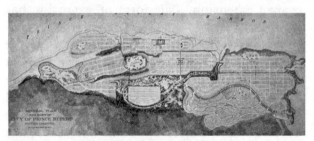

Fig. 7 Brett and Hall, Plan of Prince Rupert, British Columbia, 1909

terrain. The commercial city, which is situated on the plateau, is subdivided by a grid of streets. It is one of the few examples of a radical separation of the residential and the commercial city.

Neglected design

The common element in these urban projects lies in their neglect of design. Their construction is an undisciplined outgrowth of the urban plan. They are an inorganic accumulation of opposed elements. Their layout is determined exclusively by economic viewpoints, whose narrow-mindedness is becoming more and more apparent, thus throwing the usefulness of such urban forms into question.

City extensions

For contemporary urban planning the most important and most essential problem is the city extension. Several systems have been developed to meet this need, the most important of which are the concentric and the radial systems. The oldest is the concentric system: expansion through the installation of a new ring in the sense of a medieval city, where the circular defensive wall, if rebuilt farther out, allowed a new ring-shaped extension. This form of extension has survived even into the era of intensified traffic, yet it proves to be wholly inadequate for the metropolis. It enables not systematic growth but systematic compression. In the place of a ring formation, the radial system proposes a radial axis of development. Instead of forcing the developed and undeveloped land to conform to a belt-shaped space, a wedge-like extension allows a more intensive exploitation of undeveloped

The concentric system

The radial system

land for the population.[5] Yet this is also not a final solution but only a provisional remedy, which expires when the growing city has reached a certain size. Then this sort of extension is likewise no longer a fundamental improvement, but only an attempt at renovation made in the spirit of compromise.

The problem of the metropolis has yet to be solved in terms of residential hygiene or traffic management. For some time, one thought that the housing problem could be disregarded because this was primarily a matter of apartments for proletarians, who generally receive very little attention. For them, the worst was good enough. The traffic problem, on the other hand, soon demanded great attention. Yet both residential and traffic problems are closely connected, because the traffic of the metropolis is, of course, not an end unto itself but a means in the hands of the inhabitant of the metropolis. Thus the urban planner must consider them both at the same time, as they are the most important aspects of the entire complex of urban planning.

The sterility and unsustainable character of urban extension systems to date has already led to a new system of city extension and to a new

The unresolved system of the metropolis

[5] [Hilberseimer alludes to the wedge-like green spaces devised by Bruno Möhring and Rudolf Eberstadt as "green lungs" for Berlin in their entry for the Competition for Greater Berlin of 1910. See Rudolf Eberstadt, *Handbuch des Wohnungswesens und der Wohungsfrage* 4th ed. (Jena: Gustav Fischer, 1920), 232–33.]

The separation of districts

system of urban planning in general. Attempts have been made to create perfect housing developments through the complete separation of residential districts from centers of work. It is no accident that these attempts began in England, the country that without a doubt has the most developed residential culture. In England attempts have always been made to separate working and living quarters, which was, however, only ever possible for the upper classes. Here as well, the proletariat, the largest part of the population, was condemned to live in impossible apartments in working-class districts, which are the same in all metropolises. In a certain sense they make up the true international character of the metropolis. The rapid growth of the metropolises has only ever made these districts worse.

The satellite system

The separation or dissolution of the metropolis into residential and working quarters leads ultimately to the formation of the satellite system. Arranged concentrically around the heart of the city, the center, which in the future will only be a place of work, are self-sufficient living quarters at a sufficient distance — satellite cities of a limited population size, whose distance from the central city can be quite great given today's means of transportation, that of a rapid train system built specifically for commuters. In spite of the local self-sufficiency of these living quarters, they remain elements of a collective system, remaining closely connected with the city center, with which they form an economic and governmental unit. The residents of satellite cities work in the city center. The center will gradually become a place of work, without residential quarters, as these are to be fully excluded.

It will be objected that the transport of these great masses of people to the central city will cause extreme difficulties, even that it will be impossible, because currently it is not even possible to manage traffic within the metropolis itself. As justified as this critique is, one must keep the following in mind. Raymond Unwin, a specialist in housing at the English Ministry of Health and one of the key supporters of the satellite city system, has calculated according to statistics that 60 percent of all the workers in London work in districts different from those in which they live. Indeed, in many cases the number of workers who leave their district to go to work is the same as those who travel to the same district to work. Because these great masses of people—in New York there are three million—who must be transported to and from the central city, already live apart from their workplaces, they could just as well live outside the city in a satellite district. With systematic organization it is even possible for commuting time to be reduced and for the population to live in healthy, respectable dwellings. London already has two such satellite cities: Letchworth with 35,000 and Welwyn with 40,000 inhabitants, yet the city is working intensively on future satellites.

Masses of people

Constructing satellite cities also allows the developed area to be restricted. Building activity, which has always been distributed across the entire metropolitan periphery, can be concentrated at certain points, which will be relatively quickly developed and thereby always have a completed character. Today's urban periphery with its exposed firewalls and innumerable streets leading nowhere will disappear. The metropolis will become an organically unified figure and the necessary connection to open land will finally be established. Restricting the developed surface of the city will also be of great importance for traffic planning.

In connection with such a far-ranging urban extension, the inner city must be renovated and, accordingly, the population redistributed. By creating new residential quarters, the entire inner city will be made free for commercial life. Streets must be regulated, and narrow, unsanitary, and poorly constructed buildings and blocks must be demolished and rebuilt. Renovation must not be hindered by a sentimental consideration for history, because our task is not to conserve the past, but to prepare the way for the future. That even a medieval urban center can be reconstructed according to modern requirements is demonstrated by the sweeping renovation and redesign of Paris, which was executed by Georges-Eugène Haussmann around the middle of the nineteenth century. Even if this renovation was determined by strategic

The inner city is only a commercial city

Paris

considerations and is today outdated, its actual purpose was nevertheless to obtain a clear overview of the city and facilitate unhindered traffic by thoroughly organizing the urban center.

Martin Mächler's plan for Berlin is even more all-encompassing.[6] He has attempted to define a functional design for Berlin according to a comprehensive prognosis and has established parameters according to which his new organizational measures are to take place.

Berlin according to Mächler's plan

In order to meet the city's economic, social, and cultural tasks, Mächler allots Berlin a circular area with a fifty-kilometer radius, measured from the tower of the city hall.[7] The areas are divided according to the various requirements of economic and social life: there will be a reasonable ordering of consumer and producer groups, as well as places for work, leisure, and residence. The vital heart of Berlin is trade. The surface area defined by a six-kilometer radius from the tower of the city hall will be devoted to trade. This ring is to be surrounded by another of a ten-kilometer radius reserved for commerce.

Fig. 8

A wedge of sixty degrees cuts into this business and commercial zone from the west.

---

[6] [See Martin Mächler, "Denkschrift betreffend eine Ergänzung des Gesetzentwurfes zur Bildung eines Stadtkreises Groß-Berlin," *Der Städtebau* 15, no. 1–2 (1920): 3–12.]

[7] New York later adopted a plan for the future development of the city within a circular area defined by an eight-kilometer radius.

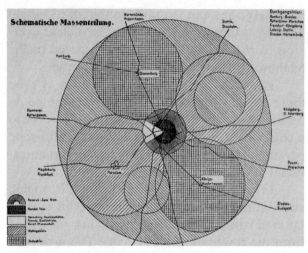

Fig. 8 Martin Mächler, Schematic distribution of Berlin's functions, 1920

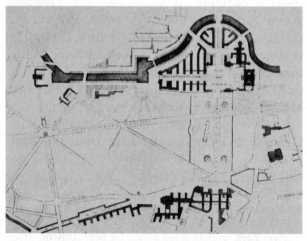

Fig. 9 Hugo Häring, Project for Platz der Republik, Berlin, 1927

Fig. 10 New York, High-rise street

Government offices, ambassadorial buildings, hotels, and institutes for art, research, and education populate this wedge from the center to the periphery.

The large outer ring contains facilities for leisure, sanitation, and agriculture.

The industrial settlements also contain space for workers' settlements because industry and the working population go hand in hand. Therefore industry must be located where it can provide workers with suitable housing.

Between the southwest and northeast industrial areas, the residential settlements are arranged along the waterways for those who work in the center.

The traffic network for Berlin

The precondition for this organization of Berlin is a correspondingly developed transportation system that will facilitate flawless traffic management. Through the creation of a central train station for Berlin, which is to be designed as a major traffic node, Mächler attempts to solve these problems. He gathers all of the rail lines that enter Berlin from all directions at two train stations at the northern and southern ends, respectively, of the city's inner periphery and directs them beneath the city by electric rail. The intersection which results will become a central train station which will be the focal point of both commuter and long-distance rail. This organization will render all terminal train stations superfluous, thereby radically solving one of the most difficult traffic problems in the center of the city.[8]

Fig. 9

Hugo Häring executed an architectural design for a detail of this comprehensive plan:

[8]   [Mächler's plan addressed the fact that most of Berlin's train stations were terminals, that is, end-of-the-line stations, which made transferring between stations and rail lines difficult, thus complicating the travel experience.]

the governmental center that is concentrated around the Reichstag. He attempts to create an entire urban space devoted to political functions, concentrating the buildings required into a political forum.

The immeasurable advantages the satellite system presents to the housing industry are offset by the above-mentioned disadvantages for transportation: such designs do not improve traffic in relation to today's traffic patterns, but neither do they exacerbate them further.[9]

By solving the housing problem only one of the most important challenges facing the metropolis is met. The problem of traffic, which is just as important, is not affected in the least by this attempt to solve the issue according to urban planning standards. The traffic within the central city will still contribute to and cause the same deficiencies. The horizontal expansion of urban land and the satellite system may be viewed as an excessive championing of horizontal urban planning. They will never offer the possibility of perfectly organizing the ever-increasing traffic in the city center of a metropolis. Everything from the outer districts will always surge toward the center, which, when a city has reached a certain size, simply cannot absorb all of the traffic. Complete chaos will ensue.

A one-sided solution

[9] [Compare to Hilberseimer's earlier advocacy for decentralization: Ludwig Hilberseimer, "Vom städtebaulichen Problem der Großstadt," *Sozialistische Monatshefte* 29, no. 6 (1923): 352–57; see this volume, pp. 42–44]

Fig. 10

This chaos in urban planning was exacerbated in America because buildings could be built at any height whatsoever until a building regulation was put in place in 1915.[10] In this way high-rises were built on urban sites that had been designed for relatively low development; a drive was created to outdo one's neighbor simply out of the desire to hold the record for the tallest building.

Disadvantages of skyscrapers

A skyscraper often creates fewer offices than the number of existing ones that it detrimentally affects by blocking the supply of light and air. Even more disastrous is the effect of tall commercial buildings on street traffic, which today defies description. When the employees of a clothing store want to go outside for fresh air during lunch they stand shoulder to shoulder. If someone needs to travel one–two kilometers in New York during business hours and is careless enough to choose a motor vehicle

[10] [Hilberseimer refers to the Building Zone Resolution adopted by the New York City Board of Estimate in 1916, which regulated the height and bulk of buildings and divided the city into three classes of districts: residence, business, and unrestricted. The resolution introduced the concept of the "zoning envelope," which limited the mass of a building according to predetermined formulas and stimulated the design of stepped-back skyscrapers. See *Commission on Building Districts and Restrictions, Final Report, June 16, 1916* (New York: Board of Estimate and Apportionment Committee on the City Plan, 1916), 223–44; Carol Willis, *Form Follows Finance: Skyscrapers and Skylines in New York and Chicago* (New York: Princeton Architectural Press, 1995), 67–79.]

as a mode of transport, he will be faced with
hour-long delays (Werner Hegemann).[11]

The impossibility of these conditions naturally increases with the height of the building.
Thus Raymond Unwin makes the following
observation on the 55-story Woolworth Build-   *Fig. 56*
ing. If an employee is allotted five square meters
of workspace, this building can contain 14,000
people.[12] If a standing employee is allotted 60
square centimeters of ground, then, if all of
these employees were gathered in front of the
building at the same time on a sidewalk six
meters wide, a sidewalk 855 meters long would
be required to accommodate these 14,000 people. But if one begins to calculate the figures for
these people in motion, then, with a necessary
surface for a walking person of 60 by 150 centimeters, a sidewalk of the same width would have
to be 2,100 meters long.

Because the Woolworth Building has but a
fragment of this sidewalk and because it is not
isolated, but between other buildings, even
if they are not as tall, one must wonder how circulation is even possible given New York's
narrow streets.

[11] Werner Hegemann, "Das Hochhaus als Verkehrsstörer
und der Wettbewerb der Chicago Tribune: Mittelalterli-
che Enge und neuzeitliche Gotik," *Wasmuths Monatshefte*
für Baukunst 8 (1924): 296.
[12] Raymond Unwin, "Higher building in relation to town
planning," *RIBA Journal* 31, no. 5 (1924): 125–50.

Street
conges-
tion

The congestion of streets for pedestrians is coupled with an even more severe situation for motor vehicles. New York's narrow streets allow only three automobiles to travel side by side, yet one is allowed to stop on both the right and left sides, leaving only one lane for unhindered motion—a condition that makes traffic obstructions ever more catastrophic. Here the consequences of neglecting the fundamental principle of urban planning—to never build a street higher that it is wide—are being felt. In America they are striving with all of their energy to solve this ever-increasing deficiency that threatens the existence of the metropolis. Under present circumstances the continued existence of the metropolis itself appears impossible.

Improve-
ment of
the street
system

*Figs.
11–12*

To ease the effects of congestion on streets caused by high-rises, the office of the state of New York has developed the Regional Plan of New York and Environs.[13] This plan attempts to create more space for vehicular traffic and to separate pedestrian and motor traffic by altering and improving the street system and by raising the level of the sidewalk above that of the

[13] [Hilberseimer refers to the New York Regional Planning Association, which was founded in 1922. The Association was not, as Hilberseimer suggests, a governmental organization. It was funded in large part by the Russell Sage Foundation and directed by the British planner Thomas Adams. See Michael Simpson, *Thomas Adams and the Modern Planning Movement: Britain, Canada, and the United States, 1900–1940* (London: Mansell, 1985).]

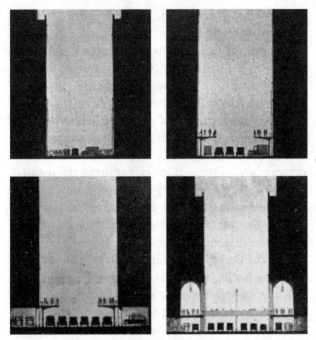

*Fig. 11 New York, Proposals for street expansions to accom-
modate traffic:* (Top Left) *Current condition;* (Top Right)
Elevation of sidewalks; (Bottom) *Elevation of sidewalks, the
use of the ground floor space of buildings for transportation,
and the enclosure of streets for pedestrian traffic*

street.[14] The City Planning Commission of Chicago is likewise attempting an urban renovation
of the inner city of Chicago, which has already

[14] [Hilberseimer refers to Harvey Wiley Corbett's design
for a system of superimposed traffic networks for lower
Manhattan. See Harvey Wiley Corbett, "Different Levels
for Foot, Wheel, and Rail," *American City* 31, no. 7 (1924):
2–6; see this volume, pp. 71–73.]

been partially executed. Though these attempts at improvement are greatly limited, they nevertheless signify a desire to bring about structural change. This is in contrast to the purely decorative attempts at concealing these problems undertaken by other cities. Some cities try to conceal the inadequacy of their urban structures through the introduction of broad avenues, which as a rule cut diagonally across the grid of the urban plan. In Philadelphia, for instance, the decorative extravagance of Fairmount Parkway in no way solves the deficiencies of the urban plan.

Fig. 13

It has yet to be made clear that in the construction of the metropolis one is faced with the organization of a new form with its own dynamics, which not only quantitatively but above all qualitatively differentiates itself from the city of the past. This is where the planlessness and chaotic character of all metropolises, which are entirely products of happenstance, derive from. As long as they have not reached a certain scale, it does not matter whether they are planned well or poorly. But their shortcomings become glaringly visible as soon as this scale is surpassed. This is the condition in which most of the so-called metropolises more or less find themselves today—first among them are the American metropolises governed by high-rises.

Metro-politan chaos

We have identified the character of the existing metropolis as a conglomeration, as an accumulation of disparate elements. Their development is a haphazard concatenation that

Fig. 12 New York, Proposal for a two-story street without intersections

Fig. 13 Jacques Gréber, Plan for Fairmount Parkway, Philadelphia, 1917

serves only immediate needs, without a higher perspective or sense of responsibility to the future. In contrast, the city of the future must have the character of a planned entity, of a fully thought-through organism. All deficiencies must be recognized and eliminated; the city must be systematically constructed according to its various elements and be designed in a completely new sense. It must embody the fundamental requirements of urban planning. The urban layout must be clear and manageable. Dwellings must be sanitary and comfortable. Enclosed residential courtyards are to be avoided. The blocks should be open and allow the circulation of air. The width of streets and courtyards must correspond to the height of adjacent buildings. Traffic must be regulated and separated according to type so that each sort of transportation mode is allocated its own respective level.

Sche-
matic
solutions

The chaos of the contemporary metropolis can only be confronted with experiments in theoretical demonstration. Their task is to develop, in the abstract, the fundamental principles of urban planning according to contemporary requirements. This will produce general rules that enable the solution of certain concrete problems. Only abstraction from the specific case is capable of revealing how the disparate elements that constitute the metropolis can be brought into an order of dense relationships. Attempts at such a fundamental analysis of the design of the metropolis have been undertaken by Le Corbusier and Ludwig Hilberseimer. Both attempt to organize everything that the population of a city of millions requires for life, labor, and leisure, with the intention of achieving a maximum amount of order, fulfilling everyone's needs for space, air, hygiene, and comfort, and of turning the city into an efficient organism.

Le Corbusier designed a plan for a city of three million inhabitants in order to demonstrate his principles of urban planning.[15] To allow absolute clarity of his intentions, he selected a completely flat terrain—a level surface without topographic hindrances, which enabled him to fully realize his geometric design.

He divides the population into three categories: the urban, the suburban, and the mixed. He calls the urban dwellers those who both work and live in the city. The suburban dwellers are those who work in the industrial zone and live in the associated garden cities. The mixed category describes those who work in the city but live in a garden city.

An urban form emerges as a delimited, dense, and concentrated organ—the center—and an extended, supple, elastic organ—the factory zone with garden cities. Between the two is an undeveloped strip of forests and meadows.

The principles of his plan include easing the pressure placed on the center, albeit with an increase of its population density, by increasing the means of transportation and increasing green space.

On a surface of 2,400 by 1,500 meters, 3,600,000 square meters or 360 hectares, in the city center stand twenty-four high-rises, which

Le Corbusier's urban plan

Figs. 14–16

Relief of the center

The high-rise core

[15] Le Corbusier, *Urbanisme* (Paris: G. Cres & Co., 1925).

Fig. 14 Le Corbusier, Ville Contemporaine, 1922; perspective

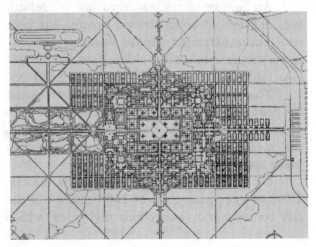

Fig. 15 Le Corbusier, Ville Contemporaine; plan

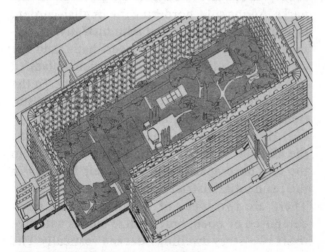

Fig. 16 Le Corbusier, Perimeter Block

occupy 5 percent of this area. They are cruciform in plan and without courtyards. They are of iron and glass and are to be sixty stories high. Every building accommodates 10,000 to 50,000 employees with an allotment of ten square meters for each. There are a total of between 400,000 and 600,000 workplaces. On average that amounts to an occupancy of between 17,000 and 25,000 employees for one high-rise, which corresponds to a density of 1,110 to 1,650 employees per hectare.

This minimal development, which occupies only 5 percent of the terrain, allows the construction of parks with playgrounds and sports facilities. Parking lots and garages are at the bottom of the high-rises. Restaurants, cafés, and luxury shops are arranged on terraces in the parks. At one side, bordering the English garden, is a forum with public and administrative buildings: museums, theaters, concert halls, and the city hall. The adjoining English garden is planned as a future expansion district for the city. To the other side of the city are docks, freight train stations, and industrial quarters.

The residential city

Insofar as they do not live in a garden city, the 400,000 to 600,000 employees who work in the city have apartments with their families in the residential district bordering the city center. There are two types of buildings. The first is composed of open, bracket-like blocks with five to six two-story dwellings stacked vertically. The density of these buildings is 300 persons per hectare with 85 percent open space. The second type is composed of closed blocks with the same density but with only 48 percent open space.

Nearly two million people live in the garden cities. Here construction is three stories high. Each dwelling has 100 square meters of living space spread over two stories and a private garden of 50 square meters. To this space is added 150 square meters of communal fruit and vegetable garden space and an adjoining 150 square meters of common recreation and sports areas.

The garden cities

In addition to residential building types, the street and rail system defines the structure of the urban plan. The spaciousness of the development permits a very favorable traffic system. The central train station is located at the center of the city. It unites all rail traffic: on the first underground level is the subway network, which has stations beneath every high-rise and residential block. On the second underground level are the long-distance lines. On the platform above the central train station is the runway for aerial transportation. Street traffic is similarly classified. Heavy vehicles and buses travel underground. All buildings stand on pillars so that the ground level is completely open. This level forms the "docks" of the buildings, where deliveries are unloaded. Light trucks, slow-moving private automobiles, and pedestrians travel on basement level. Both large, 180-meter-wide axial streets are equipped with elevated 40-to-60-meter-wide highways for fast-moving

The street and rail system

automobiles. These elevated highways are connected to street level by ramps.

Intersections and curves hinder traffic, which is why the number of streets is reduced and all of them are straight. Yet they do not only intersect at right angles, they also run diagonally. The module of street traffic is the distance between two subway stations, which is 400 meters. Thereby land parcels of 400 meters per side are created. The street loses its constricting corridor-like character due to the bracket-shaped buildings. It becomes more spacious and no longer feels closed in.

Fig. 10

Le Corbusier believes he has achieved not only a qualitative, but also a quantitative improvement of the city. The qualitative improvement is absolutely certain. His city is well organized and spacious. It is more a park than a sea of houses. The chaos of New York seems to have been overcome. Disorder has become order, insecurity has become security, disquiet has become quiet. The air is pure. Life is simplified. All the difficulties of today's metropolis have been eliminated. The entire problem has been wonderfully solved.

Critique

But if we investigate the quantitative improvement that Le Corbusier believes he has achieved, we reach a negative conclusion. The alleged enormous increase of population density of the city is based on a fiction, on the equation of incommensurable scales. The qualities of this city are not thereby annulled, but its quantitative improvement is greatly modified.

In contrast to existing cities, where streets become narrower as they approach the center, Le Corbusier places the broadest streets in the city center. How is this possible without reducing population density? Through amassing stories, which Le Corbusier increases up to sixty. This not only fails to reduce population density but even multiplies it.

The amassing of stories

The average population density of Paris is 364 persons per hectare; of London, 158; and of Berlin, 300. In the overpopulated quarters of Paris it is 533 persons per hectare; in London, 422; and in Berlin, 383. If one compares these figures with those that Le Corbusier believes he has achieved in the center of his city, 1,100 to 1,650 persons per hectare, one has the impression that, by utilizing high-rises, he has been able to triple the population density while maintaining a great quantity of open space. Upon closer inspection it turns out that he has compared incommensurable scales: the residential density of metropolises and the density of commercial occupancy.

An impossible comparison

While the ten square meters that he allots employees as workspace are quite sufficient (in America they are only allotted five square meters), this space is quite insufficient to meet the needs of a person at home. For residential purposes one should never assume an area of under thirty square meters for a single person. It therefore follows that the high level of density calculated by Le Corbusier is totally fictitious. It is founded on the impermissible equation of workspace and residential space.

As further proof, the following should be taken into consideration: we have ascertained that each of these twenty-four high-rises provides on average workspace for 17,000 to 25,000 employees. Each high-rise has a parcel of land of 400 by 400 meters (160,000 square meters, or 16 hectares) at its disposal. If one were to develop this 16-hectare area with exclusively five-story buildings, 20 to 30 percent of this area would be required in order to accommodate the same 17,000 to 25,000 employees, which would still leave 70 to 80 percent of the overall space undeveloped. Admittedly, Le Corbusier builds on only 5 percent of this 16-hectare area and intends the remaining 95 percent to be used as park and green spaces where sports facilities can also be housed.

Nevertheless, upon closer examination of these parks and green spaces, one is again led to essentially negative conclusions because there must also be sufficient street space available to the employees accommodated by the high-rises.

The demands on street space

For pedestrians alone one must allot one square meter of moving space per person. According to Erich Giese, the braking distance required by automobiles is about twenty-six square meters of traffic space.[16] Thus if each person is allotted

[16] Erich Giese, *Straßendurchbrüche als Mittel für die Lösung des Berliner Verkehrsproblems* (Berlin: Verlag der Verkehrstechnik, 1925).

an average of three–four square meters of street space, that comes to a total circulation area of 75,000 to 100,000 square meters. This spatial requirement causes the park and green spaces to shrink to such an extent that only two to three square meters are left per person. Furthermore, the vertical traffic will become downright catastrophic in these enormous sixty-story commercial buildings during rush-hour periods or in an emergency situation because, in eradicating the horizontal congestion of streets by imposing great spaciousness, Le Corbusier did nothing other than shift this horizontal congestion into a vertical congestion of high-rises.

As a result of equating residential density and the density of occupancy for commercial buildings, Le Corbusier gave the impression that he was able to triple population density. We believe we have proved that this is based on fiction. So, since it is also possible to attain the same density using buildings of only five stories, the only thing left to decide is whether one should build a city center of high-rises separated by large intervals or a city center of buildings of normal height. Vertical traffic can be reduced by increasing these twenty-four high-rises accordingly and thus the same effect with regard to density is produced using either buildings of normal height or high-rise developments. Thus it becomes clear that an economic problem has been turned into a problem of pure aesthetics.

It turns out that Le Corbusier's proposal is essentially an attempt to harmonize existing metropolises. In place of chaos he proposes the strict order of a geometric system. He does not create concentration, though initially this impression is made, but simply arranges and improves. There is no fundamental alteration or fresh reevaluation of the problem. Even the traffic problem is only restated, not newly formulated. His city center is indeed organized and spacious, but the relative increase of traffic is not thereby eliminated. The traffic problem cannot be solved by improvements that are always only relative. The traffic problem will not be solved by increasing the means of transportation but by radically eliminating the need of traffic.

The contemporary city is not dying because it is not geometric, as Le Corbusier believes, but because it is not organic. Geometric order is indeed an essential means for designing the city, but it is only ever a means, never an end unto itself.

Whereas Le Corbusier's city is essentially horizontal, despite its apparent concentration of the center and rigorous application of the theory of the satellite city, Ludwig Hilberseimer's is based on the vertical construction of the metropolis. Instead of further expansion at the ground level, Hilberseimer proposes further concentration and clustering—the construction of individual urban elements, functionally distinguished by their vertical placement. Two cities stacked vertically as it were. The commercial city and vehicular traffic lie below; the residential city and pedestrian traffic lie above. Subways and long-distance train lines lie underground.

Commercial city below, residential city above

Fig. 10

As a vertical city, it can be nothing other than a city of high-rises. Yet in contrast to the chaos of American high-rise cities, whose structure is arbitrarily defined, it must be systematically organized. The high-rise, which, like the tenement block, has long contributed to the chaos of the urban organism through the conventional subdivision of parcels of land, must be used in a completely new way. Its advantages must not be canceled out again by its arbitrary application. This is to be achieved by aggregating high-rises in blocks and through unified organization and design.

Because the residential city is located above the commercial city, everyone will live above his workplace. This aspect of the new city is similar to the city of the past. In the city of the medieval period residential quarters were placed above commercial and workspaces in a single house. What was individual in the past, in the age of manual labor, will become collective in the future, in the age of industry. Through this vertical stacking of commercial and residential cities, paths between them will no longer be traveled horizontally but for the most part vertically—taking place indeed even within the building itself, eliminating the need to ever step onto the street. Today's lengthy, time-consuming routes will disappear, simplifying both life and traffic and

Horizontal traffic, vertical traffic

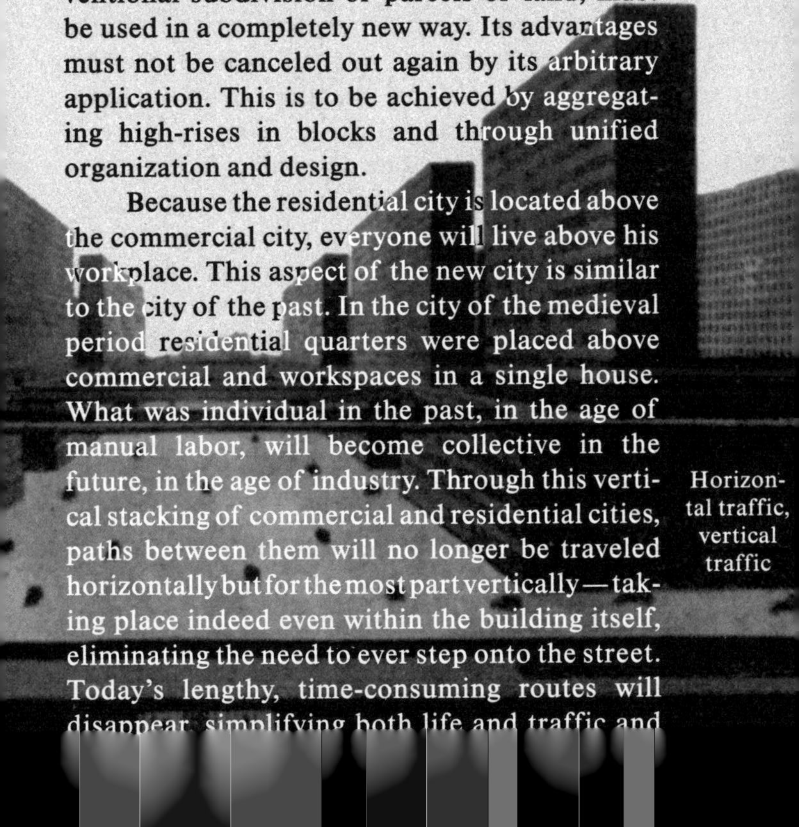

reducing the latter to the utmost. The detached house, which transformed the metropolis into chaos, will vanish. It will be replaced by the communal house, which occupies the entire block and includes apartments, work and commercial spaces, and everything else that life requires. The common street system, which is composed of numerous blocks of individual houses, which in turn produce innumerable courtyards without light or air, will disappear along with the detached house. The smallness of these blocks requires an expensive, tightly meshed network of streets, without thereby raising the quality of the apartments or functionally organizing the street system.

The new street system   The new urban form determines its street system in relation to the sun and the dimensions of streets and blocks according to the supply of light, air, and the requirements of transportation. The provision of light and air demands at minimum a distance between buildings that is equal to their height: street width equals building height. These considerations determine the width of streets and the depth of blocks because the distance between buildings inside the city blocks must also correspond to the height of the building. Block length is determined by the distance from the urban rail station. This produces blocks of extreme length but, because transverse residential structures have been eliminated, of minimal depth.

Ludwig Hilberseimer's plan, which is constructed from essential urban elements,

Fig. 17 Ludwig Hilberseimer, High-rise City, 1924; north-south street

Fig. 18 Ludwig Hilberseimer, High-rise City, 1924; east-west street

attempts to realize these requirements for a city of one million inhabitants in a purely theoretical schema without any intention of realization. The basis is a block 100 meters deep and 600 meters long that serves commercial functions in its five lower stories and residential functions in

The example

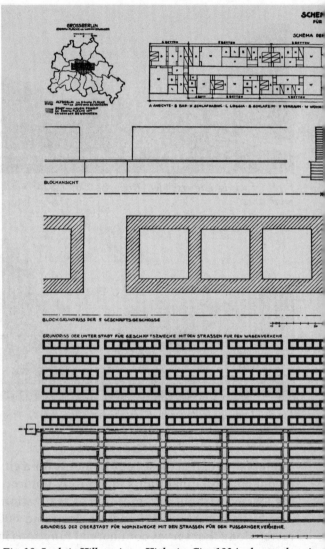

Fig. 19 Ludwig Hilberseimer, High-rise City, 1924; plans and section

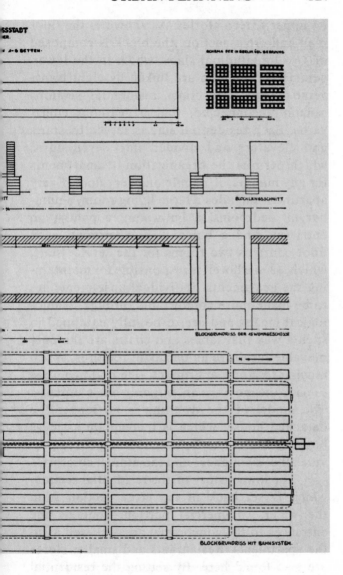

Fig. 19

its upper fifteen stories. As shown in the floor plan and cross section, the block is composed of two longitudinal slabs, which in the lower, commercial portion are linked by eight transverse wings. The upper residential sections remain unconnected, that is, without courtyards. Each residential slab is served by stairs and elevators and divided into seven units, which permits the organization of apartments for any number of people on every floor. Every apartment includes a large living room, a number of bedrooms, a bathroom, a pantry, an entryway, and a balcony. Furthermore, each floor contains two rooms for the service staff, which, as in a hotel, is responsible for maintaining the apartments. Individual apartments are to be made more comfortable through technological means and are to be fully equipped in such a way that tables and chairs are the only

Suitcase instead of the moving van

movable furniture an occupant requires. When moving to a new apartment, one no longer has to pack the moving van, but only one's suitcase. The model of the dwelling is no longer the detached house, which is inadequate as mass housing, but the hotel, which is adapted to provide all conveniences and the utmost comfort.

The lowest story of the residential section, which is set back in the cross section from the wider, commercial portion, contains the entrances to the commercial areas as well as to the apartments. Restaurants and smaller stores are also found here. By setting the residential section back from the commercial section of the block, a pedestrian path is created, which, although it is ten meters wide, only projects beyond the commercial portion of the building two meters. The elevation of the pedestrian paths requires bridges over the streets at intersections. Through this elevation today's most dangerous traffic calamity can be eliminated, that is, the crossing of pedestrians and vehicles on the same level. A sixty-meter-wide street for vehicular traffic is located in the commercial city; increased automobile traffic can develop here without issue. Most traffic must be served by the commuter rail system, however. It can only be located below ground. A system of superimposed rings that run in both directions along the main street will accommodate a system of continuously running shuttle trains. The placement of stations is of primary importance. City blocks are determined in their length by the distance from subway stations, enabling the construction of a superior urban rail system, whose stations are organized in such a way that they can be quickly reached even from the most distant point.

Long-distance trains also run through the center of the city in two directions. They are located underground as well, beneath the subway. A main train station in the center of the city, at the intersection of the two long-distance lines, enables the connection with the subway in both directions.

The schema of a city for circa one million inhabitants covering a surface of 1,400 hectares

Elevated footpaths

Circling subterranean trains

Long-distance trains

was designed on the basis of a building with fourteen residential floors that can house 9,000 people and contains circa 90,000 square meters of office and commercial space (so that every person is allotted ten square meters) on the commercial levels. If one enlarges this plan to cover a city of four million inhabitants, the approximate population of Greater Berlin, it would require an area of 5,600 hectares, which roughly corresponds to that of Old Berlin, where two million people live on 6,600 hectares.[17] Although the population density is thereby doubled, the quality of the apartments in no way decreases. On the contrary, quality will be greatly improved since all rooms receive sunlight, courtyards are eliminated, and residential slabs stand seventy meters apart. Thus these apartments are perfect and hygienically flawless metropolitan dwellings. They represent a solution to the metropolitan housing problem. Furthermore, because the traffic problem has been more or less solved by separating traffic types, but primarily by greatly reducing the traffic itself, it turns out that the vertical city, in contrast to the horizontal city, solves both of the most essential problems of urban planning.

The reduction of developed area achieved by building and population concentration also

[17] [Old Berlin refers to the city's municipal boundaries prior to the incorporation of outlying settlements into the Greater Berlin metropolitan region in 1920.]

enhances the benefits provided to urban dwellers by increasing the open and park spaces. All schools, hospitals, and sanatoriums, as well as sports and leisure areas, are to be embedded within these green spaces. Additionally, in contrast to today's urban fragmentation, which results in hours of travel in order to reach the countryside, the spatial concentration of this city enables one to reach the countryside quickly with the help of a corresponding well-developed rail system.

Advantages of concentration

These proposals should be considered neither as urban plans nor as attempts to normalize the city. Both are impossibilities because there is no such thing as the city as such. Cities are individualities, whose physiognomies depend on the character of their landscapes, populations, and functions in national and economic life. This is but a theoretical investigation and schematic application of the elements that compose the city. It is a determination of the relationships among these elements—an attempt to enable a more efficient formation of an urban organism by reorganizing and reapplying these elements.

The city as individuality

Urban planning is not an abstraction but rather the fulfillment and organization of real needs and purposes. Reality modifies every abstraction. Its conditions form the most essential factors of urban planning and therefore cannot be ignored when designing an urban organism.

In spite of each individual and unique characteristic, a city is integrated both economically

Regional
planning

and, in terms of its political temperament, intellectually into the entire nation, and the latter in turn into the entire world, wherein a city's achievements determine its rank and value. Just as the individual is only productive to society when he is able to suit his thoughts and deeds to fit society's objectives, so must the city, and even the nation, cooperate with other nations harmoniously in the building of the great human society. From this point of view, urban planning expands to become regional planning; urban planning becomes national planning. With this, Bruno Taut's theory of the dissolution of cities finally acquires actuality, especially as the progress of technology perfects radio and television and reduces traffic to a minimum.[18]

The
dissolu-
tion
of cities

But as far as the theory of the dissolution of cities can be taken, the national organism of the center—the metropolis determined by the structure of the overall population—will always be required.

The
necessity
of centers

The economic, social, and political life of a people is that of a tremendous suprapersonal individual. Even he, therefore, requires an instrument, which is continually exposed to all stimuli and is also capable of giving stimulus; an instrument that plays a similar role to the brain in the human body. The central city and

[18] [See Bruno Taut, *Die Auflösung der Städte* (Hagen: Folkwang-Verlag, 1920).]

*capital of a national organism are naturally
predestined to be physiologically equipped with
this instrument. This city is the collector, gener-
ator, and regulator of all material and spiritual
forces of a society* (Martin Mächler).[19]

Our concept of the city is for the time being
still founded on an ideology attached to the historical past. Although walls and gates have long
since fallen, their memory haunts our minds.
Urban projects, as they are currently being proposed for Paris and Tokyo, for nine million
people, or for New York, for thirty-five million
inhabitants, are based on premises entirely distinct from those to which we were accustomed
until now. They will therefore produce a new
type of city that will do away with the concept of
spatial cohesion, a concept we always used to
imagine our cities. Their great expansion necessarily leads to decentralization, which will only
be possible on the basis of the most intensive
concentration. Besides the housing problem, the
traffic problem will become the Alpha and
Omega of urban planning.

Of course a distinct separation by purpose
must exist. One will systematically group individual centers of work according to type, so
that industrial decentralization will take place

Marginalia: Historical burden

Marginalia: Decentralization and concentration

---

[19] Martin Mächler, "Denkschrift betreffend eine Ergänzung des Gesetzentwurfes zur Bildung eines Stadtkreises
Groß-Berlin," *Der Städtebau* 15, no. 1–2 (1920): 7.

alongside the establishment of concentrated points of global economic import. Or, for example, the economic and spatial connection within an industrial district will naturally grow together to form an enormous organically linked city. But this is extremely dependent on national planning. The design of the nation of the future depends on the formation of great economic complexes. It will depend on the merger of nations and nationalities into economic units. Thus, for us in particular, the unification of the politically divided European continent into an economic unit is the precondition for a productive and exemplary politics of urban planning, which will bring a solution to the as yet unresolved problem of the metropolis.

Residential Buildings

Until the middle of the nineteenth century, urban dwellings were in general the property of their inhabitants. With the introduction of freedom of movement laws and freedom of trade, a fundamental change was introduced in nearly all nations. The path to the city was suddenly opened to innumerable masses of people. Cities experienced an unforeseeable and rapid population growth, primarily in the numbers of the working class, but the number of buildings could not keep up. The sudden need for a great number of dwellings led to the construction of tenements. Since this time, the tenement has been the principal urban residential form, especially in metropolises. Other residential forms such as the small house and the cottage are of lesser importance than the tenement.

The rise of the tenement

This relatively sudden need for apartments was as surprising for architects as it was for the respective public authorities. In a free play of forces, building activity in metropolises was left to entrepreneurial builders and oriented toward mass production. The state and municipalities were helpless before these tasks, which were the results of new demands. They failed to recognize the social importance of housing and, in line with contemporary views, granted entrepreneurs absolute freedom. In this way residential construction became an object of speculation, which brought

The entrepreneur as builder

capitalists great returns to the detriment of social health. Pretentious facades often shamefully concealed multiple bleak courtyards surrounded by small apartments devoid of light and air. Pure materialism determined building plans that were mechanically designed and executed. Nobody realized that the only things being created were breeding grounds for sickness and discontent.

If these urban planners and speculators had even for one moment taken the somewhat higher ground, if they had even once viewed the masses, which were to be settled in these massive developments, not as a conglomeration of animals, but as vessels of spirit and soul, if they had but once learned to consider the settlements they created as one cell within a collective state, as an organic part of one great organism, ... then they would have seen how narrow, limited, and without insight or foresight their modes of operation actually were (Martin Mächler).[20]

The neglected residential building

Residential construction has been neglected as both a social problem and an architectural problem. It has been considered a simple job that can be taken care of on the side; at most the possibility of designing a facade was of interest. Its actual importance has not been acknowledged. Yet the residential building is the building

[20] Martin Mächler, "Das Siedelungsproblem," *Sozialistische Monatshefte* 27, no. 4 (1921): 185.

problem of the present. It is the actual problem of the architecture of the metropolis.

To date, the tenement has been built according to entirely false premises. Many have mistakenly sought to derive the building type from the individual house, which was above all conditioned by the narrow plots of land characteristic of private land ownership. Despite having exploited the land most cleverly, architects have attempted to maintain the external character of the individual house. This enterprise has led to the most grotesque deformations. It was never clear that the tenement building represents a new architectural problem, whose solution goes hand in hand with the solution of social problems. One had neither the courage nor the will to go to the source of the housing problem and tried instead to conceal the calculated uniformity of the plan and structure by uniquely designing the facade. Preoccupied by the external art of the facade, one forgot the actual problem, which is not one of form, but one of organization. Yet one believed to have exhausted the architectural problem in the design of the facade. Thus all attempts at reform have been directed to the facade, the supposed domain of the architect. The floor plan was to be monitored by the building inspectors, and the speculators and entrepreneurs had control of the most important and fundamental factors—the subdivision of parcels and city blocks. Nobody dared to intervene in this disorganized tripartite division of labor. Yet only when this state of disorganization is replaced by constructive organization can the problem of the tenement really be corrected and turned from a chaotic to an organic entity.

Since nobody truly grasped the object as such, everyone deviated from the fundamental principle of design, that is, that architectural law is to be derived from the object itself. This mistake was turned into an enduring principle. From this point of view the difference between the normal kitsch facade and a facade of tasteful classicism is relatively meaningless. On the contrary, the so-called art of facades is even worse than absolute kitsch. It strives to give the impression of culture and to turn a social problem into a formal problem. Yet it is nothing other than a tastefully executed artificial front.

Urban plan and building plan

The planning of residential buildings according to the blocks defined by the street system is of decisive importance. The site plan is closely related to the building plan. Only when both are jointly conceived can the ultimate goals of urban planning and hygienic demands be met. The self-evident north-south orientation of residential streets for low-rise settlements, which ensures the dwellings ample light, has been completely ignored when planning the layout of tenements.

Narrow, closed court-yards

The narrow, closed courtyard impedes air circulation, so that in a metropolitan apartment that which it most needs is lacking: sun, light, and air. Thus the typical street block of today, which uses buildings encircling numerous small court-yards, must be barred from use. Due to the exploitation of limited space in commercial quarters, the ample land found in residential districts is also being restricted, simply for the sake of greater returns and out of purely speculative motives. The speed of today's means of transportation can accommodate low-density construction in residential districts and their placement at great distances from the center of the city. Yet the tenement does not yet need to be forgotten and converted to a low-rise building. Residential construction in the metropolis will be able to do without cramped spaces, but, for economic reasons, not without multistory buildings.

Just as a system of streets and land subdivision has been created according to a speculative point of view, so must a system be created that takes the needs of the inhabitants into account in every way; one that considers life and general welfare. The most important requirement is to ensure that every dwelling, including the very smallest, has space, air, ventilation, and sun. Dwellings facing only to the north are to be avoided and the floor plan is to be arranged so that it meets all requirements.

The most important needs

The work of the speculator and the entrepreneur, executed without thought to planning, must be replaced by the systematic work of the consciously responsible architect, whose task is to take into account general needs as well as constructive, technical, and hygienic conditions, facts, and demands. Nevertheless one must not deny the fact that residential construction is, in large part, a question of production. It is dependent on economic factors, which cannot be ignored without cultural consequences.

The politics of land

New ground must be broken both in the organization of the overall plan and in the handling of details. In the future tenements will not be designed based on the arbitrary borders of private property. Instead, collective associations, building societies, and unions must take initiative in residential construction, or, as in the example of Holland, cities and the state itself will be involved by employing qualified architects.

It is imperative to exploit all of the advantages that arise from combining individual parcels of land into one unified block, which could contain a great number of the most ideal dwellings. Combining numerous apartments into one larger unit enables facilities to be established that are uneconomical for the standard tenement, but required for life in the metropolis. The entirety of metropolitan life is cluttered with facilities that arose to help accomplish basic household tasks, yet are today completely senseless. Just think of cooking in many individual kitchens or of laundry being done in many individual sinks.

Organized home economics

While all work is regulated by the principle of the division of labor and the combination of forces, at home the medieval form of solitary labor has persisted. The solitary person—the woman—has to perform the most diverse tasks, without ever really arriving at productive achievements, so that she is oppressed by the diversity of her work and her energies are dissipated. The reason that new forms of work are required here is twofold.

> *On the one hand is the demand to bring home economics, which is a great portion of general economics and includes the greatest portion of consumption, into harmony with the total economy and to increase its productivity, and on the other hand it is necessary to create conditions that enable women to live fulfilling lives. That means organizing household labor, that is, a systematic dismantling of the total work required within a household, and reassembling it anew, taking into account the imperatives of time and energy conservation, and, at the same time, improving labor techniques by introducing machines, which must be presupposed in the context of such a reorganization* (Meta Corssen).[21]

With a little knowledge and understanding of the restrictive factors of petit bourgeois life, which are rooted in the individual household, the amalgamation of these many costly individual tasks will not only save time and money but will also, given truly productive labor, greatly

[21] Meta Corssen, "Hausarbeit," *Sozialistische Monatshefte* 30, no. 1 (1924): 51.

simplify home life and significantly raise the standard of living.

A comfortable and practical dwelling should meet all of its inhabitants' needs while utilizing the minimum amount of space. The size and number of rooms depend on which demands must absolutely be met. Rooms for living, eating, sleeping, washing, and cooking are necessary and should be organized and arranged in the floor plan so that residential needs are met using the least possible amount of space. It is very important for the small apartment to be meticulously designed because although this is the type with the fewest means at its disposal, it is the most common form of dwelling in the metropolis.

The smallest apartment for a family with children of both sexes must have at least one living room, which is also used for meals, three bedrooms, a kitchen, and a bathroom equipped with a toilet. With an area of seventy square meters—an area that corresponds to a normal three-room apartment in Berlin—this spatial requirement can be met if functions are strictly separated. The most important requirement is that this area be organized according to purpose. The disorganization of the typical small apartment forces inhabitants to use every room for sleeping so that no real living or dining space remains. Meals must then be taken in the kitchen, which is plagued by smoke and fumes from cooking. If one organizes this area according to

purpose and limits the size of the rooms to a necessary minimum, then a type of dwelling can be
found that meets the minimum requirements of a
family of five to six people.

The dimensions of a room can be reduced
only to a certain degree. But dimensions are
defined by purpose, the number of people who
are to use a room, and the type of furniture
required. Furniture in particular, which is closely
adapted to human dimensions, will be a decisive
influence on the dimensions of rooms. The size
and placement of furnishings must be most carefully considered. Additionally, at least one room
should be slightly larger than the others because
today's economic situation limits the space allotted to a small dwelling and living in narrow
rooms becomes oppressive and cramped, while
the contrast between smaller and larger rooms
has an enlivening effect. In a small dwelling the
living and dining room, as a dual-purpose space,
must have the largest dimensions, while the
remaining rooms can have the smallest possible
dimensions. No portion of a room, even the
smallest, can go unused. Even a very small room
can be comfortably furnished and meet the
requirements of developed living standards if it
is systematically organized. A better model than
Berlin's uneconomical apartments is the furnishing of a ship's cabin, which contains all necessities
in the smallest amount of space. Or consider the
efficiency of the kitchen and furnishings in a
dining car, where in the most compact space, a

The
dimen-
sions of
rooms

great number of people work; this conveys the incredible efficiency of which an apartment is capable. Furthermore, living rooms in the rest of the world are much smaller than those we are used to in Germany.

In order for the dwelling to achieve such efficiency, all cabinets and closets for clothes, linens, luggage, dishes, etc., as well as all of the kitchen's furnishings must be built-in. When even the smallest surface area matters, then things can no longer be left to chance as was customary until now. For the cost of the space that furniture requires, one can comfortably build everything necessary in, so that in the future beds, chairs, and tables will be the only movable furniture to be dealt with.

The simplification and adaptation of interior furnishings to their proper uses and the elimination of everything unnecessary will simplify and ease domestic labor. First of all, in every house heating stoves should be replaced by a central heating system connected to a water heater. This will not only save a great amount of work, which is especially crucial in a small, narrow household, but will also be less expensive, since less fuel will be needed. Furthermore, the unclean fumes caused by stove heating will be eliminated.

The best apartment is without a doubt one that contains all that is necessary, fulfills all needs, and at the same time requires the least amount of labor. The comfort of living depends less on the size than on the functionality of the rooms in an apartment. The tenement can and must be designed in such a way, as it is unfortunately not today, so as to become a perfect organism combining the greatest comfort with the smallest expenditure of energy. Once it has freed itself from the false model of the individual house, it will become increasingly akin to a hotel outfitted with all modern conveniences, which embodies the most comfortable and freest way of living in today's world.

A fundamental change in the equipment and furnishing of a dwelling will be introduced with this economization. The ornamental complexity of furnishings customarily found in an apartment, especially in the prewar years, no longer corresponds to our way of life. These stucco ceilings, richly carved furniture, and costly wall paneling are indicators of poverty, not wealth. They correspond to the stucco-kitsch of facades and fulfill similar functions: they serve to conceal unsolved spatial problems. The design of the room can only proceed using the components of the room. Walls, floors, ceilings, doors, and windows are its most essential elements whose unresolved character one tries to conceal with pretentious luxury furniture and decorative works of art. The room and furniture are to be defined by their functions as basic commodities. Their systematic construction and design will lead to that simplification which distinguishes every strictly and objectively executed object.

Furnishings

The room and furnishings must be designed with an architectonic sensibility. Spatial relationships, illumination, and color determine a room's formal character and must produce its unity. The room is to be as neutral as possible, even in its coloration, because it is not a means unto itself but a means to meet very specific demands. It is only good when it completely fulfills those demands.

Fixed and movable furniture

By installing all cabinets and closets, furniture will be practically reduced to beds, chairs, and tables. By eliminating decorative furniture, which piles up in our present dwellings as if they were junk shops, space will suddenly be created in the smallest rooms, so that, in spite of its diminished size, the new apartment will have much more usable space than a larger standard apartment, which is however stuffed like a furniture storehouse.

Thus one will have to devote full attention to these few remaining types of furniture. Their small number will make them meaningful once more, and their full value and purpose will again be acknowledged. After all, furnishings should not be useless decorations but perfect, functional objects.

But functional organization is not enough to reduce the cost of residential construction. The uneconomical waste of space corresponds to uneconomical working methods and the uneconomical use of materials. In the future great attention will have to be devoted to both

because material costs and wages determine
construction costs. Martin Wagner has determined that by reducing the tasks carried out on
the building site to a minimum and by thoroughly
planning the working process, that is, by the
improved organization of work, building costs
can be reduced by 50 percent.[22] If one also calcu-
lates the reduction of costs offered by the
industrial production of individual building elements, then it is in no way a utopian assumption
that in the future building costs will amount to
but a fraction of current and past amounts.

Reducing construction costs

Although the problem of new materials is
being investigated everywhere, we still do not have
these new materials. We need an independent
research institute to conduct the necessary experiments and analyze the results. This new material
should by no means be a sub-standard substitute
material. On the contrary: it must be superior to
current building materials. It must perform its
tasks with greater perfection. Construction itself
will have to be given new foundations. As in the
construction of commercial buildings, in housing
construction one will also have to separate load-
bearing elements from those that merely enclose,
that is the supported elements, as Auguste Perret
attempted decades ago in his apartment house on
the Rue Franklin in Paris. The problem of the

New materials

[22] Martin Wagner, *Probleme der Baukostenverbilligung:
Ein Beitrag zur Verbilligung des Wohnungsbaues* (Berlin:
Verband Sozialer Baubetriebe, 1924).

load-bearing frame has been immaculately solved in iron and reinforced concrete in Ludwig Mies van der Rohe's exemplary and systematic application of this system of construction to the residential building.

Fig. 50

The material problem of the wall needs to be solved according to these structural premises. This problem is at least recognized today. It is evident that this requires a light material so as to not further burden the load-bearing structure. To date little attention has been paid to the proper insulating properties of walls because the prescribed thickness of brick walls, which is far more than is structurally required, offers enough protection. Today's conditions forbid such an inefficient waste of materials. Therefore one will have to search for materials that are light, have a low factor of heat conduction, allow for industrial production, and further simplify construction by no longer requiring a coat of plaster—that is, materials that are weather resistant, combine solidity with lightness, reduce noise, and provide good insulation.

Not handwork, but industry

By eliminating plaster, the entirety of interior finishing will change, especially carpentry. Even standardized windows and doors, which are indeed industrially produced, are firmly based on the principles of handwork. Windows, doors, closets, and cabinets have always been assembled from multiple pieces. This is an expensive and time-consuming task that must be replaced by economical working methods and new materials that allow for complete industrialization. Perhaps windows, doors, closets, and cabinets will be molded out of metal or out of another material that can be molded in a similar fashion.

The industrialization of construction requires that all building elements be strictly typified and all details standardized. The residential building, especially one that houses a great number of inhabitants, requires a design oriented not toward the individual but toward the collective. Due to its production methods, the entire construction industry is calling for typification. In contrast to the unique product delivered by handwork, industry produces serially and is therefore oriented toward standardization and the benefits this process provides. As in the automobile industry, industrial housing construction will achieve ever more refined forms and more perfect designs as a result of standardization and its application.

Even the development of designs and details by architects requires a great amount of unnecessary work that is of no use to housing construction, which is the central concern. This field also requires a comprehensive typification that applies not only to details, but also to the entire organism of a dwelling. By thoroughly systematizing design, typifying building elements, and standardizing details, a set of models will result that can accommodate every variation and expression, just as the letters of the alphabet, words, and the principles of grammar, in spite of

Type and norm

their apparent exhaustion, become something completely new in the hands of a creative person.

Whether one wills it or not, today's conditions demand that the entire field of construction be thoroughly industrialized. Also, the number of young professionals in specialized building trades is insufficient. This is apparent even now when very little is being built and it will be even more so when construction once again proceeds at a normal pace. Then the conditions themselves will inspire new methods, preparing the way for the industrialization of residential construction. Then houses will no longer be built, but put together from ready-to-assemble components and made suitable for habitation in the shortest time.

Funda-
mental
solutions

Fig. 20

The
American
tenement

The Chicago architect Frank Lloyd Wright is among the first to have attempted to fundamentally solve the tenement problem. His designs for the Lexington Terraces, which are based on the Francisco Terraces built in 1894 in Chicago, seek to solve the problem of the rental apartment through centralization. Three-, four-, and five-room apartments are brought together in the form of a unified block that is composed of internal and external groups of apartments. The internal group of apartments is separated from the external group by a narrow courtyard. The streetside group has three stories, while the courtyard group has two. Every apartment has two entrances, one from the street and another from the courtyard for service, which is provided

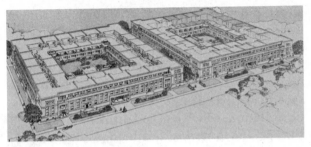

Fig. 20 Frank Lloyd Wright, Lexington Terrace Apartments, 1901; bird's-eye view

by building staff. The narrow courtyard onto which the bedrooms look must be considered a deficiency, yet it is determined by the peculiarity of American conditions.

Wright's smaller apartment buildings are distinguished by courtyards that open onto the

Fig. 21 J. J. P. Oud, Tusschendijken Apartments, Rotterdam, 1920–21

street, a typical feature of American apartment buildings that improves ventilation. Wright's apartments are oriented toward extreme economy. Rooms are differentiated according to functions. All cabinets and closets are built-in to save space. The complete renunciation of stylistic imitation, which has had disastrous effects in Europe and America, has here produced, from the task of building itself, exemplary works of a certain perfection.

The Dutch tenement

Fig. 21

The Dutchman J. J. P. Oud followed Wright in attempting to design a block of apartments as an integral unity. His apartment blocks in Rotterdam contain small dwellings and a systematically executed economization of living area. The floor plan is organized so as to allow variation in the size of apartments. A dwelling is composed of a living room, a kitchen, and, according to need, two to five bedrooms. The construction of these blocks is distinguished by architectural purity and unambiguity—through precision and clarity. Neither arbitrary interruption nor unmotivated arrangement is present. Only the windows, arranged on each floor-level and in the stairway as perfectly cut-out recesses, affect the undisturbed cubic mass of the block. This economical and functional use of space and distribution, which express securely defined living habits, stands in contrast to the arbitrariness of German spatial order and application, which necessarily leads to wasted space and fails to make dwellings more comfortable or livable. The scarcity of funds and the general decline in prosperity of the postwar years have, however, led to extensive efforts at economy, which have greatly reduced the amount of living space allotted to a single person, indeed making it seem insufficient.

For example, the city of Vienna has prescribed an area of thirty-eight square meters for a small apartment, which is far too little for a large family. Nevertheless, Anton Brenner was successful in finding a very useful distribution of this small area using extreme economy and functionality. Every stairwell serves four apartments, which are separated from one another by a half story. The apartments have an entryway, a bathroom with washing facilities, a kitchen, and a living room with folding beds for the children, and a bedroom for the parents. The living room and the parents' bedroom are separated by a wall of cupboards. The kitchen has been compacted into four square meters and contains a built-in cupboard, gas stove, and dishwashing equipment, yet there is still enough room to work.

Adolf Rading has also attempted to reduce living space to a minimum in a design for a communal house. The imperative of spatial compression led to the idea of combining the living room area from each apartment, which had become far too small, thereby giving the inhabitants more freedom of movement. To do this the inhabitant would have to forgo the private dwelling and preserve only the bedroom as space reserved for him and him alone. Rading has

Viennese residential construction

Communal house

Fig. 22

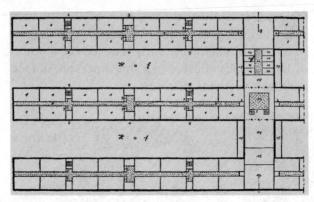

Fig. 22 Adolf Rading, Communal house, 1924; floor plan

shown that the floor plan of a standard six-bed-
room apartment can be divided into three
apartments of two bedrooms each, of which
only one would be equipped with a small kitch-
enette while the second would have a sleeping
alcove and at least a small section of living space;
the final apartment has only a space for sleeping.
But, in exchange, the inhabitants have numerous
communal rooms at their disposal—a central
kitchen, dining room, recreation room, a parlor,
music room, and reading room—and as a result,
life would be conducted as if in a hotel.

Excessive   Yet these attempts to conserve living space
spatial   have gone too far. They are only valid as tempo-
demands   rary emergency measures. The means to a true
economization is to be found not in the shrinking
of rooms, which makes both the apartment and
the inhabitant suffer, but primarily in a reasonable
economy of finance and real estate and in

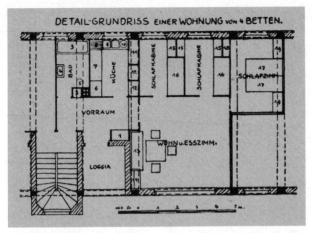

Fig. 23 Ludwig Hilberseimer, Four-bedroom apartment, 1923; floor plan

a systematically executed process of typification, which would enable the industrialization of residential construction. Only here can true savings be made and a great reduction of total costs achieved without detriment to the apartment as such. For it is precisely the metropolitan small apartment which requires, in the interest of social health, the most perfect design and especially the separation of rooms according to function.

Guided by these demands, Ludwig Hilberseimer has attempted to design a small dwelling and to create a typology of rooms for a tenement. His plan variations for three, four, five, six, and seven inhabitants are each based on identical spatial elements and satisfy the corresponding spatial requirements. The fundamental elements

Floor-plan variations

Figs. 23–24

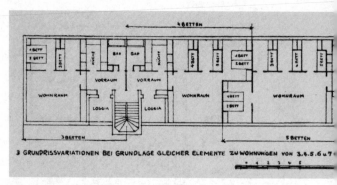

Fig. 24 Ludwig Hilberseimer, Variations of identical floor-plan

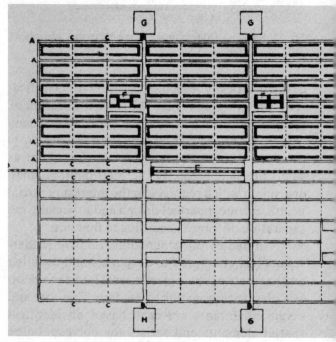

Fig. 25 Ludwig Hilberseimer, Residential City, 1923; plan

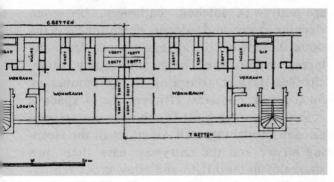

elements for apartments of three, four, five, six, and seven beds, 1923

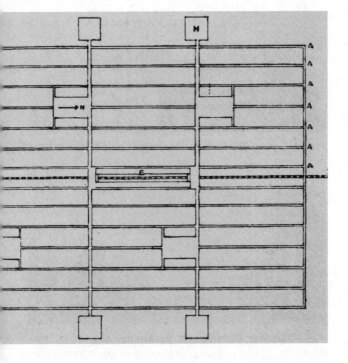

are entryway, kitchen, bathroom, bedroom, sleeping alcove, and balcony, which appear in the same dimensions in all apartments. Only the largest room, the living and dining room, changes its size according to the number of inhabitants. The most efficient use of space is achieved through built-in cabinets, closets, and kitchen furnishings. All rooms, even the sleeping alcove and the entryway, have their own source of natural light and allow cross ventilation. The two-story buildings at the northern

Fig. 26 Ludwig Hilberseimer, Residential City, 1923; perspective

Fig. 27 Ludwig Hilberseimer, Residential City, 1923; view of street

and southern ends of the block that contain stores lend the otherwise unformed mass a cubic form. They provide an animated contrast to the residential wings, open the block structure, and reveal its three-dimensional character. The arrangement of the block front is augmented by the slightly protruding stairwells as well as the balconies, which are deeply recessed, and this feature, in conjunction with the stairwells jutting out, creates taut three-dimensional accents. In the corresponding schematic plan of a residential city these elements are used to organize an entire city (satellite city) of circa 125,000 inhabitants, composed of large, open, and ventilated blocks. The north-south streets are residential streets, while the few east-west streets are intended for commerce and traffic. The two train stations that connect to the city center are located so that they may be rapidly reached from any point in the residential settlement without requiring any other means of transportation.

Schematic plan of a residential city

Figs. 25–27

In contrast to these attempts to organize the rooms of an apartment according to their respective purposes and to permanently define the distribution of functions, there is also the possibility of allowing the tenant to divide the available space according to his own needs. This is made possible by introducing movable partition walls, or rather wall components, which can easily be fastened to the ceiling and floor and which, as a result of their maneuverability, will

Flexible layout of rooms

allow rooms to be divided up in any way at any time without issue.

Figs.
28–29

Mies van der Rohe realized these ideas for the first time in the apartment house he built for the Stuttgart Werkbund exhibition.[23] The floor plan of this apartment building is based on a sys-

Fig. 28 Mies van der Rohe, Apartment building, Weissenhof-siedlung, Stuttgart, 1927

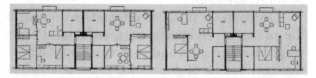

Fig. 29 Mies van der Rohe, Apartment building, Weissenhof-siedlung, Stuttgart, 1927; floor plan variations: left, *enclosed rooms;* right, *open rooms*

[23] [Hilberseimer refers to the building exhibition "Die Wohnung" (The Dwelling) at the Weissenhofsiedlung in Stuttgart in 1927.]

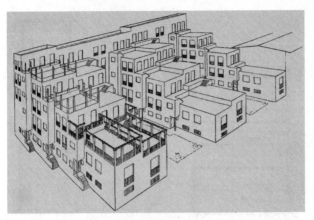

Fig. 30 Adolf Loos, Terraced apartment building, 1924

tem of pillars and party walls between the individual apartments. The walls surrounding the kitchen, bathroom, and stairwell are the only fixed walls. All other subdivisions are made according to the wishes of the tenant through movable wall components. With six to nine such wall components every spatial variation is possible, as the floor plans demonstrate, without thereby exhausting the variety of possibilities.

Tenements that provide each apartment with direct access to the street, in spite of the high number of individual dwellings, represent a special type. The gallery structure of Michiel Brinkman in Rotterdam includes 262 living units that are arranged in a four-story block in such a way that each individual apartment has its own entry. The apartments of the ground floor and the first floor have direct access to the street. The

Direct street entry

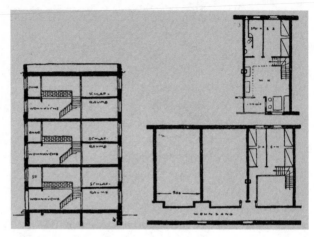

Fig. 31 Heinrich de Fries, Apartment building with split-level apartments, 1919; section and plan

upper apartments are reached by a second-story gallery. These upper apartments are of two stories. A living room and a kitchen occupy their lower quarters, while the upper story contains three bedrooms.

Two-story apartments in England

The Stepney House in London by Harry Barnes and W. R. Davidge is an arrangement of enclosed two-story apartments (maisonettes) within one large block. Its ten floors contain five vertically stacked two-story living units, which are each accessible from a gallery running the entirety of each floor. Each apartment has a hallway with a stair leading up, a living room, a kitchen, and a balcony in the lower portion. The upper story has three bedrooms and a bathroom. The very functional distribution of minimal space shows that even in mass housing the best elements of English residential culture can be maintained.

Heinrich de Fries has further developed this idea of the two-story apartment.[24] By differentiating between the heights of the floors, he exploits space effectively and achieves strong spatial contrasts. His fundamental theory is as follows: a cubic, relatively tall apartment structure is vertically cut into two parts widthwise. The wider front section takes up the entire height and contains the living room, or rather, the kitchen, which includes dining and living facilities. The shallower rear portion is divided into two half-stories containing bedrooms and other rooms. The upper portion of the living room has a gallery connecting it to the building's main stairwells, which, as a result of this design, are only required at great intervals, meaning that many apartments can be accessed by one or two staircases. Entering the apartment from the naturally lighted and well-ventilated corridor, one steps onto the interior gallery, passing two doors to the upper bedrooms and then using a small stairway to reach the large living room. The living room is equipped with an alcove for the stove, a window seat, and a balcony. From this level one enters the rooms of the lower half-story: the third bedroom, a room for washing dishes and laundry, and the

Two-story apartments in Germany

Fig. 31

---

[24] [See Heinrich de Fries, *Wohnstädte der Zukunft: Neugestaltung der Kleinwohnungen im Hochbau der Großstadt* (Berlin: Verlag der "Bauwelt," 1919).]

bathroom. The disadvantage of this distribution is that the cooking facilities are in the living space. It is a shame that the large living room must also serve as a kitchen. If the room for washing dishes were enlarged slightly, cooking could take place there too. De Fries did actually incorporate this idea into a later proposal.

Two-story apartments in France

Le Corbusier proposes a similar distribution, which, like de Fries's system of full and half-stories, is also based on the differentiation of ceiling heights. But in contrast to de Fries, who reacted to the demands posed by a small apartment, Le Corbusier's designs are based on more extensive requirements. Le Corbusier attempts to give the tenement some of the advantages of the hotel and at least a few of the merits of the villa. Each apartment is to have the advantages of a communal dwelling: common domestic servants, common social rooms, and a central kitchen, all of which provide the same freedom as a good hotel; that is, generally applying the hotel system of maintenance, meal services, and management to the private dwelling.

Figs. 32–33

His design for a building is composed of two residential wings that are connected by two transverse structures containing rooms for communal purposes. In total, the block houses 120 private apartments stacked in five layers. The floor plan organizes rooms according to need and purpose. Each apartment has two stories; the living room takes up the entire two-story space, the single-story spaces contain the

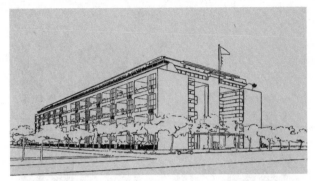

Fig. 32 Le Corbusier, Immeubles-Villas, 1922; perspective

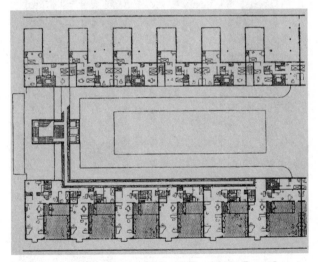

Fig. 33 Le Corbusier, Immeubles-Villas, 1922; floor plan

kitchen, dining room, bathroom, and bedrooms.
Each apartment also has a large balcony extend-
ing to both stories, which is to be used as a private
garden. The deep recesses of the large balconies

Fig. 34 Ludwig Hilberseimer, Boarding house, 1926; perspective

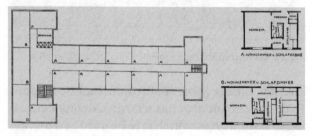

Fig. 35 Ludwig Hilberseimer, Boarding house, 1926; floor plans

create the strong three-dimensional character of the building, lending this apartment house its unique form.

High-rises will also become a possibility for the new way of life. In America buildings of ten to fifteen stories already exist, the so-called apartment houses. They combine every imaginable service and supply every comfort in the smallest amount of space. American apartment houses are furnished practically and are occupied especially by single people and couples without children where both members of the couple are employed. In general they comprise a living room that is equipped with a bed that folds away into a ventilated storage space, making it possible to use the space as a bedroom at night, a dressing room, a bathroom, and a small dining room with an attached cooking alcove. This cooking alcove is a furnished meticulously. It has a gas stove with an oven and a range, counter space for washing dishes, an icebox, a garbage chute, and all of the labor-saving domestic appliances.

An example of such an apartment house is the Surf Apartment Hotel in Chicago. It has nineteen separate very comfortable apartments on each of its nine floors. The ground floor contains the common social rooms. Service is conducted as in a hotel by building staff. In contrast to these apartment houses, which are designed for long-term occupancy and which are probably the future metropolitan way of life, are the actual hotels. America has also developed

The apartment house

Figs. 34–35

The American hotel

exemplary models of the hotel in terms of over-all organization as well as in the design of individual rooms.

The tasks to be fulfilled by such a hotel are far more numerous and encompassing than any European variant. Its grand foyer is a sort of public leisure space, which is also used by visitors who are not guests at the hotel. Hundreds do business, read newspapers, use rooms for dictation and writing, and take advantage of telephones, telegraphs, information desks, barbershops, shoe cleaners, and cafés found here. Single rooms and entire suites can also be used for exhibitions. Traveling doctors and other privately employed individuals schedule their visiting hours to be held in hotels for weeks at a time and use certain hotel employees as if they were their private secretaries and personal staff.

The lower portions of the building serve these various functions while the upper portions contain guest rooms. Guest rooms are all quite similar in their dimensions and furnishings. They consist of a bedroom, a bathroom with a toilet, and a dressing room. The number of guests in large hotels can reach the thousands. The Palmer House hotel in Chicago by Holabird & Roche can hold 4,000 guests in nineteen stories, while the five lower stories of the twenty-four-story building serve other purposes.[25]

[25] [Hilberseimer drew on Richard Neutra's detailed description of the Palmer House; see Richard Neutra,

The conditions of the metropolis have given rise to the small urban house as well as the tenement. The urban house's small scale seldom permits its construction as a freestanding building. For economic reasons, they are often built in pairs, groups, or in rows as local site conditions and the need for garden space permit. This form first appeared in English and American settlements intended for workers and civil servants in large industrial centers. Since they usually are the products of an individual or of a private, defined group, they always display a certain completeness and uniformity that is usually absent in tenements.

The small house

The first projects of this sort were, like most metropolitan undertakings, unsystematically executed. As in tenement blocks the crucial factor was always the pressing daily need, that is, the creation of the greatest number of buildings. In this way bare, long, dingy rows of houses emerged as can be seen in London and in German and Belgian industrial centers. Ebenezer Howard sought to improve this situation through the Garden City movement.

The English garden city

With the smallest amount of money possible for obtaining plots of land and erecting houses, a great number of reasonably sized apartments are to be created on a defined area, which must never-

Wie baut Amerika?, Die Baubücher, Bd. 1 (Stuttgart: J. Hoffmann, 1927), 24–43.]

theless remain undeveloped to such an extent that it can still meet all requirements of modern hygiene for air and light, enable a certain joy of life and leisure, and provide individual private gardens and a parcel of arable land to all inhabitants.[26]

Port Sunlight near Liverpool provided a model. A certain perfection was achieved at Letchworth and Hampstead. Architects such as Lutyens, Parker, Unwin, and Scott have played a great role in the design of garden cities.

English projects maintain a certain strictness of architectural design in spite of their adaptation to site conditions, while German settlements are more picturesque but lack an architectural design. More exemplary in the latter respect are the projects by Danish, Belgian, and especially Dutch architects, which are based on a more fundamental understanding of the problem of the garden city than are the German projects.

Together with Heinrich de Fries, Peter Behrens made an important contribution to the problem of the settlement in a work titled *Vom sparsamen Bauen* (On Economical Building), in which they attempted to fundamentally solve the issue.[27] It is clear that any such attempt must

[26] [Citation from an unidentified source. Howard's book *To-Morrow: A Peaceful Path to Reform* (1898), which inspired the English Garden City movement, was translated into German in 1907; see *Gartenstädte in Sicht*, trans. Maria Wallroth-Unterlip (Jena: Diederichs, 1907).]

[27] Peter Behrens and Heinrich de Fries, *Vom sparsamen*

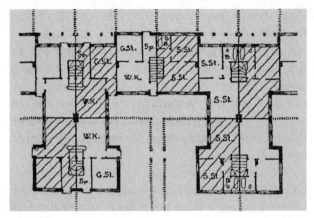

Fig. 36 Heinrich de Fries and Peter Behrens, Clustered row houses, 1918; floor plans

focus first on the question of economics. The factor that increases the cost of small house construction, excluding labor costs and land prices, is the cost of installing streets, sewers, and other utility lines, which is more expensive due to the yard space required for a single home. To economize the latter costs, de Fries and Behrens propose constructing houses in groups. Six or seven houses, according to the size of the housing types, are to be grouped in pairs, one behind another, so that the street frontage will only be used by four or five buildings. Using this layout in the development of an eleven-hectare area allows the construction of thirty-eight more houses on the same amount of developed area

Building in groups not in rows

Fig. 36

Bauen: Ein Beitrag zur Siedlungsfrage (Berlin: Bauwelt, 1918).

than would have been possible using simple row housing. Furthermore, this method also requires significantly less street frontage due to the relatively narrow space required for each house, thus resulting in a great reduction in the costs of utilities installation and other related ancillary costs. The architectural advantages of this method are also superior to those of simple row housing.

Common row houses have an amorphous, completely flat character, which architects have tried to counter with borrowed, purely decorative motifs such as oriels and gables. By gathering individual houses into groups, a three-dimensional arrangement of masses emerges as a result of the projection and recession of the houses themselves; that is, a powerfully accentuated corporeality becomes possible. Thus, by systematically fulfilling economic requirements, not only is money saved, but also the product of such systematically executed typification is a form that, as the embodiment of an organism, allows borrowed decorative motifs to be eliminated.

Until now settlements have been designed primarily with linear perspectives in mind. Rows of houses form narrow strips of buildings along the street, emphasizing its linear quality. In order to create contrasts, squares were added and streets were widened. These were often the result of a misguided reliance on urban forms of the medieval period; like oriels and gables, these designs were also used as decorative motifs

Plastic organization

intended to break up the monotony of the street and to lend corporeality to the linear, two-dimensional street form. In contrast, the method of building houses in groups also leads to an altered concept of the effects of streets and space. Space no longer translates into widening roads and sidewalks; rather, space signifies the open room between structures regardless of whether it is also being used as a place of traffic. Our old concepts of the street and space must thus be definitively reevaluated. By moving a portion of a housing group's allotted garden space to the front yard of the buildings, a spaciousness between individual housing groups is achieved, which puts an end to the uncomfortable closeness of multi-family housing arrangements and offers the advantage of making the area of the entire development available for useful purposes.

A change in the concept of space

Jan Wils produced an excellent example of the relaxed block front in his Daal en Berg settlement through the skillful manner in which he interlocked the individual houses. By employing projections and recessions across the entire building mass he creates an extremely animated cubic design and produces a strong contrasting effect.

Relaxing the block structure

Figs. 37–38

Victor Bourgeois successfully relaxed the building structure in a different way. In order of avoid the north-south orientation of houses in an east-west street of the Cité Moderne in Brussels, he sets them on an axis of forty-five degrees to that of the street, thereby creating a serrated development which receives sunlight from the

Sunlight in an east-west street

Fig. 39

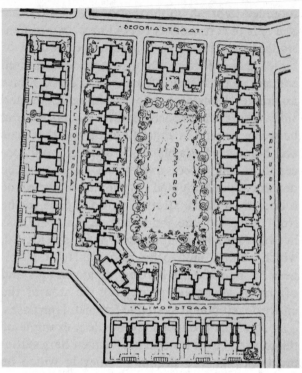

Fig. 37 Jan Wils, Papaverhof, "Daal en Berg," The Hague, 1919–22; site plan

Fig. 38 Jan Wils, Papaverhof, "Daal en Berg," The Hague, 1919–22

northern east-west and the southern east-west sides; at the same time, this design eliminates the rigid form of the street.

Ludwig Hilberseimer has also applied his typification and functional separation of rooms to designs for row housing and the small house. The floor plan is organized so that smaller rooms are arranged in the shape of an "L" and occupy one story, wrapping around the open two-story living room. The main floor contains the office, dining room, kitchen, and entryway. On the upper floor, which has a terrace above the living room,

Typification of spaces

Figs. 40–41

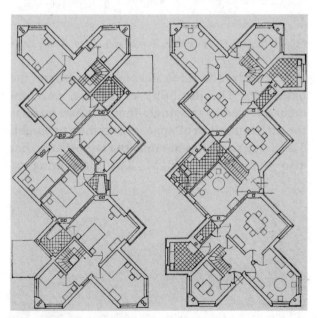

Fig. 39 Victor Bourgeois, Cité Moderne, Brussels, 1922–25; floor plans

Fig. 40 Ludwig Hilberseimer, Row houses, 1924; perspective

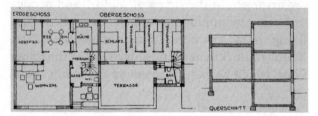

Fig. 41 Ludwig Hilberseimer, Row houses, 1924; floor plans

are the bedroom, three sleeping alcoves, and the bathroom. The flexibility of vertical development allowed by the single-family house enables the differentiation of spaces according to height. The living room has not only the largest area, but also the greatest height. The alternating of

Fig. 42 J. J. P. Oud, Hoek van Holland workers' housing, 1924

one- and two-story spaces produces a decisively three-dimensional construction, which is emphasized when arranged in rows.

In Hoek van Holland, J. J. P. Oud built a group of row houses particularly distinguished by its remarkable floor plan. This floor plan represents the perfect solution for the tenement. By exchanging narrow and broad room components, the apartment size can be altered in any way. Apartments are made up of one large living room, a kitchen, and, depending on their size, one to three bedrooms. At the corners of the blocks and in the courtyard-like recessions of the buildings are shops, whose special design lends a lively contrast of space and materials to the simple form of the block.

Fig. 42

Changing apartment sizes

Le Corbusier has made many attempts at perfecting the form of the small house. His most remarkable is the Maison "Citrohan," which in spite of its small area provides a very comfortable dwelling. The main living room has a double ceiling height; the dining room, kitchen, and the bedrooms, etc., are vertically stacked in three stories. Thus a strict differentiation of spaces emerges, not only in the rooms themselves, but also in their organization. Le Corbusier has devoted special attention to the problem of the typification and serial production of the small house. In the Pessac settlement near Bordeaux he had the opportunity to realize his proposals for the small house. This settlement is composed of single, double, triple, and row houses with

Spatial differentiation

Fig. 43

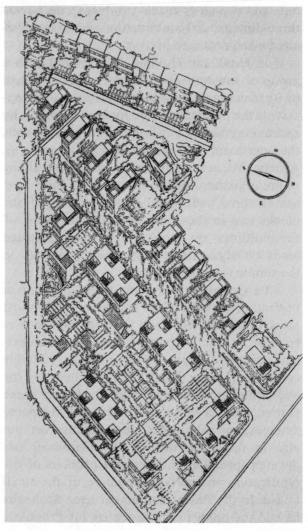

Fig. 43 Le Corbusier, Modern Frugès Quarter, Pessac, 1924–26; general axonometric view

small apartments. All of the buildings use the flat roof as a garden. Stairs are located on the exteriors of the single and double houses. The relatively narrow apartments, which extend back rather deeply, contain a kitchen, living room, a small and a large bedroom, and a bathroom. At the ground level, space is often left mostly open and undeveloped. This feature and the long strips of windows cause the houses to assume an ethereal quality, producing a light, almost floating effect. All of the houses are constructed with reinforced concrete and completed using serially produced building elements.

The Pessac settlement by Le Corbusier, the Törten settlement near Dessau by Walter

Fig. 44 Walter Gropius, Törten Settlement, Dessau, 1926–28; general axonometric view

An attempt to industrialize construction

Fig. 44

Gropius, and Praunheim near Frankfurt am Main by Ernst May are the first general attempts to industrialize construction.

In order to avoid the danger of uniformity, which can be seen in English suburban housing, Walter Gropius has attempted to typify individual building elements, not entire buildings. Various house forms can then be developed from these elements. Gropius believes that repressing individualism is wrong and shortsighted. His

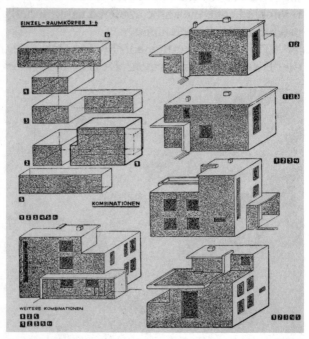

Fig. 45 Walter Gropius, "Life-size building blocks," 1923; building components

"life-size building blocks" can be put together into various types of houses, accommodating even the smallest details of building plans and any number of inhabitants and their various needs. Individual houses can thus be adapted to every need and allow infinite variations, while the construction itself, in spite of being made out of serialized elements, allows a rich diversity of appearance.

Building blocks

Fig. 45

By investigating functions that until now have been associated with the window—illumination, ventilation, and views—Hugo Häring has achieved a functional separation of these three purposes. A room is best illuminated by a skylight, while cross ventilation, occurring directly below the ceiling, is the most efficient ventilation technique. Views are best provided through clear single-sheet sliding panes of glass; that is panes without grilles, as in a Pullman rail car. When illumination comes from a skylight and when only a few windows are required for looking outside, the design of the floor plan obtains a great flexibility. However, illumination by means of a skylight requires that a building be only one story, but this does allow expansion on three sides, permitting a compact form of development. This is a significant result that ensures small and individual houses an existence in the immediate vicinity of a metropolis. One will perhaps raise the objection that the only rooms with a view are the living rooms, a prejudice that is based

Light from above for living rooms

Fig. 46 Ludwig Hilberseimer, Single-family house, Weissen-hofsiedlung, Stuttgart, 1927; general view

purely on ignorance. On the contrary, bed-rooms require no view, and secondary rooms most definitely do not; rather they need venti-lation and light, both of which will be provided to a greater degree than before.

The country house

Villas and country houses have always displayed more architectural value than the tenement, yet here even greater absurdities led to disasters in design. The villa and the country house are more or less luxury buildings. Their respective characters are influenced by individ-ual desires, and thus they are not to be developed as types, but rather given a distinctly subjective

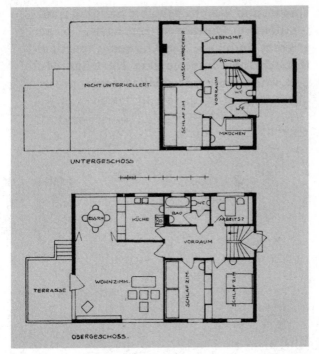

Fig. 47 Ludwig Hilberseimer, Single-family house, Weissen-hofsiedlung, Stuttgart, 1927; floor plans

character. The old private house has served as the model for the villa and the country house, and the traditional mode of building has produced valuable examples everywhere. This is true above all in the northern countries, especially England, where a distinct bourgeois residential culture has been developed, which is clearly demonstrated by the design of the floor plan. In the buildings of Lutyens, Scott,

English residential culture

Unwin, and Wood a valuable building tradition is still alive. These architects have also exerted a great influence on Germany, particularly through their intermediary Hermann Muthesius, who attempted to realize similar projects.[28]

Yet most of these buildings demonstrate a dispassionate character of schematic abstraction and rigidity, and they rarely display a trace of contemporary vibrancy. The impression and influence of traditional models have been so great that only a few architects have dared to take the leap into the present and to tackle the problem at its roots. The

The contemporary country house

contemporary country house distinguishes itself from that of the past through an entirely new mode of use. While in the past it was essentially determined by its opulent character, today it is more oriented toward functionality and providing comfort to its inhabitants. Thus it renounces in the first place any imposing axial arrangements,

Figs. 46–47

which place great restrictions on the spatial organization of a small building, and attempts, rather, to render the internal spatial organization legible on the exterior of the building.

The country house is unsuited for an arrangement in consecutive rows, in contrast to the tenement, whose isolation, even when it is

[28] [Hilberseimer refers to the English architects Edwin Lutyens, M. H. Baille-Scott, Raymond Unwin, and Edgar Wood. Hermann Muthesius popularized English domestic design in his influential work *Das englische Haus* (The English House); see Hermann Muthesius, *Das englische Haus* 3 vols. (Berlin: Ernst Wasmuth, 1904–05).]

intentional, is countered by the dynamics of the street layout. Country houses have an organic spatial relationship to the surrounding garden; their relationship to the street is only secondary. Therefore these buildings are well suited to exhibit originality; their relationships and spatial distribution are often modified by the uniqueness of the terrain—a quality that the country houses of Frank Lloyd Wright clearly display.

Wright's country houses demonstrate a completely new form of design in the manner in which their rooms are arranged, which corresponds to the American way of life. The living spaces are arranged next to each other virtually without any partition walls so that the principal common floor is one large, continuous room, which is nevertheless broken down according to the most various purposes, without ever being distinctly divided. This sort of spatial arrangement corresponds to a form of living that is entirely different from the European form.

Figs. 48–49

The contiguous living space

Their exterior construction demonstrates similar originality. In spite of a distinctly horizontal organization, it achieves a light, almost floating character through broad openings, great projecting terraces, and flat roofs. The extreme variety in the height of different parts of the building allows the rooms to be lighted by high-set side windows, groups of windows, or windows arranged in strips running along entire sections of the building. At the same time, these disparate heights serve to produce a lively cubic

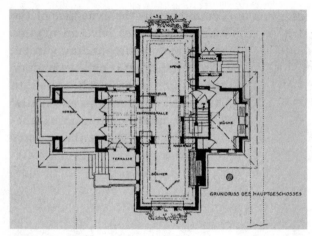

Fig. 48 Frank Lloyd Wright, Martin House, Buffalo, 1905; floor plan

Fig. 49 Frank Lloyd Wright, Martin House, Buffalo, 1905; general view

Emphasis on the horizontal organization of the structure. While American architecture, like German architecture, is generally vertical, Wright emphasizes the horizontal. He extends the flat roofs of his houses as well as balconies and terraces, creating contiguous, horizontal divisions, and he uses the horizontal to strengthen the vertical progression of his distinctly terrace-like houses. He also incorporates the environment of his buildings into the architectural design. The surrounding footpaths run parallel to the horizontals of the structure. The projections of the roof, the terraces, and other elements produce partially corporeal entities that effectively transition the indifferent quality of the air space into the corporeal determinacy of the building, whose weight is however simultaneously nullified optically. The influence that Wright has exerted can hardly be measured. Nearly all modern European architects are under his influence. In particular, Holland's vibrant architecture is unthinkable without Wright's example.

By exploiting the constructive possibilities of reinforced concrete, Mies van der Rohe also broke new ground in country house construction. Attempts to use reinforced concrete as a material for residential construction have been made many times, but for the most part they have been misguided. In general, architects simply tried to create stone buildings out of concrete. The advantages of the material were not recognized and its disadvantages not avoided. The principal advantage of reinforced concrete construction is found in its material economy, which is made possible by strictly separating load-bearing from non-load-bearing elements. Mies van der Rohe attempted to solve the problem of

New paths

Fig. 50

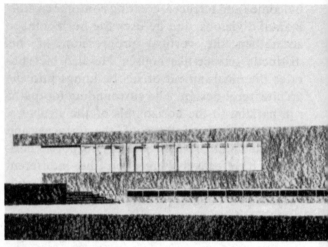

Fig. 50 Mies van der Rohe, Concrete country house, 1923

Fig. 51 Mies van der Rohe, Brick country house, 1924

the reinforced-concrete house in a design for a country house. The main residential portion is supported by a double-stem truss system. This system is enclosed by a thin layer of reinforced concrete forming both the walls and the ceiling. Openings are cut in the walls where required for lighting and views. The fact that the wall is freed from its former load-bearing function allows openings to be placed anywhere, creating stunning effects. The heavy corporeality of the building mass is dissolved and a floating lightness is achieved.

Games of form

While Mies van der Rohe systematically developed this effect from the mode of construction itself, many have tried to outwardly imitate these forms at great cost without, however, grasping the constructive sense of the new possibilities of form or the new organism. Mies van der Rohe's distance from such games of form is clearly shown in his brick country house. While it is a great departure from standard models, it also complies with its own constructive principles and the materials used. It is a new formation, created by a new spatial organism, not by a misuse of materials.

Fig. 51

Commercial Buildings

Centralization is one of the principal requirements of circulation in the metropolis. The need
to be able to manage various business matters
within a limited space gave rise to the principle
of the city center.[29] The new form of centralized
business operations led to the emergence of new
building types: department stores, commercial
buildings, and office buildings. These building
types require well-lighted working and sales
spaces, the ability to change the size and formats
of rooms, an unhindered flow of traffic, and the
complete exploitation of the building site. The
organization of these requirements produced a
new building type, in which the typically load-
bearing walls were reduced to pillars and the
building enclosed by walls was transformed into
a skeletal structure. Two possibilities for architectural design emerged: emphasizing the
vertical by turning the walls between the pillars
into plate glass or emphasizing the horizontal by
installing contiguous bands, between which windows are stretched, to strongly demarcate the
separate floors.

A new
building
type

The department store in particular, which is
the organizational form of a new business concept, has developed both vertical and horizontal

[29] [Hilberseimer uses the English word City in the original; see note 2, p. 89.]

Fig. 52 Alfred Messel, Wertheim department store, Berlin,

1896–1912

types. Alfred Messel's Wertheim department store in Berlin consciously emphasizes the vertical quality of the pillar system. It is a unique mix of daring construction and standard conventions: the new constructive principle is subtly framed by historical reminiscences. Established concepts of form are schematically applied and ornamentally exaggerated in the corner arcade building with its cathedral-like tapestry room. All of this betrays a certain tentative lack of confidence. Messel sensed rather than acknowledged the architectural consequences of the constructive principles he applied. This corner building, with its tall, narrow windows, has produced innumerable variations. See for example the Tietz store buildings designed by Olbrich in Düsseldorf or by Kreis in Cologne. Both still employ steep ornamental gables, required by such an emphasis on the vertical, to break up the crowning horizontal component; they overemphasize disjointed and disconnected qualities and signify a further vertical disintegration of the building mass.

Peter Behrens applied this principle with relative success to the small engine factory of AEG in Berlin. This "factory building" is essentially modeled after the Wertheim building. After everything superfluous was removed and the most essential qualities emphasized, the same basic rhythmic idea emerged: a simple arrangement in rows. This was executed with clarity, strength, and precision and the rows were architectonically connected. These exemplary characteristics are apparent despite the inorganic roof, required for usage and to comply with building ordinances, and despite the frieze that connects the pillars and the references to classicism.

Fig. 53 V. A. and A. A. Vesnin, Mostorg department store, Moscow, 1925

Horizon-
tality

American
depart-
ment
stores

French
depart-
ment
stores

Emphasizing horizontality offers more perfect solutions. The easily attainable cubic corporeality avoids the danger of dissolving the cubic component into pure linearity, which is what occurs when the vertical quality is overemphasized. The horizontal articulation of floors allows the expression of self-supporting, vertically stacked cubes. Such a design, which alludes to the principle of weight, does not contain the danger inherent in the systematic application of the vertical component, which is that the form itself will be disrupted. In addition, horizontal organization corresponds to the vertical stacking of floors. This is why, despite their historical reminiscences, the Louvres, Printemps, and Bon Marché stores in Paris produce greater architectonic effects than the vertically oriented German department stores. The same is true of such American department stores as Daniel Burnham's building for Butler Brothers or George Nimmons's for Sears, Roebuck & Co. in Chicago, both of which are based on a principle of horizontal design but are nevertheless completely romantic in an architectural sense. In contrast, Louis Sullivan's Carson, Pirie, Scott & Co. department store in Chicago and Otto Wagner's Neumann department store in Vienna, in which the horizontal stacking of stories is clearly expressed architectonically, are executed with greater consequence. Wagner's department store has the special characteristic that in his building, like the Tietz department store in Berlin designed

Bernhard Sehring, stories are defined by large contiguous panes of plate glass. These buildings were the first to realize the new structural possibilities offered by steel construction, which, just like reinforced concrete, allows pillars on the building front to be entirely eliminated by using instead projected horizontal constructive elements as load-bearing components. Thus, in place of an exterior wall pierced by windows or a front divided by pillars, there emerges a great plate-glass surface subdivided horizontally by metal strips. The same constructive principle was applied to a department store in Moscow designed by the architects V.A. and A.A. Vesnin. In this instance as well the front, without pillars, is composed of plate glass set in metal frames.

Fig. 53

Yet in the end these enormous plate-glass panes are nothing other than a new material romanticism. Shelves for goods are placed directly behind the panes of glass, so that their true function of providing better illumination for the rooms inside is partially nullified.

Material romanticism

In contrast, Erich Mendelsohn has taken account of this fact in his Schocken department store in Nuremberg by placing the bands of windows above the shelving units.

Office and commercial buildings have developed more slowly but with greater architectural logic, leading ultimately to the high-rise. Thus Messel's commercial buildings in Berlin are in great part based on the floor plans and construction of Renaissance palaces. Nevertheless

The office and commercial building

Messel has given windows and pillars equal weight by reducing the size of the pillars. The opposite is true of Ludwig Hoffmann's entirely decorative governmental buildings, where windows are relatively small and offices receive insufficient light due to Hoffmann's emphasis on historical architectural forms.[30]

Despite the presence of historical forms, in Richardson's and Sullivan's buildings the window becomes the most important element, thereby allowing the need for light to greatly influence the design of the building.

Reorganization of the floor plan

Fig. 54

The floor plan of the administrative building of the Mannesmann-Werke in Düsseldorf designed by Peter Behrens is organized according to the requirements of business operations. With this he achieves new possibilities for architectural design, which are, however, nullified by his classical orientation. In order to facilitate universal functionality, he has avoided permanently separating central working spaces. The main walls of these workrooms are subdivided by numerous identically shaped and narrowly spaced pillars. Through easily removable,

[30] [Ludwig Hoffmann was the Stadtbaurat (City Building Councilor) for Berlin from 1896 to 1924. Hilberseimer's remark reflects the opinion, which was shared by a number of progressive architects, that Hoffmann directed a conservative building department during his tenure; protest against his influence led indirectly to the foundation of the Ring of modern architects. See Dörte Döhl, *Ludwig Hoffmann: Bauen für Berlin 1896–1924* (Tübingen: Ernst Wasmuth, 2004), 177–82.]

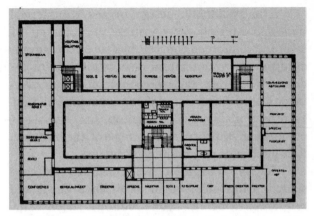

Fig. 54 Peter Behrens, Office building of the Mannesmann-röhren-Werke, Düsseldorf, 1910–12; floor plan

double-layer, soundproof partitions the size of the rooms can be altered at any time according to need. Thus rooms can range from the small two-window room to enormous halls accommodating many workers and with as many windows as desired. Built-in filing cabinets in the walls of the corridors perfect this practical usage.

Frank Lloyd Wright took into account the business operations of large organizations even more systematically. His administrative building for the Larkin Company in Buffalo is comprised of one single light-flooded space. Open workspaces on each floor surround the central light court. No partition walls hinder supervision and communication. Everything is functionally equipped. A unique form was logically developed based on what was needed.

Open work-spaces

The systematic design of the commercial building utilizing the constructive potential of steel and reinforced concrete has paved the way for entirely new architectural possibilities. As in the department store, skeleton construction has overtaken wall construction in the commercial building. Ensuring maximal illumination has decisively conditioned the form and purpose of the building, thus creating a new building structure.

Skeleton construction

Beyond that, the tectonic character of construction has changed in its essence. Steel and reinforced-concrete constructions have surmounted the old load and support system. Both enable the building mass to protrude beyond its supporting pillars. Thus, recalling medieval wooden construction, Hans Poelzig built his Breslau (Wrocław) commercial building in such a way that each story juts out beyond the one below it.

Overcoming the old system of load and support

Erich Mendelsohn has devoted his attention to the same problem, particularly in his expansion of the Mosse building in Berlin, though he addresses the issue indirectly rather than pointedly, and, to an extent, paraphrases it symbolically. He strives to articulate his independence from load-bearing vertical elements through the lateral and diagonal cantilevering of individual stories.

Mies van der Rohe has recognized the design possibilities of the new constructive theories with unique consistency; his design for an office building represents their architectural solution. A double-stem frame measuring eight

Fig. 55 Mies van der Rohe, Concrete office building, 1923

meters wide with a peripheral cantilever of four meters was established as the most economical construction system. This frame carries the ceiling panel, which at the end of the cantilevered section forms an upward right angle and becomes the interior wall, serving as the back wall for the shelving units, which have been removed from the central space and placed on the peripheral walls for the sake of clarity. Above the shelves is a strip of windows that runs to the ceiling unbroken by visible walls or supports. The horizontal stacking of the multistory building is thus dynamically emphasized and made a defining principle of the design. The design of the building is based on the essence of the task and it employs the means of our time. Form and construction have become an immediate unity.

The efficient system of construction

Fig. 55

High-rises

The development of the high-rise

The steadily increasing concentration of business life in America has logically led to the high-rise. With the high-rise, America has produced a building type whose daring construction contains the kernel of a new form of architecture. The first high-rises appeared in the 1880s in the commercial district of Chicago, a small area bounded by Lake Michigan, the Chicago River, and the terminal train stations of the central rail lines. Business operations that were concentrated in this small area took on ever-greater dimensions. Nobody wanted to forsake the economic advantages that resulted from such concentration. Increasing the number of stories in a building became the only way to accommodate the pressing need for space. At first additional stories were added to existing buildings; eventually high-rises were built and their advantages soon recognized. High-rises were therefore erected not only where space was scarce but also where the technical and economic advantages of concentration were found. They soon appeared in great numbers in nearly all larger American cities. They rose completely haphazardly and without consideration for urban planning perspectives; one-sided, ephemeral interests reigned.

The physiognomy of these cities was quickly and fundamentally transformed. In place of the extended, moderately contoured horizontal character, which still defines the silhouettes of European metropolises, richly formed urban silhouettes with potent accents appeared in America—towering masses separated by deep ravine-like gaps.

But the effects of these high-rise cities are based on pure happenstance; they lack a consciously planned design. Attempts at conscious planning have been made repeatedly without success. The problem of the individual building can only ever be solved in conjunction with the problem of the city. With regard to the high-rise, which exerts such great influence on the plan of an urban area, the latter is of great importance. Like every building, the high-rise is but a cell, a component of the urban organism, and it must be systematically connected to the latter.

A lack of planning, however, is one of the characteristic features of the capitalist economic form. This is also naturally expressed in the urban form that capitalism has produced, that is, in the metropolis.

Lack of planning

In America, the classic nation of the liberal capitalist economy, this disorganization has been pushed beyond all bounds. In the mountain ranges of buildings in New York the material convictions of our time have found their most powerful expression. While in Europe this excess remains limited, in America the drive of speculation has functioned unchecked and produced total urban disorganization. Eliminating this situation has become a pressing question of survival.

Fig. 10

Fig. 56 Cass Gilbert, Woolworth Building, New York, 1913

Fig. 57 McKim, Mead & White, Pennsylvania Hotel, New York, 1919

The inability to recognize the new in its early development also led to grotesque deformations in the construction of high-rises. Architects attempted to neutralize the unusual appearance of high-rises by decorating them with stylistic features derived from past ages, degrading them to the level of an Italian pseudo-palazzo. The aggregation of forms, instead of conscious formation, became the principle of design. Yet the inherent elemental characteristics of these buildings survived such clever mock architecture.

Aggrega-
tion
instead of
formation

Architecture is based primarily on the form of construction that makes its existence possible. Recent architecture in particular has nearly achieved a state of pure construction as a result of its founding principle of rationalism; in the architecture of the past, sacred and religious requirements outweighed rational purposes.

The first high-rises were originally built like all residential buildings since antiquity. They were composed of perimeter load-bearing walls and pillars. Yet with the increasing number of stories, the disadvantages of this form of construction became increasingly clear and its unsuitability increasingly apparent. The thickness of the walls grew with the number of stories, swallowing up space. The load-bearing limits of the land were quickly surpassed by the monstrous masses of material required. At first builders separated the ceilings from the walls, supporting the former with steel support beams. From here it was only a short step to an independent system of steel supports able to bear great loads and forces with relatively small cross sections and enabling the separation of load-bearing and non-load-bearing elements. This reduces the permanent load, allowing both a greater number of stories and faster construction.

Separating load-bearing and non-load-bearing elements

It is characteristic of American architecture that, apart from a small number of exceptions, the structural support system has been entirely ignored in formal design. The constructive implications were understood, but not the implications for form. The structural skeleton was covered in various mock architectural styles; memories of what Americans saw on European tours were grotesquely distorted. Renaissance forms had the most prestige, but medieval forms were also used. For instance, Cass Gilbert succeeded in destroying the elemental greatness of his Woolworth Building, the tallest building in the world, by adding Gothic stylistic elements of pressed metal.

Disregard for the support system

Mock architecture

Fig. 56

American architecture is strongly influenced by the academicism of the French Renaissance. Nevertheless, it must be recognized that forms are applied with taste and logic to the extent possible. The architects of these buildings have delivered proof that antique forms, which until now have been adapted to every form of building, or rather, have controlled every shift in constructive principles, are also suitable as decorative elements for the high-rise. Despite the importance of such buildings as

Academi-
cism

Fig. 56

The do-
minance
of the
functional
concept

Ernest R. Graham's Equitable Building, McKim, Mead & White's Pennsylvania Hotel in New York, and even Albert Kahn's General Motors Building in Detroit, they are still only academic achievements that carry no value for the future. The design of their masses is their only valuable and new element. They are based on a floor plan employing wings that places courtyards and light wells on the street side of buildings, thus allowing a cubic vertical organization of the building and favorable lighting conditions.

However, the vast majority of other high-rises depart from these and similarly tasteful buildings. American high-rises do, in general, still exhibit the same constructive principles, which, however are greatly modified as a result of the unbridled sway of the elementary concept of function; indeed these constructive principles are manipulated *ad absurdum*. In these buildings no consideration is given to the decorative elements found in the wealth of classical forms. The forms used are applied only out of pure convention. Their removal would reveal a naked functional building. This is surely an advantage but still not a solution. Yet these are precisely the buildings that have contributed most to the realization that details based on the dimensions of normal rooms become absurd in a high-rise. They have made it clear that a systematic application of the concept of function also creates new architectural forms that no longer require a decorative shell. Decisive for the design of a

high-rise are only the new needs and require- The
ments related to technology and spatial design
relationships, as well as the new materials: steel,
reinforced concrete, and glass, which have all
proved to be very effective for high-rises.

The only American architect to recognize The first
and grasp these facts, besides Sullivan, was John experi-
Root, who implemented them in his Monadnock ment
Building in Chicago constructed in 1891. It is *Fig. 58*
astounding that this high-rise, which is one of
the earliest high-rises ever built, has yet to
be surpassed by another in its "correctness."
Though it does belong to an era in which the support system had not yet been invented, what
distinguishes this building is that it revealed that
the problem plaguing all architecture is a cubic
and rhythmic problem; that it revealed this in a
new way and took contemporary conditions into
consideration. The desire to replace creative
inability with overblown material accumulation,
that is, the embarrassing path taken for most
later buildings, was here instinctively avoided.
An unmistakable sense of proportion gives this
building an inner consistency and logical form.
Root abandoned metered design, axial emphasis, and the combination of separate elements
into higher-order formal compositions. The
mass was successfully designed as an organism.
Architecture ceased to be an ill-fitted mask.
Root gave American architecture a foundation
and a goal with this building: he attained libera-
tion from European taste; he formulated the

Fig. 58 Burnham & Root, Monadnock Building, Chicago, 1891

American principle of style that Frank Lloyd Wright universally outlined. The new that has arisen in this way has nothing to do with banal functionality; rather it is simultaneously the greatest coherence and concentration. Root has shown that new types of expressive forms must be found to satisfy the conditions of his country and the requirements of the present.

The new form

There has been no lack of attempts to alter the unsustainable conditions resulting from the haphazard erection of high-rises in America's high-rise cities. A new building law, the "zoning law," the fundamental principles of which were already assumed by Sullivan in his Chicago high-rises, attempts to improve the amount of light received in individual high-rises.[31] Provisions vary from urban district to urban district. Thus, in some districts the first setback must occur at a height of two and a half times the width of the street; in other districts, it must take place lower, at a height of two times the width of the street. A tower may only be erected when it covers no more than one quarter of the total area to be developed. The Shelton Hotel in New York was built by A. L. Harmon according to these principles. A design by Hugh Ferriss shows how an entire city block can be designed according to these regulations; New York, an intense upward dissolving of building masses. This is surely a great improvement but

Zoning

Fig. 59

---

[31]   [See note 10, p. 106.]

Fig. 59 Hugh Ferriss, Proposal for the development of a block according to the zoning law, 1925

it does not provide any advantages for the flow of traffic.

High-rise and traffic

Fig. 14

Le Corbusier attempted to solve the traffic problem by placing high-rises at large intervals from each other. This proposal had already been made by Perret.[32] Raymond Hood, the designer

[32] [Hilberseimer refers to Auguste Perret's projects for a city of towers of 1921–22. See J. Labadié, "Les cathédrales de la cité moderne," *L'Illustration*, 12 August 1922, 129–36.]

of the Chicago Tribune Tower, has recently revisited this problem in a design for high-rises that expand only in the upper stories and occupy a relatively small area.[33] But the broad, open spaces foreseen by these proposals are at odds with the concept of the high-rise because if the interstitial terrain were developed at regular building heights, it would provide the same amount of usable space.

The high-rise is outdated in its contemporary form, especially when it appears as a row house, as it does in most American metropolises. That which has already been proved to be inadequate for the tenement, that is, an unsuitable urban plan, applies even more to existing high-rise cities. The urban plan is not an abstraction: it depends fundamentally on the type of constructive development. All existing metropolises are based on the medieval system of the individual house. But the individual house has in the meantime become a house for the masses. The urban plan, conditioned by the relationships of private ownership, has yet to overcome the stage of the individual house. This is an impediment to the systematic design of housing for the masses because the latter depends entirely on the design of the urban plan—they are mutually

Development and urban plan

Fig. 10

[33] [Hilberseimer refers to Raymond Hood's proposal for a series of skyscrapers with small building footprints. See Raymond Hood, "Tower Buildings and Wider Streets: A Suggested Relief for Traffic Congestion," *American Architect* 132, 5 July 1927, 67–68.]

dependent. This is why, as a result of an insufficiently organized urban plan, the advantages offered by the high-rise are for the most part nullified. As a solitary building, the high-rise should only be constructed at certain points in the urban plan, at points with sufficient light and air. Where it appears as a row house, the high-rise must be systematically designed as such, as Ludwig Hilberseimer has done in his schema for a High-rise City. Here the high-rise is applied in a completely new way; it is integrally bound to the urban plan, thereby creating an organic entity from the chaotic disadvantages of past high-rises with regard to traffic, hygiene, and lighting.

In Europe the question of the construction of high-rises has also recently been raised. Indeed, architects already considered the possibility of high-rise construction before the war, especially in Berlin, where the constantly growing need for commercial space and timesaving concentration made the high-rise a necessity. Building ordinances, however, did not permit their construction. Building ordinances have been treated blandly and schematically, turning Berlin into a faceless city. The city's overextended horizontal character demands compact vertical elements and calls for the vibrancy produced by alternating building masses, which, in a metropolis, is only to be achieved by high-rises. If, for this reason, European cities are to build high-rises, the only suitable sites are those required by need and permitted by the

The high-rise as row house

Figs. 17–19

The schematic treatment of building ordinances

considerations of urban planning, because the European high-rise has a completely different urban function from the American variant, whose narrow arrangement has led to a complete lack of light in offices and thus practically destroyed the true advantages of the high-rise. The American high-rise is inherently a row house, without however being properly designed as such. In spite of all its stylistic masquerades it retains no individual effect. In order to achieve such an effect, its location would need to be isolated; the location would have to dominate certain streets and squares and bring order and simplicity to the street system. The European high-rise can to a great degree fulfill these requirements. The high-rise is therefore to be purposefully erected where it accentuates and focuses the dynamics of a street or square, giving movement an aim and direction. Yet it should not strive for false monumentality, such as that seen in the building proposed by Otto Kohtz for the Reichshaus on the Platz der Republik in Berlin, whose pathos recalls far too distinctly the happily conquered past, or even the pseudo-monumentality of Bruno Möhring's designs.[34]

False monumentality

[34] [Hilberseimer refers to the proposals made by Kohtz and Möhring from 1920 on. See Otto Kohtz, "Das Reichshaus am Königsplatz in Berlin," *Stadtbaukunst alter und neuer Zeit* 1 (1920): 241–45; Bruno Möhring, "Über die Vorzüge der Turmhäuser und die Voraussetzungen, unter denen sie in Berlin gebaut werden können," *Stadtbaukunst alter und neuer Zeit* 1 (1920): 353–57, 370–76, 385–91.]

Fig. 60 Mies van der Rohe, High-rise in iron and glass, 1922

The floor plans of these designs are characteristic. In order to achieve the most compact building mass, they enclose narrow, entirely surrounded courtyards—complete nonsense in a high-rise. In contrast to these decoratively oriented designs, such proposals as Richard Döcker's for Stuttgart proceed from the considerations of urban planning. In order to lend the muddled urban silhouette of Stuttgart some character, Döcker proposes high-rises in the valley (which correspond to existing towers in their height) and a continuous development of the ridge— vertical development by embedding building masses, not elevating them.[35]

With his high-rise of iron and glass, Mies van der Rohe attempted to turn the daring structural concepts that are explicitly expressed in typical high-rises into the foundation of artistic design. Relinquishing traditional forms entirely, he sought to design the object from the very essence of the new task. The peculiar form of the floor plan is based on the recognition that the glass house is not dependent on the interaction of light and shadow, but on the rich interplay of reflected light. The curves of the floor plan were determined according to the needs of interior lighting, the effect of the building mass on the street, and the interplay of reflected light.

The high-rise in iron and glass

Fig. 60

[35] [See Richard Herre, "Hochhäuser für Stuttgart," *Wasmuths Monatshefte für Baukunst* 6, nos. 11–12 (1921–22): 375–90.]

Halls and Theaters

Extrava-
gance of
form

The need for halls and theaters in metropolises offered the architects of the nineteenth century, who erringly strove for false monumentality, the opportunity for the most luxurious extravagance of form. Exterior wealth was required to conceal inner poverty. The uncomfortable impression of these magnificent buildings is caused primarily by the senseless use of historical stylistic elements. Travel and historical research enriched stylistic eclecticism with exoticisms, fusing classical principles with ornamental elements of all peoples and periods. Joseph Poelaert's Palace of Justice in Brussels; Charles Garnier's Grand Opera in Paris; Gottfried Semper's museums and theaters in Vienna and Dresden; Paul Wallot's Reichstag in Berlin; Henri-Adolphe-Auguste Deglane's Grand and Charles-Louis Girault's Small Palais in the Champs-Elysées; Gabriel Davioud and Jules Bourdais's Trocadéro in Paris; and Friedrich von Thiersch's Festival Hall in Frankfurt am Main are all spirited characteristic examples of the extreme ornamental orientation of the time. An uncertain will and arbitrary games of form disturbed the clarity of building principles, which, in the end, in the hands of imitators, were fully nullified by bombastic monumentality.

And yet, with their distinct differentiation of rooms and rich shifts in cubic construction, these

are precisely the types of buildings that could lead
to an architecture internally formed according to
its inherent characteristics, to the creation of spatial organisms, whose exterior is purposefully
defined by the internal organization of spaces. J.
P. Berlage's stock exchange building is a clear
demonstration of this.

For events such as concerts, exhibitions, **Halls**
gatherings, and celebrations a building type has
developed that is usually composed of two
interconnected halls, both surrounded by foy-
ers, checkrooms, and stairs. Earlier building
techniques were generally sufficient for their
construction. Thus their architectural appearances were influenced by the corresponding
eclectic forms of past ages. Even in the application of the newest constructive tools, that is,
steel and reinforced concrete, one was never far
removed from eclecticism, not even in the case
of large halls such as the Albert Hall in London, the Trocadéro or the Grand Palais in Paris,
or the Festival Hall in Frankfurt, to name but a
few examples.

Though the new mode of construction
allowed large-dimensioned rooms, it was for the
most part applied in a most antiquarian fashion,
for example to imitate historical vaulted forms in
iron and glass. Architects sought to impede the
form-shaping capabilities offered by the new
constructive options with any means necessary.
Similar to what happened in the construction of
train station halls, here the elementary power of

form inherent in the construction is often concealed behind poorly executed historicisms. The immediacy of this elementary power has been inhibited; the direct unity of structure and form has been ignored.

However, at the beginning of this line of development is a work that intentionally departed from the practices of stone construction: an exhibition hall in London, a building of iron and glass that was the ingenious work of the gardener Joseph Paxton. It was constructed for the international industrial exhibition in London in 1850.[36] In 1852 it was dismantled and re-erected in 1854 with even greater dimensions in Sydenham near London as the Crystal Palace.

The
Crystal
Palace in
London

It is composed of an extended structure interrupted by lateral pavilions that contain entrances and provide architectural accentuation. The continuous half-cylinder ceiling forms a welcome contrast to the otherwise common rectilinear forms employed. The Crystal Palace is a building of glass and iron of the most primitive type that has nevertheless clearly and purely become form. It is a building of glazed iron latticework—a pure pattern of lines and surfaces—that dissolves the structure's true weight. The traditional contrasts of light and shadow that affected proportions of form in past architecture have disappeared here, making way for

[36]   [Hilberseimer refers to the Great Exhibition of the Works of Industry of all Nations.]

evenly distributed light and creating a space of shadowless luminosity.

Max Berg and the reinforced-concrete company Dyckerhoff and Widmann constructed the Centennial Hall in Breslau (Wrocław) exclusively of reinforced concrete. This building has the greatest unsupported span of any solid construction to date. Its construction is reminiscent of the Pantheon in Rome, whose dome is also constructed of load-bearing ribs and rests on a cylindrical base. The hall's lower portion is pierced by four large load-bearing arches to which apsidal extensions are attached, expanding the space. The challenge in the construction was to strike a balance between the play of forces in the supporting arches of the cylindrical drum and the flying buttresses of the apses. As flying buttresses of a Gothic cathedral divert the loads of the vaulting, so here the flying buttresses of

The Centennial Hall in Breslau

Figs. 61–62

Fig. 61 Max Berg, Centennial Hall, Breslau (Wrocław), 1911–13

Fig. 62 Max Berg, Centennial Hall, Breslau (Wrocław),

1911–13; interior

the apses divert the load of the four large arches that support the central dome—a spatial construction of rare daring and powerful energy.

Wooden construction, like steel and reinforced concrete, has also been subject to designs emphasizing economization and proper engineering. In contrast to older primitive modes of building, which were based on the beam structures used by carpenters, new methods of building in wood are based on the flow of forces. This enables even wooden construction to span large spaces without intermediary supports and to thereby fulfill new spatial requirements in a manner not unlike that of iron construction.

Engineered timber construction

Among the many attempts that have been undertaken in this field, those of Carl Tuchscherer and Company are the most remarkable. The trade fair hall in Breslau (Wrocław) and above all the Westfalenhalle in Dortmund are massive constructions of rare daring and novel spatial effects.

Westfalenhalle in Dortmund

The floor plan of the Westfalenhalle is elliptical, corresponding to athletic requirements. The distance between supports is seventy-eight meters and the trusses are placed at twenty-meter intervals. The trusses themselves are made of a pressed wooden band with wooden relieving supports above these. The weight of the roof of the elliptical space is carried by a continuous band of purlins that run parallel to the long axis at both narrow ends. Thus a constructive and satisfactory spatial effect was achieved. The light provided by rows of windows set above the trusses gives the space the daylight required for sporting events.

In addition to arranging the floor plan, the architectural challenge in theater construction is to uniformly align the contradictory constructive spaces of the stage and auditorium, which are determined by the interior organism; that is, to design spaces, whose disparity is continuously augmented due to the increasing technical demands of the stage, as one unit. The traditional theater contained both the stage and audience hall beneath one roof. Georg Moller must have been the first to attempt to arrange the building masses of a theater according to their actual requirements. In his City Theater in Mainz the audience hall, a half cylinder, is placed in front of the cubic stage portion. The building was clearly and unambiguously given the character of a theater. In spite of an excess of details, the exterior of Garnier's Grand Opera in Paris expresses the purpose of the building as well as its interior organization. The foyer, audience hall, and stage are clearly emphasized; the stage is powerfully summarized by an enormous gable. Gottfried Semper developed the essential form of the theater even more purposefully. In the Opera House in Dresden and in the Court Theater in Vienna he maintained the cylindrical form of the audience hall for the surrounding foyer as well, creating stark contrasts in the building mass by placing the entry pavilions and approaches laterally.

The traditional theater

Despite his elemental creative energy, Semper was not able to escape eclecticism. Though he fought against the "impotence of half-bankrupt architecture," he nevertheless fell victim himself to this bankruptcy with his ornamental motifs.[37] Certain concepts of form and reminiscences of art history seemed indispensable to him.

Technical perfection   The theater progressed further on the path to technical perfection in the buildings of Max Littmann and Heinrich Seeling, though it was still restrained by the straitjacket of stylistic limitation. In line with contemporary taste, the decorative arts were applied to theater buildings: a different way to avoid pure design by employing a novel ornamentality; see, for example, Martin Dülfer's and Oskar Kaufmann's theaters in Dortmund and Berlin.

The Cologne Werkbund Theater by Henri van der Velde is architecturally more

[37] [Semper did not use this precise phrase. Hilberseimer cites a popular misquotation of Semper's "preliminary remarks" of 1834 on polychrome architecture in antiquity. The "half-bankrupt architecture" Semper had in mind came from the students of the Schachbrettkanzler (chessboard chancellor) Jean-Nicholas-Louis Durand at the Ecole Polytechnique and the students of the Ecole des Beaux-Arts. See Gottfried Semper, "Vorläufige Bemerkungen über bemalte Architektur und Plastik bei den Alten," in Kleine Schriften, eds. Manfred Semper and Hans Semper (Berlin, W. Spemann, 1884), 216–17; translation in The Four Elements of Architecture and Other Writings, trans. Harry Francis Mallgrave and Wolfgang Hermann (Cambridge: Cambridge University Press, 1989), 45–46.]

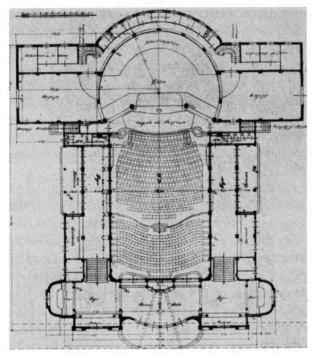

Fig. 63 Henri van de Velde, Werkbund Theater, Cologne, 1914; floor plan

Fig. 64 Henri van de Velde, Werkbund Theater, Cologne, 1914

The
Werk-
bund
theater in
Cologne

*Figs.
63–64*

purposeful. It is a small building and yet it is one of the most unique creations of contemporary architecture. It is free of reminiscences and historicisms and is designed as a most suitable solution to the requirements of space. With this a spatial fantasy becomes creative; a fantastically animated building has come into being; the dead building mass has been revived by rhythmic motion, assembled into three-dimensional masses.

All of these theaters, with the exception of van der Velde's, are based more or less on the courtly hierarchical theater. This explains the historicism of their architecture. Architects attempted to democratize the theater originally created for the court by increasing its scale—a genuine aim of the parvenu and entirely characteristic of the intellectual spirit of the nineteenth century. But it is not possible to adapt an organism that has a well-defined sociological basis to a completely different set of sociological conditions simply by enlarging it. With complete disregard of his duty, this is what Oskar Kaufmann did with the Berlin People's Theater, turning an architectural and sociological problem into a formal and decorative one. The new theater, the actual people's theater, can only become the new theater if the new requirements are also architectonically fulfilled in a purposeful manner.

The fundamental requirements are the creation of seats that are as equal in value as possible; the abolition of the traditional picture-box stage, which is enclosed on three sides; and the unity of audience hall and stage. The multi-level theater and the traditional picture stage are closely related; they have a common sociological cause—to serve the illusionistic pleasures of a hierarchically structured court society. The new theater dismisses both divisions according to social ranking and the illusionistic stage. This leads to the new spatial problem, that is, the unity of audience hall and stage.

The fundamental requirements

The form of the amphitheater offers the most seats of equal value. They are differentiated only through the varied distances from the stage, which is unavoidable. By organizing seats in the form of an amphitheater, the differentiation of height is also kept to a minimum, benefiting the stage, which can only be of a certain height.

The Amphitheater

The American single-level theater represents a doubling of the amphitheater, as it were. It was created with the intention of providing the greatest number of seats of as equal value as possible. It arranges thirty-five or more rows of seats successively in the parquet and in the balcony.

The American single-level theater

The pronounced tendency toward height in the European multi-level theater gives the upper-most balcony a very steep viewing angle. The single-level theater reduces this angle, in spite of the great height of some seats, thereby creating a much better field of vision.

The Americans have removed the disadvantageous spatial effect of deeply recessed parquet seats beneath the balcony by breaking through the ceiling of the parquet and making the great space beneath the balcony accessible as a so-called *promenoir*. This eliminates the oppressive claustrophobic character of the rear parquet seats, creating at the same time a very useful promenade corridor for the balcony.

The new theater   The traditional picture stage can only be overcome by a stage space that is designed in three dimensions and spatially arranged. The stage must be divided according to height, with individual levels stacked successively one behind the other. The front of the stage must project into the audience hall; it must connect directly to the first rows of seats. Because this is the true setting of action, it represents the connection between the audience hall and the stage. Thus a spatially and architecturally unified space will appear, one that will become the true architectural center of gravity of the building.

Transportation Buildings

The train station connects street and rail traffic, thus acting as an architectonic link between the most diverse forms of transportation. The actual hall of the train station, the space for arriving and departing trains, is in general an iron hall whose construction is determined by the type of truss employed. As a rule, this space has a very rational character in contrast to the hall's peripheral buildings: the switch room, waiting halls, luggage rooms, administrative offices, all of whose dimensions allow them to be constructed using the constructive tools of the past. This is why there is such a discrepancy between these spaces and the halls, which are often enormous and built using new methods. This discrepancy has led to extreme deformations. A misguided pursuit of monumentality sought to transform the actual building mass, the steel hall, into a stone construction, either by using stone cladding—as in Anhalter Station in Berlin; Frankfurt am Main, Central Station; Gare du Nord, Paris—or by attempting to surpass and eliminate the elemental effects of the iron hall through theatrical architecture—Hamburger and Antwerpener Stations—or finally, as seen in the new Leipziger Station, by making the hall disappear entirely behind enormously proportioned ancillary buildings.

The new form of engineering construction is only wholly apparent in the unornamented and architecturally neglected rear portions of the actual halls—particularly in Hamburg, Frankfurt, Dresden, and Antwerp—where these forms develop freely; it is also apparent in the interiors of the train halls, which are wide-span, illuminated spaces of rare majesty.

The revolution of transportation

The radical change in the conditions of transportation, particularly in American metropolises, has not been without influence on the design of train stations. Not just local lines, but also long-distance lines are now directed through tunnels into the center of the city, a feat made possible through the introduction of electricity.

By placing the tracks underground, street traffic can flow unhindered above ground. This has also resulted in the disappearance of the characteristic train station hall. For instance, at the new terminal station of the New York Central Railroad in New York City platforms are vertically stacked in three subterranean levels.[38] They are directly connected to each other and to the entry building through tunnels, so that transfers to every train are possible. An elevated street, which surrounds the entry building and slopes down at the rear of the site, makes the train station accessible to automobile traffic on two levels, ensuring the quickest

Three-level track installation

[38] [Hilberseimer refers to Grand Central Terminal in New York City, designed by Reed & Stem and Warren & Wetmore, 1903–13.]

possible flow of traffic to and from the station. Unfortunately this systematically organized organism and its exterior appearance do not correspond: a bombastic building in Alexandrian-American style encloses the entire complex.

If the architecture of these buildings has until now served to conceal the alleged unseemliness of the new forms of construction and to create mock works meant to be ostentatious representations, several new designs for train stations are based on the objective preconditions of the train station complex. A train station complex is essentially a conductor of traffic: the most comfortable and functional connection of rail and street traffic requires a rational order and design of traffic routes.

Three types of rail complexes result from local conditions and various traffic requirements: the terminal station, the through station, and the transfer station.

Three types of train stations

The terminal station of Rush City by Richard J. Neutra is connected to a similar station at the northern side of the city by four subterranean through lines for passenger traffic and two rails for cargo. This enables the connection of long-distance and urban traffic.

The terminal station

Fig. 65

Just as the train station with its commuter rail lines connects directly to subway lines, trams are routed to the train station in such a way that no traveler needs to cross a street in order to reach the train station. The proposed hotel at the

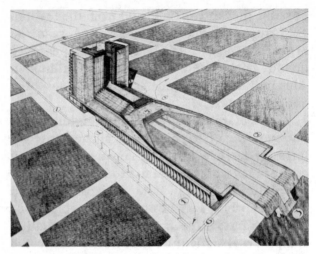

Fig. 65 Richard Neutra, Terminal Station, Rush City, 1926

end of the train station is directly connected to the station platforms.

The through station

Figs. 66–67

In contrast to the terminal station, whose rails are placed beneath street level, the rails of the through station designed by Mart Stam for Geneva are raised significantly above the street. The platforms are accessible through a mezzanine concourse set perpendicular to the platforms. The need to overcome these differences in height creates special conditions for the layout of the arrival and departure hall. Stam connects the street to the level of the concourse with a ramp, thus creating a direct connection between the street and platform. Because the corridors and ticket-counter rooms are not enclosed by doors or vestibules—they

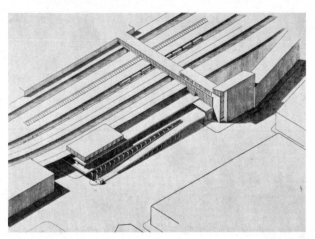

Fig. 66 Mart Stam, Project for a train station in Geneva, 1924

Fig. 67 Mart Stam, Project for a train station in Geneva, 1924; perspective

are considered elements of the connecting route between the street and the platform—this direct connection between the interior and exterior is intensified.

In connection with Martin Mächler's proposal for the redesign of Berlin, Ludwig Hilberseimer designed a main train station which, as a transfer station, is the central point

The transfer train station

Fig. 68 Ludwig Hilberseimer, Central train station for Berlin,

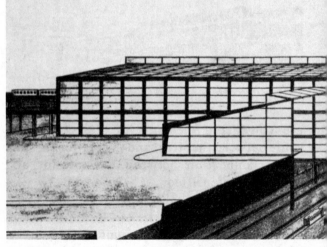

Fig. 69 Ludwig Hilberseimer, Central train station for Berlin,

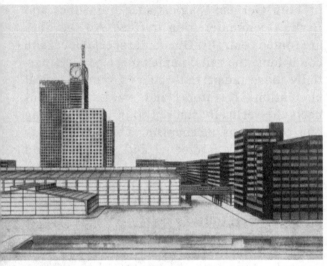

1927; perspective

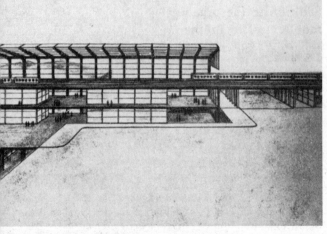

1927; perspectival section

Figs.
68–69

of both German long-distance train lines and Berlin's commuter train traffic.[39] All the lines are routed centrally. Due to the special local site conditions, the rail complex must be built partially above and partially below ground. Vertical circulation—elevators and escalators—connects the vertically stacked train lines, creating one continuous mechanism. Thus a radiating traffic network is created and a rational and intensive flow of traffic is made possible.

The growth of street traffic

The difficulty of managing street traffic grows along with the size of a city. Besides such fixed lines of traffic as urban and commuter trains, streetcars, and elevated and subterranean trains, the free traffic of automobiles acquires ever-greater importance. This applies both to the systematic network of buses and to the independent form of the private automobile. In addition to the organic incorporation of automobile traffic in the street network and the creation of arterial and through streets, the construction of mass garages will also become an

[39] [Hilberseimer's project for a central train station in Berlin was intended for the site of the former Lehrter Bahnhof—where Berlin Hauptbahnhof currently stands—and was designed as a complement to Mächler's project for the reorganization of the city of 1917–19; both projects were exhibited at the Große Berliner Kunstausstellung in 1927. See Ludwig Hilberseimer, "Struktiver Städtebau," *Das Kunstblatt* 11 (1927): 267–71; Max Berg, "Der neue Geist im Städtebau auf der Großen Berliner Kunstausstellung." *Stadtbaukunst alter und neuer Zeit* 8, no. 3 (1927): 41–50.]

unavoidable necessity, primarily because the automobile is ceasing to be a luxury item and is becoming a standard commodity in both America and Europe. With this development, the number of private drivers—the actual users of mass garages—is growing. The mass garage will become a new concept in our traffic life and will lead to new architectural designs. A mass garage must not only include parking spaces for cars but also car-washing facilities, repair shops, gas stations, and lodgings for chauffeurs. For reasons of profitability, one will quickly move beyond the single-story arrangement of parking spaces around a courtyard and begin erecting garage buildings in which parking spaces are arranged in vertically stacked rows. The transportation of automobiles onto the upper stories can be accomplished either by ramps or elevators. The lack of suitable parking spaces in the center of metropolises will also require the creation of underground garages. This need will primarily arise as a practical way to park cars that would otherwise have to be left on the street. Because such an underground garage is often only intended to provide short-term parking for automobiles, a means of rapid entry and exit is of great importance.

The mass garage

Underground garages

The method and manner of accommodating cars is of the greatest importance for mass garages. For the time being individual parking compartments are preferred, for which a variety of perpendicular and diagonal systems have been developed.[40] Yet developments are leading to open parking, as is already common in America and France. The advantages of this sort of parking, which occurs in large, open hall-like spaces, are enormous since both partition walls and doors are eliminated. The total space required is greatly reduced and the lanes can become much narrower. By eliminating the time-consuming opening and closing of doors, overseeing the complex will become significantly more simple and clear.

Airports The ever-increasing amount of air travel will create entirely new tasks. Like the train station, the airport will become a vital organ of the urban body. Therefore the placing of airports must proceed with the greatest care. The most important precondition is a prime location connected to the city.

Both existing airport facilities and the airplane of today were developed primarily for military purposes. Yet they remain the standard models of aerial transportation. For this reason air traffic facilities, like the passenger airplane, are relatively undeveloped.

Initially, the minimum size of an airfield was calculated to be 700 by 700 meters. As airplanes increased in size, so too did the size of airfields, so that even now a size of 1,000 by 1,000 meters seems too small.

[40] [Hilberseimer refers to the use of parking compartments with individual doors and operated like small, private garages.]

Berlin's central airport is apparently the only airport based on purely technical considerations of transportation. Exemplary for today's conditions is also its relationship to the city and its direct connection to the subway. Its airfield has an area of 1,000 by 1,300 meters; it is set within an open area that is zoned to prohibit further construction and which includes a 500-meter border between the airfield itself and the boundary where construction is again permitted.

Figs. 70–71

Today little can be said with certainty about the future development of airport complexes. Technological advancements, primarily the shift of take-off and landing procedures from the horizontal to the vertical, will result in fundamental changes in the design of the airport. Yet these will also affect future urban planning in ways unimaginable today.

In contrast to true architectural structures, bridges do not design space, but traverse it. They are not finite, stand-alone structures but connecting structures. Their task is to span a depth—to connect two separate points using a linear system. They are essentially determined by structural requirements. Therefore the dependency of form on construction and calculation is nowhere so striking as in bridge building. Here the elements of design are identical to the elements of construction, so that design in the figurative sense is fundamentally impossible. Still, the perfect design incorporates both the

Bridges

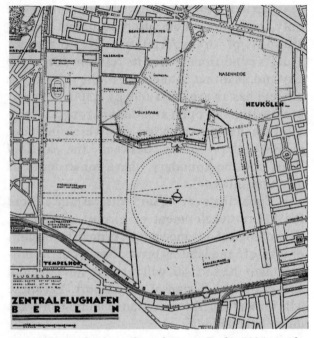

Fig. 70 Heinrich Kosina, Central Airport, Berlin, 1926; site plan

technical-constructive and aesthetic solution. Only when both requirements are met is the solution perfect, rational, and tectonic. The optical impression of a bridge is determined primarily by the placement and layout of the road. The latter is the essential element of the organism of a bridge; it is to be borne, supported, and held. The forces necessary for this, tectonically formed and connected, transition from support to support, and from pillar to pillar, in a straight line, oscillating between concave or

The optical impression

Fig. 71 Heinrich Kosina, Central Airport, Berlin, 1926; airplane hangars

convex lines, or in all these lines, uniting into one compound linear system.

There are three fundamental bridge systems, which correspond to various systems of support and the transference of weight to

Fig. 72 John Fowler, Bridge over the Firth of Forth, 1890

supports: girder bridges, which transfer loads vertically; arch bridges, which transfer weight at angles; and suspension bridges, which also transmit loads vertically but in an entirely different way. In the latter, the roadway of the bridge is no longer supported from below, but suspended from above. All of these unique systems can also be united into one composite system.

Girder bridges

The simplest and most primitive form of the bridge is the pure girder bridge. This type, however, can only be applied to narrow spans. Larger spans require a more complex support system, commonly a lattice structure with horizontal girders, which are fastened by fixed diagonal bracing.

Cantilever bridges are a variety of girder bridges which are, so to speak, composed of halves of two arch bridges joined in an abutment, thereby vertically transferring the diagonally oriented pressure of both pieces to the middle. This type of construction is seldom applied as it was in the construction of the Stößensee Bridge near Spandau built by Karl Bernhard. More commonly this form is used as the foundation of a composite system that incorporates elements of the suspension system, as seen in the bridge over the Firth of Forth.

Fig. 72

Arch bridges

The appearance of arch bridges varies with the placement of the road. It can be placed above the structure, as in the Washington Bridge in New York; within the support structure, as in the Treskow Bridge in Berlin; or beneath the structure, hung from the latter so to speak, as in the Czerny Bridge in Heidelberg.

In the latter arrangement, the horizontal thrust is accommodated by the bridge itself since the ends of the arches are securely connected to the road. The pressure is then no longer exerted diagonally, but rather transferred horizontally, whereby the arch construction becomes a type of girder bridge.

The transfer of diagonal pressure in arch bridges requires that the abutments be sturdily designed. Ballast structures, such as those employed in the Grünental High Bridge over the Kiel Canal, can become necessary. Normally however, these constructions provide an occasion for decorative excess as at the Pont d'Alexandre in Paris, a low arch bridge over the Seine. The latter was an attempt to imitate the compactness of stone bridges in iron, also out of purely decorative motifs. The bridge is composed of screwed, cast-steel elements instead of riveted, rolled-iron components.

In suspension bridges the road is not supported from below but suspended from above. The structure required for this type of bridge has created a new tectonic entity characterized by tall pillars and the descending upper curve, forming a lively contrast to the ascending curves of girder and arch bridges.

Suspension bridges

The design of the load-bearing pillars is decisive for this construction. They can be executed in stone as in the Brooklyn Bridge in New

York by John and Washington Roebling or even more systematically in steel as in a design for a bridge for Cologne by Peter Behrens.

The composite system

The construction of bridges based on composite systems is diverse. This is demonstrated especially in the counter-motion of the extended, crisscrossing double-curves, exhibited for example in the pedestrian bridge built over the Spree in Berlin-Niederschöneweide by Heinrich Müller-Breslau, which is composed of girder and suspension bridge elements. Another example is the robust bridge over the Firth of Forth in Scotland with its 500-meter free span. This bridge is based on a unique cantilever construction with upper suspenders ascending in a straight diagonal line, curved lower arches, and arch beams hung in between. Its powerful effect and its elemental stability are particularly expressed by the straightness of the upper suspender construction. It is a work of rare forcefulness and the most elementary impact.

Bridges in reinforced concrete

Bridge building has also become a broad field for the application of reinforced concrete. Its structural advantages, short production time, minimal maintenance costs, and technological and economic advantages have prompted the rapid introduction of this method. Many structures of this type, primarily girder bridges and arch bridges, have already been realized. The structural and technical foundations are the same as those in steel construction. The difference is merely in the material, which, in contrast to steel construction, requires a more compact mass. At the same time, the danger exists that materials will be misused, that stone bridges will be imitated. This was the case with Wilhelm Kreis's design for the Friedrich-August Bridge in Dresden in which a misguided desire to conform to the urban image produced a concrete bridge that imitates a bridge of stone. In the process, its exterior surfaces were covered with an ornamental cut-stone shell, just like the Max-Josef Bridge in Munich by Theodor Fischer, which also ornamentally imitates stone forms and the structural character of masonry by inserting joints into the surface.

The misuse of materials

Thus the more significant reinforced concrete bridges are those that clearly express the uniqueness of the material and the skeletal character of its structure while uniting structural necessity and design of form. I mention the Hundwilertobel Bridge by Eduard Züblin and Company in the Swiss canton of Appenzell, whose thinly structured features completely correspond to the material and whose form perfectly expresses the constructive principles of this building technique.

Skeletal character

Industrial Buildings

The new principles of building have been most freely realized in industrial construction. In fact, the designs of engineering structures are virtually determining the peculiarities of form of our age. Buildings have been created for new industries and purposes. These structures are entirely without prior models in terms of typology, structure, and dimension. Thus these new buildings could be realized without inhibition. In solving these tasks, the pure constructive element, and thus the activities of the engineer, took precedence, which at first resulted in clarity and awareness of objective needs. Then the increasing performance demands restricted the engineer to the purely objective, functional-constructive element. Industrial corporations, set on obtaining extreme economy, demanded spaces and buildings of the greatest functional capacity. By indiscriminately emphasizing functional construction, engineers were able to achieve completely new architectonic results. Architects, on the other hand, caught in the spell of their traditional concepts of form, ignored the new possibilities; they were either unable able to free themselves from traditional constructions and forms or they used the new structural possibilities to realize incongruous monumental and representational effects. For instance, although Gottfried Semper both recognized the suitability

No models

The engineer

The architect

Gottfried Semper's mistake

of iron as a new structural material and understood the ideal of its systematic application—invisible architecture, the possibility of
creating maximum functionality using a minimum amount of material—because he was
unable to liberate himself from stone construction, he demanded at the same time that iron not
be applied independently.[41] It was only to be
used to increase the spanning capabilities of
more compact constructions; that is to say, he
subordinated a new constructive principle to a
principle derived from the concepts of form of
the past.

Peter Behrens, led astray by the imperialist
consciousness of power of the prewar era and
limited by classical influences, believed it was
necessary to place a facade on the front of his
AEG Turbine Hall, which is otherwise a robust
structure, in Berlin-Moabit. He designed the corners of this iron hall as mighty ashlar blocks with
the intention of creating a material and static
contradiction—an architecturally effective contrast—and of achieving an imposing effect.

Yet these masonry corner pillars, which
produce a hieratic, imposing effect, are in fact

The
symbol-
ism of
facades

Fig. 73

[41] [Hilberseimer refers to Semper's remarks on the "cast-
iron style"; see Gottfried Semper, *Der Stil in den technischen
und tektonischen Künste* 2 vols. (Munich: F. Bruckmann,
1860–63), translated as *Style in the Technical and Tectonic
Arts, or, Practical Aesthetics* ed. Harry Francis Mallgrave,
trans. Harry Francis Mallgrave and Michael Robinson
(Los Angeles: Getty Research Institute, 2004), 658–59.]

Fig. 73 Peter Behrens, AEG Turbine Hall, Berlin, 1909

not pillars at all. They are, as shown in the floor plan, composed of a thin shell of reinforced concrete. They represent an attempt to use new technological means to achieve archaic effects — a typical aspect of facade architecture, a desire to symbolize uncertain sensations of nonexistent forces, a desire to subordinate organic features to representational tastes.

Pure engineering works

Industrial buildings that constitute pure works of engineering are more significant. Their astounding architectonics are based not on a vague aesthetic sensibility but on powerful originality, on a naïve sense of architectonics. They prove that great functionality includes not only the most practical designs but also the most aesthetically perfect solutions. Only by completely meeting all needs can impressive, typical solutions be found and new building types created.

Despite the heterogeneity of industrial buildings, which derives from their diverse purposes, their common characteristics include precise objectivity and the strictest fulfillment of economic and technological necessities. These characteristics are the basis for a perfectly functional design — for works of convincing self-assurance.

The diversity of industrial buildings

Industrial buildings are characterized by their extremely large, functionally defined diversity. Buildings and rooms are differentiated according to size and the type of object to be handled, in accordance with the production processes. The relationship of individual buildings and rooms to

Fig. 74 Karl Bernhard, Silk-weaving Factory, Nowawes (Babelsberg), 1912

Fig. 75 Erich Mendelsohn, Red Banner Textile Factory, St. Petersburg, 1925; model

each other is determined by the coordinated flow of raw materials and partial and completed goods through the course of production. Counteractive and reverse movements of materials lead to a lack of space and raise production costs.

Spatial requirements vary according to function. Workshops and production rooms may require large, small, high, or low formats. They may have to be at ground level, elevated, or below ground. They may also have to accommodate production processes in which work flows vertically in stacked production rooms. In the metropolis the high price of land forces the use

Fig. 76 Wayss & Freitag, Maizena grain silos, Barby an der Elbe, 1922–24

Fig. 76

of multistory buildings, even for production processes which could be accommodated in a horizontal building. Beyond single and multistory buildings there are production processes that require great height, making halls a necessity primarily when overhead cranes are required. For the accommodation of fluids and gasses, for the storing of ore, coal, cement, and grain, container structures and silos are necessary.

In contrast to stone constructions, which use only lateral force and vertical compression, constructions in steel and reinforced concrete use tension and curvature, whereby structures of astounding daring and completely new spatial forms are enabled: extended, horizontally covered workshops; enormous, broadly spanned halls; tall, skeletal structures; cantilevered constructions; and thin-walled container and silos. Because of the inherent possibility of placing windows everywhere and at any size, all-day illumination can be achieved even in low-rise buildings constructed on large developed spaces, since the light can enter through skylight sheds or lanterns. In order to achieve the most unhindered horizontal extension of a structure while maintaining suitable lighting conditions, wide-span train platform roof trusses are commonly employed, which, at the ends, become large perpendicular skylights in the form of gabled roof structures, thus also considerably influencing the external character of a building. If wide-span spaces whose entire height is needed for operations are required, this can be accommodated by a new structural system, which places the truss inside the overhead lantern system that runs along the roof in a caterpillar-like fashion, enabling a level ceiling and a space that can be used in all of its dimensions.

A hall is required when both spaciousness and great heights are necessary. The cross section for halls allows many variations, all of which are determined by the intended use. Trusses and supports are both the structural and

Means of construction

Fig. 74

Low-rise buildings

Halls

space-defining elements, determining both the interior and exterior of a building. In these hall structures the specificity of new structural systems and new spatial principles are expressed with rare force and elementary power.

Multi-story buildings

In contrast to halls and single-story buildings, which can be lighted from above, only lateral illumination is possible for multistory buildings. The depth of rooms is therefore dependent on the lighting required, which is in turn determined by the size of the windows and the heights of the ceilings. Among multistory industrial structures, the Fiat Automobile Factory by Matté Trucco in Lingotto near Turin is of particular interest. The roof of this extended building is constructed as a twenty-four-meter-wide, one-kilometer-long car track, designed to enable the testing of automobiles before delivery. The extreme ends of the track are curved and elevated to a height of six meters in order to allow automobiles to turn at maximum speed.

Function is always legible in mining complexes, with their characteristic shaft and conveyor structures, and in metal and concrete container structures. In a similar fashion, blast furnace complexes, containers for ore and coal, and cement and grain silos speak for themselves. Only gas and water containers have been converted into mock architectural works by completely disregarding their characteristic appearance and concealing it behind a wall. Gasometers enclosed by walls and dressed as monuments at great expense and water towers disguised as a city gates have long since become outdated and are today left with their characteristic appearances.

What distinguishes industrial buildings is the diversity of building types produced by their various purposes. Tall, steep buildings or large, wide-span halls are connected to large, extended single-story structures—with contrasts between cubic corporeality and finely structured iron construction. The piping systems and apparatuses of blast furnace complexes or chemical industry buildings create strange contrasts with the simple cubic building shapes. The task of design is to creatively control this diversity and to form it as one unit, that is, to express the necessary with unrelenting logic.

Architects, with few exceptions, have almost never taken the process of production into consideration in designing industrial buildings. Their decorative orientations have led them to create facades as a way to avoid the problem. Instead of organically designing a factory complex according to its needs, architects, misjudging their true task, believe they have fulfilled their obligations with cheap ornamentation. But only the most extreme differentiation of structures according to the requirements of production processes and the creative accommodation of all conditions can create a living organism, one that lives not from borrowed beauty but from its own characteristic and inherent features.

Variation of building types

Fig. 75

Consideration for production processes

In the future the architect will have to relinquish both the desire to superficially beautify the work of the engineer and to impose monumentality on engineering structures. For the sake of a unity of a higher order he will cooperate with the engineer to put architectonic interests at the service of structural problems. The new can only be built on the foundation of the constructive and the functional. The constructive idea must be infused with the architectonic spirit. The engineer's drive toward characteristic solutions must not be annulled by preconceived concepts of form. The architect, through the force of the division of labor and through his ignorance, has lost

The creative mastery of means

control of constructive elements. Only when the architect recovers control and creatively masters them, will he emerge from the sterility of his epigonism and achieve truly creative output. Although artistic will will indeed always be decisive, this will must nevertheless be characterized by the fact that it excludes no element that contributes to the definition of unity.[42] Calculated construction and an instinctive feeling for masses and forms must be one; contradictory elements must be designed as a unity. Mathematics and aesthetics are not opposed; they are equal tools, the absolute basis of architecture.

[42] [Hilberseimer uses the phrase *künsterlisches Wollen*, which approximates Alois Riegl's concept of *Kunstwollen*, or artistic volition. Hilberseimer incorporated the concept of *Kunstwollen* into the earliest drafts of *Großstadtarchitektur*. See this volume, p. 58.]

Building Trades
and the
Building Industry

"Metropolisarchitecture" is distinguished from the architecture of the past primarily through changed sociological and economic premises.[43] New functional requirements have produced peculiarities of form that have come to completely define metropolisarchitecture. Today we need not cathedrals, temples, or palaces, but rather residential buildings, commercial buildings, and factories, which, however, have been built to resemble cathedrals, temples, and palaces. In addition to designing the city as such, one of the most important tasks of metropolisarchitecture is to sensibly design the residential building, the commercial building, and the factory. Pure models of these building types have yet to emerge. They must first be created. The homogeneity of the intended use enables comprehensive standardization and thus an industrialization of the entire building industry. This is a necessary task for which not even the first step has been taken today. The industrialization of production,

[43] [Hilberseimer uses the word *Großstadtarchitektur* for the first time here. The term is rendered as "metropolisarchitecture" in order to convey the immediate relationship between the metropolis and architecture in Hilberseimer's theory of the city. See this volume, p. 12.]

the standardization of production processes, the typification of the products of production, and generalization to the point of universality are today the tasks of every industrial firm.

Resis-
tance

Until now, the building industry has shied away from industrialization, normalization, and the mode of analysis associated with these processes, which are the foundations of all industry. It still rests on individual, manual foundations, while the entire present is based on collective, industrial conditions. Business and industry have essentially altered the environment. Every field of labor has been affected by the strict division of labor, creating corresponding production processes that meet new requirements. Industrial collectivism has replaced manual individualism. Only the building industry continues to operate using manual labor. It has remained essentially unaltered through all of these changes in production. Today it still applies the working methods of antiquity and the Middle Ages. This is a strange discrepancy, for which architects are mainly responsible.

Mock
architec-
ture

The architecture of the past century was retrospectively oriented. It was fully alienated from its most fundamental elements and ignored every invigorating contemporary development. Architects hoped to remedy this problem with all kinds of mock forms. Even in their best achievements, architects were not able to free themselves from the urge to conceal necessity with "beauty." Instead of demanding from engineers, chemists, and industry new structures and materials to create new, more rational modes of building, architects absurdly used the new structures and materials offered to them as substitute materials. For example, reinforced concrete was used to imitate cut stone, and iron structures were disguised with stylistic elements from all past ages. The academic stylistic tradition hindered the complete recognition and utilization of new constructive possibilities. Through their conservatism, architects have impeded or rather inhibited the implementation and exploitation of new methods and modes of working in all branches of the building trades, thereby frustrating the fruitful effects that industry has delivered in every other area of practice for architecture.

Imitations

Because manual construction has stubbornly persevered, architects have not yet realized that the machine is only a tool with greater potential than manual labor. The fruitful effects of mechanical production processes on form have not yet been recognized. For the meantime, one sees in the machine only schematization and an impediment to the process of creation. The precise opposite is actually true. By mechanizing tools we will achieve a greater freedom of creation; it will not hem in a creator's intentions, but rather stimulate them. Because, like a laborer's tool, the machine is a tool in the hands of the creator. It is by no means an end in itself, but only a means to an end, an executing organ of a superior will.

The machine is a means, not an end in itself

Freedom of creation

Metropolisarchitecture

Architecture of the past and of the present

The metropolis, with its entirely new demands and functions, has produced a new type of architecture, which is in many ways diametrically opposed to the architecture of the past. Despite a certain dependence on social, commercial, and productive forms, the architecture of the past had essentially cultic and religious origins. Metropolisarchitecture lacks such associations entirely. It is born of real needs and defined by objectivity and economy; material and construction; and economic and sociological factors. It is therefore independent of historical architecture, which arose from fundamentally different relations, and it cannot, as is often attempted, be derived from architecture of the past. It is illogical, absurd, and contradictory to try to apply the forms of historical architecture, detached from their premises, abstractly, indiscriminately, and without distinction.

Metropolisarchitecture is a new type of architecture with its own forms and laws. It represents the design of today's operative economic and sociological conditions. It seeks to free itself from all that is not immediate. It strives for reduction to the most essential elements, to achieve the greatest development of energy, the most extreme possibilities of tension, and ultimate precision. It corresponds to contemporary human life; it is the expression of a new awareness of life that is not subjective-individual but rather objective-collective.

Architecture is the creation of space. Its foundation is the sense of space. Through material objectification the sense of space is made perceptible—material substance is formed according to an idea. The formation of material substance according to an idea also entails the formation of ideal substance according to material laws. Architecture is created through the union of both factors in a single form. Architecture is therefore just as dependent on a spatial idea as on the space-enclosing material. It only emerges through their indissoluble unity; it is realized in the process of design. To a much greater degree than the other arts, architecture is rooted in material, the formal design of which is one of architecture's central tasks.

Architecture is the creation of space

External form and interior space are mutually dependent. The organization of the interior determines the design of the exterior, just as, vice versa, interior space depends on essential features of exterior design. Exterior form and interior space share a common border in the external surface of a structure. These surfaces, as a concentration of both spatial conditions, constitute the actual architectonic form. The universal agreement of interior and exterior creates the proportionality necessary for perfection. In single-room buildings this agreement is easy to achieve. The relationships become more complicated as the number of rooms and floors

The relationship between exterior and interior

increases. A horizontal design of a structure will arise on its own as a result of the layering of floors, while an exclusive emphasis of vertical elements in a horizontally layered building is nonsensical.

The floor plan

The relationship of interior to exterior is essentially determined by the floor plan. Thus the floor plan is of the greatest importance for the general design of a building. The plan should be discernible from the building's external appearance and vice versa. The floor plan introduces the third spatial coordinate, depth, to the horizontal and the vertical elements; thus it must be systematically integrated. It represents the horizontal projections of the structure, which, along with the vertical projections (sections and elevations), geometrically define and establish the building.

Style as result

The sum of the most characteristic features of a period's total artistic creation is labeled its style. Our time has until now searched in vain for its style. It has summoned neither a general will nor directed creative people to concrete problems of design. Under the suggestive influence of the past and the characteristic historicism of the nineteenth century, our time has believed that it had to be imitative in order to be effective. Misjudging the most important style-forming factors, our time has considered the architectural problem to be one of pure form and sought to hide its creative inability behind decorative stylistic masks. In seeking style, the absence of style was achieved. Because, like form, style can never be an objective but only a result—style is never an end in itself but always the result of the creative permeation of the entirety of sociological, economic, and technical conditions and demands; style embodies their harmonization and artistic expression. The secondary, form, has been placed before the primary, organic unity. But the individual form, the detail, is not independent and detachable, as academicism would have us believe, but rather is always dependent on the total design, a relation of the latter. Today it appears as if this academicism has been overcome. In architecture a fundamental renewal is making itself felt, particularly in response to the building tasks of the metropolis. This movement is working toward the essential, toward recognizing and designing the immediate and the necessary.

The new architecture, which is now being formed, has finally found the basis on which its activities can become fruitful. Like every work, architecture must also be connected to the overall whole and defined by necessity. It has finally been recognized that architecture can only be formed in itself, can only be based on its own fundamental elements, only shaped out of itself. A striving for clarity, architectural logic, and inner truth will lead to an austere unification. All works, as diverse as they may be, must emanate from a unified spirit. The architect must be in accord with the principles of the engineers, of their creations: machines and ships, cars and airplanes, cranes and bridges, which are always connected by the spirit of unity and represent the expression of a common will.

The basis of the new architectonic

Rational thinking, accuracy, precision, and economy—until now characteristics of the engineer—must become the basis of the new architectonic. All objects must be complete in themselves, reduced to their ultimate essential forms, organized reasonably, and led to their ultimate consummation.

Like every discipline, architecture is also confronting the requisite need to provide clarity regarding the means on which it is based and which are at its disposal. In this context, painting has provided valuable preliminary work. It was painting that first drew attention to the fundamental forms inherent in all art: geometric and cubic elements that permit no further objectification. The simple cubic bodies—boxes and spheres, prisms and cylinders, pyramids and cones, purely constructive elements—are the fundamental forms of every architecture. Their corporeal clarity demands clarity of form, bringing order to chaos in the most realistic manner.

The problem of architecture

The problem of architecture, apart from the practicality of materials and their appropriate use, is the spatial design of masses, which encompasses the organization, visualization, realization, and formation of a vision. The corporeality of architectural masses is produced by the rhythm of light and shadow. The whole design lives as a result of light. The entire rhythm receives its vitality through it. The weight or lightness of architecture depends on the effects of light and shadow, on the surface that receives and controls both. "In order to use light and shadow according to their essential properties and intentions, the architect has only certain geometrical combinations at his disposal. What tremendous effects he can create from limited means ... Might the effects of art be greater the more simple the means?" (Auguste Rodin).[44]

The architect must forget the entire ballast of forms with which he has been burdened by a scholarly education. The economy of a train car or an ocean liner provides an example superior to any diagram of stylistic ornament. The architect must develop solutions to new tasks organically, taking intended use, construction, and material into consideration. In the process of design he must remember the fundamental architectural elements: structure, surface, color, window and door openings, balconies, loggias, and chimneys. Working with these elements, he will arrive at an architecture that emerges out of its own principles. He will be able to eliminate ornamental decoration and other adornments because adornments are nothing but shells hiding unsolved architectural problems concealed

---

[44] [Auguste Rodin, *Die Kathedralen Frankreichs* (Leipzig: K. Wolff, 1917), 4. Hilberseimer cited the German translation of Rodin's French text; see this volume, pp. 59–60.]

by ornamental plaster and neutralized by decorative design. Only designing the truly functional will lead to a pure architecture. The constructive function must be viewed as architecture: the tautness of functional relationships, construction itself, must overcome its own materiality and become architectonic form. Metropolisarchitecture is considerably dependent on solving two factors: the individual cell of the room and the collective urban organism. The solution will be determined by the manner in which the room is manifested as an element of buildings linked together in one street block, thus becoming a determining factor of the city structure, which is the actual objective of architecture. Inversely, the constructive design of the urban plan will gain considerable influence on the formation of the room and the building as such.

The room, its constitutive elements of floors, walls, ceilings, windows and doors, material and color, furniture and its arrangement, produce a large complex of new creative possibilities. Through a new conception of space, new spatial relationships are created, new forms and proportions. Through the organization of individual rooms in the floor plan, the functional building that encompasses an entire street block is born. In doing so, extensive relationships of form are produced. A comprehensive synthesis of form is made possible.

In addition to the cubic mass, which is determined by the shaping power of the floor

Individual cell and urban organism

The elements of the room

plan, the number of floors, and the silhouette of the building, the partitioning of the building surfaces and their perforation are of essential importance. The architectonic problem in this instance lies in developing projections, setbacks, and recesses that emerge organically from the structure. The projection assumes a positive function in the composite surface; the recess, with its darkness, a negative one. As organizational factors, both spatial functions determine the rhythm of the structure. Thus entrances, windows, loggias, pillars, and the like are the actual exponents and bearers of rhythm. The sharpness and precision of rhythmic accentuation depend on the relationship of the form to light; they are based on the contrast of the lightness of the surface and the darkness of the recessions that penetrate it.

The bearers of rhythm

Even large openings, deeply recessed spaces, and entrance alcoves must not be neutralized by decoratively applied pillars or columns. As space-forming elements, they are to be organically incorporated into the building. They are not to be narrowed; they are to become true space-forming elements. They must be transformed from form-destroying elements into form-building elements.

A shift in the relationship of window to surface is of great importance for large buildings that occupy entire city blocks or for high-rises of many stories. In historical architecture the window was always an autonomous element, a factor

Windows and surface

of division, accent, or axial order. It was a penetration of the wall, and, as such, it had a negative surface function to fulfill in contrast to the surrounding surface features of the building mass. In an apartment block or high-rise, the window is entirely divested of this significance as an autonomous building element. As a result of its frequent occurrence, the window no longer contrasts with the surface but instead begins to assume some of the surface's positive functions; it becomes a part and component of the surface itself. The window no longer interrupts the wall surface but rather invigorates it evenly. From this shift in meaning, a new unifying element is acquired, created from purely functional purposes because the window, applied in a wide variety of ways, could easily become dangerous in a long or multistory building.

The identity of construction and form

The identity of construction and form is an essential precondition of architecture. While construction and form may seem to be opposed, architecture is founded on precisely their points of contact, their unity. Construction and material are the physical preconditions of architectural design, and they are always interrelated. Thus Greek architecture is based on the interplay of verticals and horizontals, as dictated by stone construction, and uses all the possibilities of cut stone while maintaining the unity of the material. A Greek temple is a perfect work of engineering in stone. Through the construction of arches and vaults the Romans greatly enriched the simple interplay of the vertical and the horizontal. Yet the Romans abandoned the unity of materials in the separation of structural ribs, infill, and revetment, which to this day has created a characteristic composite mode of construction, above all in the framing of openings and the covering of floors with cut stone. From the superimposition of several stories organized in columnar orders emerged the standard horizontal organization of multistory buildings, a principle that Michelangelo was the first to break. He was the first to combine several stories into one single order. With this development, the absolute ornamentality of building forms derived from antiquity was born. The forms gradually lost their sense of structural design until they finally became mock beings in their entirety: the architecture of the nineteenth century.

As a result of its new structural tasks, metropolisarchitecture was the first to make new construction and new materials an inevitable demand. Only building materials that allow for the greatest use of space and combine increased resistance to wear and weathering with great solidity are to be used in metropolisarchitecture. Iron, concrete, and reinforced concrete are the building materials that enable the new types of structures needed to meet metropolitan demands: horizontal or vaulted enclosures for large-span spaces and great cantilevered, self-supporting projections.

Concrete and reinforced concrete are building materials that place very few restrictions on

Metropolisarchitecture

Iron and reinforced concrete

the fantasy of the architect. We do not mean their malleability; i. e., the possibility of overcoming all physical impediments through casting. On the contrary: their constructive consequences, the possibility of creating a completely homogeneous structure, the combination of supporting and supported parts, the pure enclosure of masses, and the rendering superfluous of every kind of covering and trimming.

Overcoming the old support and load systems

Through the constructive possibilities of iron and reinforced concrete the old support and load system, which only permitted building from bottom up and from front to rear, has been overcome. Both enable cantilevered construction and projection beyond supports. They make possible the complete separation of supporting and supported parts and the reduction of the supporting construction to a minimum of points. The structure is separated into a load-bearing skeleton and its enclosing and dividing walls, which are no longer load-bearing. From these properties emerge new technical and material problems and especially new architectural and optical problems—a complete change of the apparently well-founded static visual form of a structure, so that when a cantilevered construction is applied and large plate-glass surfaces covering entire stories are used, a new architecture of floating lightness comes into being.

Horizontal articulation

With the disappearance of walls and supports at the front, the horizontal layering of multilevel buildings will be emphasized.

Horizontal design has until now been completely ignored due to the decorative use of pillars, yet it is one of the most important characteristics of a multistory building.

Along with reinforced concrete construction, the application of glass and steel as primary building materials is of great importance. Paul Scheerbart correctly recognized that glass offers completely new architectural possibilities.[45] His writings, however, have led Expressionist architects to use glass construction for anti-architectural, decorative fantasies. They ignorantly flouted the structural preconditions of steel and glass buildings.

Because this is a question of entirely new materials for spatial formation, the possibilities of this combination of materials must first be investigated in a purely experimental manner. The relationship of the sense of space to such combinations of materials and spatial forms must be investigated. Initially preference will be given to the corporeality and solidity of the stone wall over the steel-framed glass wall of the same statistical solidity.

No material can be used contrary to its own properties. Therefore a building of steel and

Glass and steel

[45] [Hilberseimer refers to Paul Scheerbart's concept of "glass architecture," which Expressionist architects championed. See Paul Scheerbart, *Glasarchitektur* (Berlin: Verlag der Sturm, 1914); Ludwig Hilberseimer, "Paul Scheerbart und die Architekten," *Das Kunstblatt* 3 (1919): 271–74; this volume, p. 31.]

glass requires a different technical treatment than a compact building. One will have to consider the relationship of transparent glass to lighting because glass structures seem to absorb more light than they reflect. The glass building without windows or other openings also requires a new structural and metric design than that commonly used until now in a standard compact building that is pierced by openings. In particular, the receptivity to color and simultaneous transparency of glass contain material possibilities that make Scheerbart's suggestions appear as more than merely utopian visions.

For the time being, however, we are still far from a planned and logical study and application of this new building material. Nearly everyone concerned with glass and steel construction has either overlooked or ignored the principles of this new type of construction, seeing in it instead a new means for exploring decorative possibilities.

Color

The element of color has been handled with great indifference in the past. A general underestimation of color was followed by its application in a hypertrophic and completely undisciplined way during Expressionism. It was applied only superficially to surfaces and buildings without an organic connection to material or form; without becoming one of their features. In architecture, color can never be applied as color as such, but only as the color of building materials. The coloration of architecture is always determined by the coloration of the material as one of its properties. Thus the element of color and its relationship to light are of the greatest importance.

Evenness, consistency, intensity of light, rate of change, and air humidity and temperature are the elements that unify the optical image of architecture according to definite laws. The haze of the air hovering over the metropolis dilutes any clear color. That is why the primary color of every metropolis is an undefined grey, the very color of haze. Yet coloration can contribute greatly to the intensification of architectural aims. Monotone coloration can become a unifying element, while multicolor schemes can become invigorating, even compositional elements—by employing color, both single buildings and multi-building projects can be more tautly brought together, heightening their cubic effect.

Color can also be used to emphasize individual parts of a building, to differentiate parts, to create or support a hierarchy, or to direct the eye to the flow of the principal lines. Yet color must never be an added element but always a property of the building material.

The relationship of building materials to light is also of great importance. The transparency and opacity, smoothness and bluntness, hardness and softness of materials, sharp lines and edges, and transitions from raised to recessed surfaces are decisive for the refraction of light, the reduction of brightness, and therefore for

The relation-ship to light

color. They determine the variable degree of corporeality and the degree of independence among individual parts. As unifying and isolating elements of the compositional material, they are of greatest import.

The general law

The distinctiveness of an organism can be seen in its individual organs, which embody this distinction. The general law, in its universality, is represented in the entire organism, the details demonstrating only the specific case. This is why the difference of the metropolis from other urban forms must also be displayed in individual buildings. Just as the metropolis is not a traditional city on a larger scale, the metropolitan building is not a conversion of older forms to larger dimensions.

New structural and spatial needs and demands, altered requirements and different uses have led to new constructions and materials, thus producing new forms.

The metropolitan structure, as a cell, and the metropolitan organism, as a part of a unity, must contain essential architectural characteristics that are conditioned by the nature of the metropolis. Because the preconditions of past architectural practice no longer apply, their means of expression cannot be maintained. The decorative schema of the Renaissance cannot be transferred to an apartment building, a warehouse, or an office building if these buildings are not to lose their meaning—it was due to this sort of nonsense that the offices of Ludwig

Hoffmann's new municipal administration building in Berlin receive so little light.[46]

All details applied at the scale of individual rooms become absurd if their intensity and motivating force cannot incorporate the entire building; that is, where they are by nature intimate details. Therefore options for incorporating organizational details are greatly reduced in metropolisarchitecture. Ornament in particular is entirely absurd. Everything surges toward a powerful design of the profile, of the floor plan, which determines the contours of the building. In a decisively cubic construction details recede into the background. The general design of masses and the laws of proportion that govern them are the decisive factors.

The necessity of creating a law of form that is equally valid for every element, for an often monstrous and heterogeneous mass of material, requires that architectural form be reduced to the most concise, most necessary, and most general characteristics and restricted to the geometric cubic forms, the fundamental elements of all architecture.

Accordingly, the most essential qualities of the architect—his sense of mass and proportion and his organizational ability—acquire greater importance. To form great masses by suppressing rampant multiplicity according to a general

---

[46] [Hilberseimer refers to Hoffmann's Stadthaus in Berlin (1900–11). On Hoffmann see note 30, p. 198.]

law is Nietzsche's definition of style: the general case, the law is respected and emphasized; the exception, however, is put aside, nuance is swept away, measure becomes master, chaos is forced to become form: logical, unambiguous, mathematics, law.[47]

[47] [For Hilberseimer's reference to Nietzsche's definition of style, see this volume, pp. 62–63.]

Selected Essays

The Will to Architecture

"Der Wille zur Architektur," *Das Kunstblatt* 7 (1923): 133–40.

The art of the past decades fled from reality. Because one could not cope with the facts of societal life, one turned to mysticism. The present and its tasks were forgotten in favor of metaphysical speculations. All will to design life was absent. Due to irresponsibility, to a deficient desire for life, refuge was sought in an artificially idealized past. And yet, unlike most other periods before, the present found itself obligated to grapple with the realities and agitations of this world. It forced a creative rationalism, called forth a revolution of spiritual means: politics, science, art. And thus after many experimental attempts, art discovered the path to reality. It reduced illusionism, the sole aim of art since the Renaissance, to absurdity; it created a new appreciation for the objects of our environment. Today it is no longer essential to simply paint paintings, sculpt statues, or create aesthetic arrangements. Rather it is crucial to design reality itself. It is not important to paint reproductions, but to form entities, to apply the constructive laws of art to the room, to the object, as reality. It must be attempted to take all those forces that today still operate in a reproductive fashion and connect them to productive labor process, to methodically spur them to efficacy. Because the objective is to order the world and human relationships, to induce responsible actions, to regulate the most important and essential conditions of life.

Only by concentrating all artistically creative strength in one defined area, by setting the most resolute aim, will we achieve the output required. Architecture is the artistic field that can solve the most problems today. This explains the efforts of all modern artistic genres to connect to architecture. First the image surface was rendered architectonically. Thus as early as Expressionism a clarification of the means of design was discerned. The construction of the image took place according to structural principles. But Expressionism did not extend beyond the domain of the emotional. Subjective arbitrariness and emotional obfuscation hindered the logical expression of form.

Conscious of the fundamental elements of all design, Cubism reverted to foundational geometric-cubic forms. Cubism is the first stage on the path from illusion to autonomous formation. It recognized the identity of material and form, attempted to design with conscious, stylistic will, yet ended like Expressionism in subjective speculation. The problem of anthropomorphic figuration continued to absorb it far too much. It is no coincidence that precisely Picasso and Archipenko initiated a new Classicism.

Abstract art was the first to transcend the narrow boundary of the subjective in order to reach the objective, the typical. It relinquished the compositional principle in favor of the constructive. With Suprematism it achieved its ultimate effects. Abstract idealism reached its apogee; everything still materialistic in some way was destroyed. The conclusion of an artistic phase was reached, the way made free for new creative possibilities.

The Constructivists strode this path—the path to reality—purposefully. Their provisional, as yet non-utilitarian constructions reveal the unmistakable will to possess reality. The world itself became the material of their design; every object was drawn into their domain. From the construction of painting, the Constructivists transitioned to the construction of objects, to architecture in the most all-encompassing sense of the word. The Constructivists most lucidly recognized the new aim, putting their entire creative power at its disposal.

Rational thinking, accuracy, precision, and economy—until now characteristics of the engineer—must become the basis of this comprehensive architectonic. Because Constructivism is no new ornamentality, no new formalism. It grips objects themselves, permeates and suffuses them with spirit, reduces them to their essential forms, organizes them reasonably, leads them to their ultimate consummation of form.

In the end, the works of the Constructivists are only experiments of material; they are attempts to become acquainted with and shape material and its possibilities; attempts to fathom the potentials of assembly and interdependencies, to explain contrasts of material and form, to work deliberately to solve the modern problems posed by the latter. These newly discovered laws of form will achieve an all-encompassing influence on modern architecture. They are certainly modified by different requirements and purposes. Every new object will always embody the law inherent to itself. But as disparate as these objects may be, they will always be connected through the laws of clarity and economy.

The experimental character of Constructivist works excludes from the start that they are ends unto themselves. They are only works of transition, intended for utilitarian architectural constructions. A well-disciplined training in architecture is the ultimate objective.

Like every art, architecture is also confronting the requisite need to provide clarity regarding the means upon which it is based and which are at its disposal. In this context, painting has provided valuable preliminary work. It was painting that first drew attention to the fundamental geometric-cubic forms inherent in all art. The simple cubic bodies: boxes and spheres, prisms and cylinders, pyramids and cones, purely constructive elements, are the fundamental forms of every architecture. Their corporeal clarity demands clarity of form. Architecture originates from geometry. When geometric entities become proportioned bodies, architecture emerges, revealing diversity within great unity. The central axis takes precedence over details. Particulars retreat fully before the decisive cubic composition. The standard is set by the general design of masses, the law of proportions to which it is subject. The most heterogeneous material masses require a law of form applicable for every element in equal measure. Thus structural forms are reduced to their most essential, most general, most simple, most unambiguous. Rampant multiplicity is suppressed; formation occurs according to a general law of form.[1]

The architecture of the present distinguishes itself from the architecture of the past primarily through its sociological and economic premises. Technical particularities that are absolutely definitive for today's architecture result from new function-oriented requirements. These particularities are new and exhilarating elements, which constitute, through their shapes, the artistic moment of today. Today we need not cathedrals, temples, or palaces, but rather residential buildings, commercial buildings, and factories, which, however, were formerly built to resemble cathedrals, temples, and palaces. One of the most essential tasks of architecture today is to sensibly design the residential building, the commercial building, and the factory. Pure

[1]   [Although Hilberseimer does not mention it here, his discussion of the reduction of form and the suppression of multiplicity draws on his reading of Friedrich Nietzsche's concept of style. See this volume, pp. 62–63.]

models of these building types have yet to emerge. They must first be created. The homogeneity of their intended uses enables comprehensive standardization, a necessary, constructive task for which not even the first step has been taken today. Until now, architecture has shied away from normalization, the process on which all industry is based. It still rests on individual, manual foundations, while the entire present is based on collective, industrial conditions. Ignoring necessities has always led to rigidity. And what is more rigid than the architecture of the present? But creativity reveals itself precisely by comprehensively addressing given conditions, by seeking an adequate shape for them.

Today's architecture is considerably dependent on solving two factors: the individual cell of the room and the collective urban organism. The solution will be determined by the manner in which the room is manifested as an element of buildings linked together in one street block, thus becoming a shaping factor of the city structure, which is the actual objective of architecture. Inversely, the constructive design of the urban plan will gain considerable influence on the constructive formation of the room and the building as such.

The room and its constitutive elements of floors, walls, ceilings, openings in the walls, material and color, furniture and its arrangement, and the connection to neighboring rooms produce a large complex of creative-constructive possibilities. Constructivism generates a new conception of space, creates new spatial relationships, new forms and proportions. By organizing individual rooms in the floor plan, the functional building that encompasses an entire street block is born. In doing so, extensive relationships of form are produced. A comprehensive synthesis of form is made possible. In addition to the cubic mass, which is determined by the floor plan and the number of floors, of essential import is the partitioning of building surfaces and their perforation. The technical problem in this instance lies in developing projections and recesses that emerge organically from the structure. The projection assumes a positive function in the composite surface, the recess, with its darkness, a negative one. As organizational factors, both functions determine the rhythm of the structure.

What the room represents on a small scale, the urban structure is on a large one: an all-encompassing organization of reciprocal needs and relationships. A number of factors must be taken into account, some of which extend far beyond the spatial nature of the city. These are dependent on the economic and sociological structure of the state. The distinctiveness of an urban organism can be seen in its individual organs, which embody this distinction. The general law, in its universality, is represented in the entire organism; the individual building demonstrates one particular case. New technical and

Fig. 77 Ludwig Hilberseimer, High-rise factory project, 1922

spatial needs and demands, which result from altered requirements and different uses, lead to new applications of material and to new kinds of forms. Their constructive character expresses the singularity of our age.

The work of the engineer is completed by producing rational output. That of the architect begins where the latter left off. For the architect, a rational solution is the material of design. A comprehensive conception of form takes precedence over the rational solution. The latter is merely a means for lending corporeality to an idea, for actualizing it in space.

Proposal for City-Center Development

"Vorschlag zur City-Bebauung," *Die Form* 5, nos. 23–24 (1930): 608–11. Republished in *Moderne Bauformen* 30, no. 3 (1931): 55–59.

One of the most important and current problems for urban planning today is the reorganization and reconstruction of the city center. Today the center is a hybrid residential city and business city. As such it is functional as neither one nor the other. Thus all residences must be removed from the city center so that it can be systematically rebuilt for its purpose. Like the city center itself, its structures also comprise a mixture of residential and commercial buildings. The commercial building of today evolved from the apartment building as partition walls were removed from floor to floor and larger windows were knocked out. If one building was no longer sufficient, a second and third would be annexed, until one day the complexity of this product of happenstance forced, in the interest of rational business management, the construction of a new building. But further development and expanding operations would soon render this newly constructed building insufficient—especially in the case of the department store—and thus additional new buildings would be required, which, despite being adeptly attached to the old buildings, retained in principle the disadvantages—though on an improved foundation—as the original apartment buildings that had been successively annexed and converted for commercial purposes.

One example of how a large department store has been created from successively annexed components is the Wertheim department store in Berlin on Leipziger Platz, which today covers an entire street block of considerable dimensions.[1] When, more than thirty years ago, the first component was designed and executed, no one imagined that the space required by the Wertheim building would amount to what it is today.

Fig. 52

A further phase of this development is represented by the Tietz department store on Alexanderplatz in Berlin. In this instance, a building complex of approximately the same size as the Wertheim department store was created all at once according to a specific plan, not piecemeal as a result of successive expansion.[2] In doing so, all the advantages facilitated by a clear design naturally benefited operations. Not only the department store, but also the office building has gone through this phase of development. For

[1] [The Wertheim department store was built in four stages from 1896 to 1912. Alfred Messel designed the first three; Heinrich Schweitzer, the fourth. No longer extant.]

[2] [The Tietz department store at Alexanderplatz was designed by Wilhelm Cremer and Richard Wolffenstein and opened in 1905; a new atrium was added in 1912. No longer extant.]

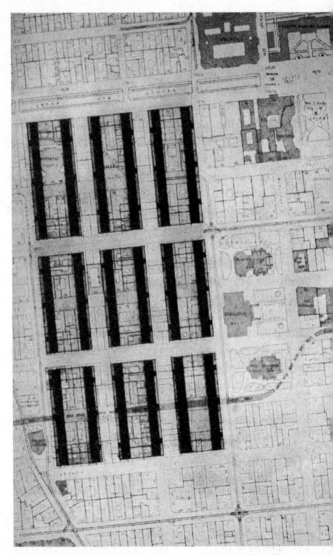

Fig. 78 Ludwig Hilberseimer, Proposal for City-Center

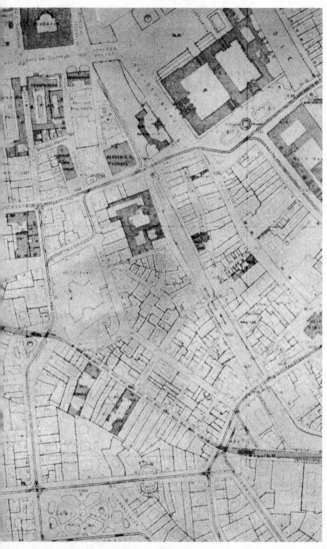

Development, 1928–30; site plan

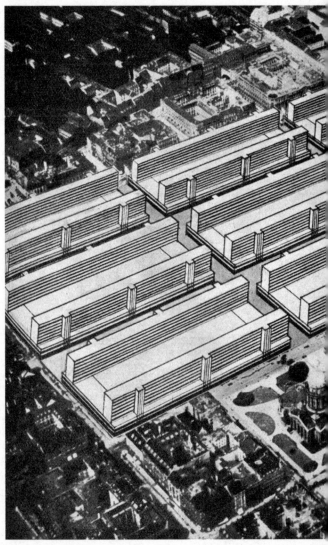

Fig. 79 Ludwig Hilberseimer, Proposal for City-Center

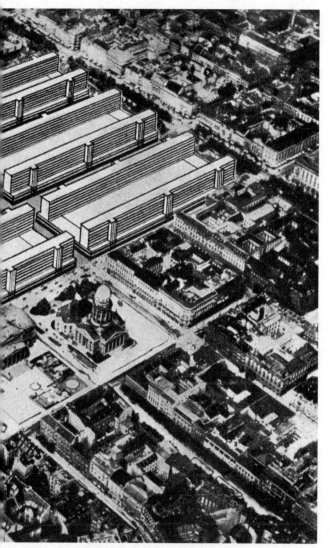

Development, 1928–30; photomontage of aerial view

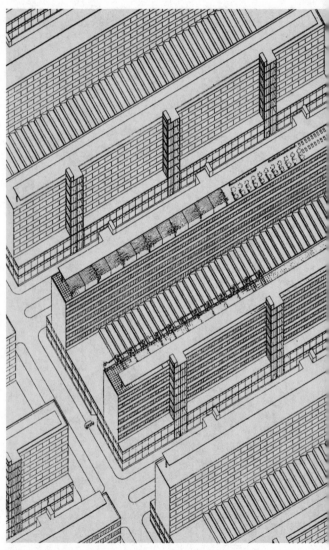

Fig. 80 Ludwig Hilberseimer, Proposal for City-Center

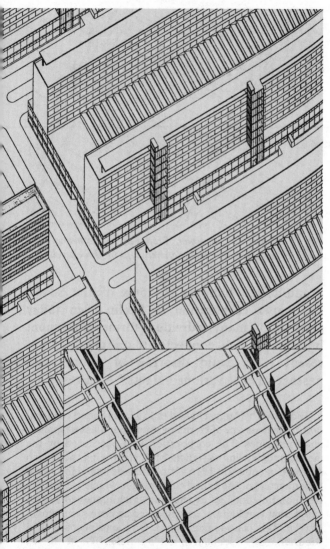

Development, 1928–30; axonometric view

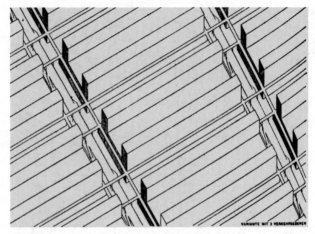

Fig. 81 Ludwig Hilberseimer, Proposal; axonometric view, detail of variant with circulation networks on three levels

example, the building complex of the Scherl newspaper corporation in Berlin even today consists of many individual former apartment buildings, which, connected to one another, represent a fantastic disarray of rooms and passageways at various heights.[3] As a result of

[3]   [Founded by August Scherl in 1883, the Scherl corporation published some of Germany's most popular newspapers and magazines. The corporation was purchased by the media mogul, industrialist, and right-wing politician Alfred Hugenberg in 1916. Otto Kohtz designed the initial headquarters of the Scherl corporation, which was built in 1928, and planned an expansion, which remained unexecuted, that would have encompassed an entire city block. The building is no longer extant. On the project see Otto Riedrich, "Die Neubauten der Fa. Scherl G. M. B. H., Berlin," *Deutsche Bauzeitung* 63, no. 42 (1929): 369–76.]

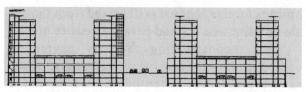

Fig. 82 Ludwig Hilberseimer, Proposal; transverse section

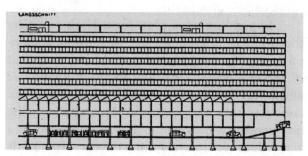

Fig. 83 Ludwig Hilberseimer, Proposal; longitudinal section

the associated difficulties, the Scherl corporation has already begun constructing a new building. It is relatively simple for larger companies to meet their space requirements by constructing new buildings. This is not the case for smaller businesses, which are forced to rent space in old office buildings where rooms are often very impractical. In order for such an office building to fulfill its purpose, the building must be able to provide, in addition to the rooms used directly by small businesses, communal rooms for conferences and the like for individual tenants, who would not otherwise be able to afford them. The office building can best meet these requirements, and thus offer entirely different options for use, when it is liberated from the single building and instead covers an entire block.

By reconstructing the city center, an option that is becoming increasingly necessary, these demands can be easily met, and at the same time existing objectionable conditions can be eliminated.

Expanding on a plan for a High-rise City that was formulated in 1924, this proposal demonstrates the reorganization and redevelopment of the city center.[4] Without increasing land use and solely through an alternate distribution and concentration of building masses, it allows the city center to be developed and improved in a way that completely meets the standards demanded by a business quarter. For this new city center it is entirely possible to employ the high-rise as the exclusive structural form because it is to be constructed on an urban plan that corresponds to this building type. Unlike the high-rise cities of America, it is not based on the system of the individual building, which descends from medieval times. This urban plan, which is aligned with the high-rise, enables not only a controlled flow of traffic but also the necessary supply of light and air by ensuring sufficient intervals between buildings, avoiding courtyards, and orienting the buildings toward the sun. The necessarily large intervals between

[4] Ludwig Hilberseimer, *Großstadtarchitektur*, Die Baubücher, Bd. 3 (Stuttgart: J. Hoffmann, 1927), 17–20. [See this volume, pp. 125–130.]

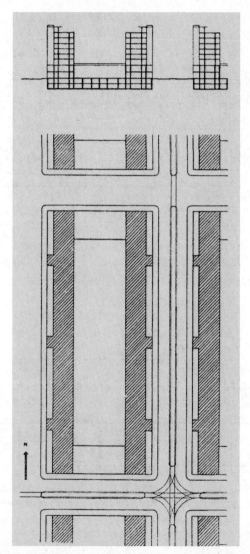

Fig. 84 Ludwig Hilberseimer, Proposal; proposed block structure

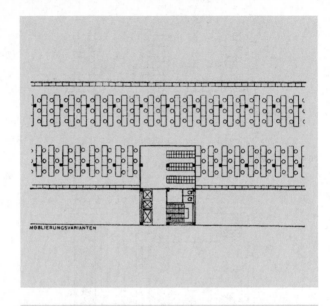

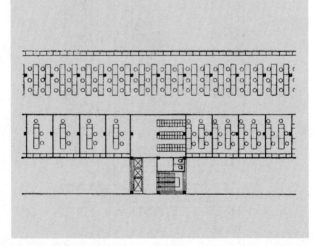

Fig. 85 Ludwig Hilberseimer, Proposal; floor plan variations

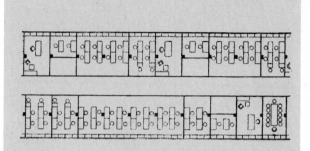

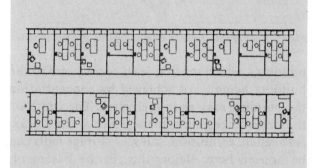

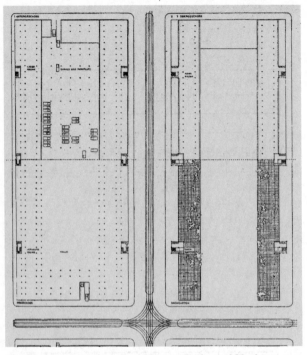

Fig. 86 Ludwig Hilberseimer, Proposal; plans of block structure

buildings, which must at least correspond to the building height, are achieved by concentrating the building masses in high-rises. The width of the street corresponds to the width of the blocks. As needed, exhibition, sales, or storage halls can be housed here. Below this, in the basement, garages and parking lots for automobiles can be situated, thus efficiently solving the problem of parking automobiles, which poses an extraordinary challenge for the metropolis.

This proposal has intentionally left the existing building density unaltered. Building masses have simply been distributed differently. An increase in height by several floors is already being considered in the city center for the sort of buildings existing today, but with this proposal an increase in height can be readily implemented. It can be executed in this case under far more favorable conditions than with existing building types since, through the elimination of small courtyards, the structures in this proposal offer superior working spaces, light conditions, and ventilation.

Such a city center is also of great significance for transportation planning. Should it become necessary, it allows for a street system to be designed on multiple levels and thus a complete separation of pedestrian traffic from vehicular traffic. Furthermore, vehicular traffic can be separated by the allocation of a second vehicular traffic level, facilitating street crossings without intersections. These vehicular traffic levels can be connected to each other by ramps. Mass public transportation occurs without the use of trams, employing instead the subway and buses, whose stations connect to pedestrian traffic levels by elevators and escalators.

Visual Documents

1   The cover of *Großstadt-architektur* conveys both Hilberseimer's interest in typological analysis and his understanding of the essentially typical nature of architecture in the metropolis. He juxtaposes his project for a Residential City (upper right) with the structural skeleton of an unidentified skyscraper (upper left). A visual rhyme links the blocks of his project to the Portland cement factory in El Paso, Texas, pictured in the center. At lower right, the grand hall of Tony Garnier's slaughterhouses of La Mouche in Lyon (1909–13) symbolizes the metabolism of the metropolis, while Le Corbusier's Cook House, at lower left, signals Hilberseimer's simultaneously reverential and critical relationship to the single-family house as a type and to the Franco-Swiss master as a designer.

LUDWIG HILBERSEIMER

BAUBÜCHER BAND 3

GROSS
STADT

ARCHITEKTUR

JULIUS HOFFMANN
VERLAG / STUTTGART   MIT 229 ABBILDUNGEN / KART. M 9.50

in Philadelphia der Durchbruch des Fairmount Parkway, dessen dekorativer Aufwand die Mängel des Stadtgrundrisses keineswegs beseitigt.

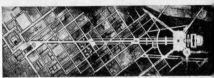

Abb. 15. Philadelphia, Durchbruch des Fairmount Parkway. Nach Unwin

Man war sich bei dem Ausbau der Großstädte nicht klar darüber, daß man einen neuen, durchaus eigengesetzlichen Körper zu gliedern hatte, der nicht nur quantitativ, sondern vor allem auch qualitativ von der Stadt der Vergangenheit unterschieden ist. Daher die Planlosigkeit, der chaotische Charakter aller Großstädte, die völlige Zufallsprodukte sind. Solange sie nicht eine bestimmte Größe erreicht haben, genügen sie so gut oder schlecht wie möglich. Ihre Unzulänglichkeit tritt aber eklatant in Erscheinung, wenn diese Größe erreicht oder überschritten wird. Ein Zustand, in dem sich heute alle sogenannten Großstädte mehr oder weniger befinden. Vor allem aber die durch Hochhäuser beherrschten amerikanischen Großstädte.

Wir haben den Charakter der bestehenden Großstadt als den eines Konglomerats erkannt: als eine Häufung disparater Elemente. Ihre Entwicklung als eine planlose, nur das Tagesbedürfnis befriedigende Aneinanderreihung, ohne höhere Gesichtspunkte, ohne Verantwortung für das Kommende. Im Gegensatz dazu muß die Stadt der Zukunft den Charakter eines planvollen Gebildes, eines völlig durchdachten Organismus haben. Alle Mängel müssen erkannt und beseitigt, die Stadt planvoll auf Grund ihrer Elemente aufgebaut, in einem völlig neuen Sinn gestaltet werden. Sie muß die städtebaulichen Grundforderungen verwirklichen. Der Stadtplan klar und übersichtlich

Großstadtchaos

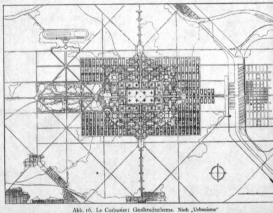

Abb. 16. Le Corbusier: Großstadtschema. Nach „Urbanisme"

12

Abb. 17. Le Corbusier: Großstadtschema, Ansicht. Nach „Urbanisme"

Die Wohnungen gesund und bequem. Abgeschlossene Wohnhöfe vermeiden. Die Blocks offen und durchlüftbar. Die Straßen- und Hofbreiten den Gebäudehöhen entsprechend. Der Verkehr muß geregelt, nach Verkehrsarten getrennt sein, so daß auf gleicher Ebene nur gleiche Verkehrsmittel verkehren.

Dem Chaos der heutigen Großstadt können nur theoretische Demonstrationsversuche gegenübergestellt werden. Ihre Aufgabe ist es, rein abstrakt, fundamentale Prinzipien des Städtebaues aus den aktuellen Bedürfnissen heraus zu entwickeln: zur Gewinnung von allgemeinen Regeln, die die Lösung bestimmter konkreter Aufgaben ermöglichen. Denn nur die Abstraktion vom besonderen Fall erlaubt es zu zeigen, wie die disparaten Elemente, die eine Großstadt ausmachen, in eine beziehungsreiche Ordnung zu dieser gebracht werden können. Versuche zu einer solchen grundsätzlichen Auseinandersetzung

mit dem Gestaltungsproblem der Großstadt wurden von Le Corbusier und Ludwig Hilberseimer unternommen. Beide versuchen eine Ordnung der Dinge, welche die Menschen einer Millionenstadt zum Leben, zur Arbeit und zur Erholung brauchen. Mit der Absicht, ein Höchstmaß von Ordnung zu erreichen. Jedem einzelnen seine Ansprüche an Raum, Luft, Hygiene und Bequemlichkeit zu erfüllen. Die Stadt zu einem leistungsfähigen Organismus zu machen.

Um seine Prinzipien des Städtebaues zu demonstrieren, hat Le Corbusier den Plan zu einer Stadt für etwa 3 Millionen Einwohner entworfen. (Urbanisme, Paris 1925.) Um seine Absichten klarer entwickeln zu können, hat er ein völlig ebenes Terrain angenommen. Eine plane Ebene ohne topographische Hindernisse, die es ihm ermöglicht, seine geometrische Planung konsequent durchzuführen.

Die Bevölkerung unterteilt er in: Städter, Vorstädter und Gemischte. Städter nennt er die, die in der Stadt arbeiten und wohnen. Vorstädter die, die in der Fabrikzone arbeiten und in den dazugehörigen Gartenstädten wohnen. Die Gemischten sind die, die zwar in der Stadt arbeiten, aber in einer Gartenstadt wohnen.

Dadurch ergibt sich für die Stadtanlage ein begrenztes, dichtes, konzentriertes Organ: das Zentrum, und ein ausgedehntes, schmiegsames, elastisches Organ: die Fabrikzone mit den Gartenstädten. Zwischen beiden liegt ein unbebaubarer Wald- und Wiesengürtel.

Die Prinzipien seiner Planung sind: Entlastung des Stadtzentrums, trotzdem aber Zunahme seiner Bevölkerungsdichtigkeit. Zunahme der Verkehrsmittel und Zunahme der bepflanzten Flächen.

In der City des Zentrums befinden sich auf einer

(marginal notes:) Le Corbusiers Stadtplan Abb. 16 u. 17

Entlastung des Zentrums

Abb. 18. Le Corbusier: Hochhausgrundriß

13

problem of the metropolis,
not a fundamental solution.

Abb. 46. Bruno Taut: Siedlung Britz bei Berlin

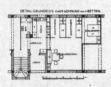

Abb. 47. Martin Wagner: Siedlung Britz bei 'Berlin

Abb. 48. Bruno Taut: Siedlung Britz bei Berlin,
Grundriß

Abb. 49. Ludwig Hilberseimer: Grundriß einer Wohnung von 4 Betten

Vorraum: 1 Garderobeschrank, 2 Gasmesser usw.
Bad: 3 Wanne, 4 Waschbecken, 5 W C.
Küche: 6 Gasherd, 7 Tisch, 8 Abtropfbrett, 9 Abwaschtisch, 10 Ausguß-
becken, 11 Speiseschrank, 12 Geschirrschrank
Wohn- und Eßzimmer: 13 Sofa, 14 Anrichte
Schlafkabine: 15 Kleiderschrank mit Tischplatte, 16 Bett
Schlafzimmer: 17 Bett, 18 Wäscheschrank, 19 Kleiderschrank

Abb. 50.
Ludwig Hilberseimer:
Grundrißvariationen
bei Grundlage
gleicher Elemente
zu Wohnungen von
3, 4, 5, 6 und 7
Betten

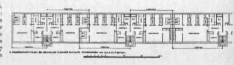

32

3　　In these pages, Hilberseimer compares his projects for mass housing with realized structures: Bruno Taut and Martin Wagner's Horseshoe Settlement in Berlin. The comparison manifests Hilberseimer's belief in the power of theoretical

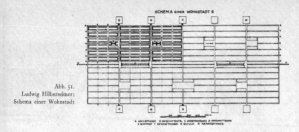

SCHEMA einer WOHNSTADT B

Abb. 51.
Ludwig Hilberseimer:
Schema einer Wohnstadt

A WOHNSTRASSE B GESCHÄFTSSTR. C VERBINDUNGS D ERHOLUNGSBAHN
E BAHNHOF F VERKEHRSBAHN G SCHULE H KRANKENHAUS

Abb. 52.
Ludwig
Hilberseimer:
Blockansicht

Abb. 53.
Ludwig Hilberseimer:
Schema einer Wohnstadt,
Straßenansicht

entsprechend der größeren Zahl der Bewohner. Durch den Einbau aller Schrankmöbel und der Kücheneinrichtung ermöglicht sich die größte Nutzbarmachung des Raumes. Alle Räume, auch die Schlafkabine und der Vorraum sind direkt beleuchtet und lassen Querlüftung zu. Im Aufbau bekommt der sonst ungegliederte Block dadurch eine kubische Gliederung, daß die nach Norden und Süden zu liegenden Kopfbauten mit Läden usw. nur zweigeschossig sind, damit einen lebhaften Kontrast zu den fünfgeschossigen Wohntrakten bilden, den Baublock öffnen und seine Struktur plastisch sichtbar

Abb. 52

Abb. 88. Victor Bourgeois: Cité Moderne, Brüssel. Vgl. Abb. 87

erzielt, die die Enge des Nebeneinanders vergessen läßt und den Vorteil bietet, den Flächenraum der Gesamtplanung wirklichen Nutzzwecken dienstbar zu machen.

Auflockerung des Blocks Abb. 84—86

Eine solche Auflockerung der starren Blockfront hat Jan Wils bei einer Siedlung „Daalen Berg" im Haag durch eine geschickte Verschachtelung der Einzelhäuser erzielt. Durch das Vor und Zurück des Baukörpers gewinnt er eine außerordentlich lebendige kubische Gliederung, erreicht er starke Kontrastwirkungen.

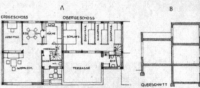

Abb. 89. Ludwig Hilberseimer: Reihenhäuser, Grundrisse und Schnitt

Abb. 90. Ludwig Hilberseimer: Reihenhäuser

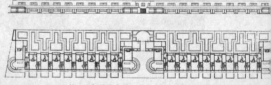

Abb. 91. J. J. P. Oud: Reihenhausanlage in Hook van Holland

44

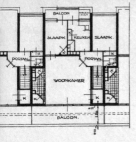

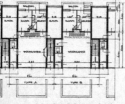

Abb. 92–93. J. J. P. Oud: Reihenhausanlage in Hook van Holland, oben: Obergeschoßgrundriß, unten: Erdgeschoßgrundriß

Auf eine andere Art hat Victor Bourgeois die Auflockerung des Baukörpers erreicht. Um bei einer gegebenen Ost-West-Straße der Cité Moderne in Brüssel die Nord-Süd-Orientierung der Häuser zu vermeiden, läßt er deren Achse unter 45 Grad die Straßenachse schneiden und gewinnt durch die sich so ergebende sägeförmige Bebauung nicht nur eine Nord-Ost-West- und Süd-Ost-West-Belichtung, sondern auch eine Aufhebung der starren Straßenfront.

Die bei seinem Miethausentwurf durchgeführte Trennung nach Zwecken und Typisierung der einzelnen Räume hat Ludwig Hilberseimer bei seinem Entwurf für Reihenhäuser auch auf das Kleinhaus angewandt. Der Grundriß ist so organisiert, daß sich um den eingeschossigen Hauptraumkörper, den Wohnraum, L-förmig in zwei Geschossen die anderen kleineren Räume legen. Im Hauptgeschoß: Arbeitszimmer, Eßzimmer, Küche und Vorraum. Im Obergeschoß, wo über dem Hauptwohnraum eine Terrasse angeordnet ist, liegen um dieselbe herum Schlafzimmer, drei Schlafkabinen und Bad. Die Freiheiten, die das Einfamilienhaus hinsichtlich seiner Höhenentwicklung erlaubt, ermöglichen auch eine Differenzierung der Räume der Höhe nach. Der Hauptwohnraum hat nicht nur die größte Bodenfläche, sondern auch die größte Höhe. Durch den Wechsel eingeschossiger und zweigeschossiger Bauteile ergibt sich ein ausgeprägter plastischer Aufbau, der durch die Reihung wesentlich verstärkt wird.

In Hook van Holland hat J. J. P. Oud eine Reihenhausgruppe erbaut, die besonders durch die Art

Besonnungs-möglichkeit einer Ost-West-Straße
Abb. 87 u. 88

Raum-typisierung
Abb. 89 u. 90

Abb. 91–94

Abb. 94.
J. J. P. Oud:
Reihenhausanlage in
Hook van Holland

45

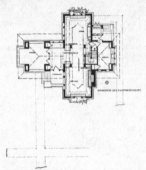

Abb. 116. Frank Lloyd Wright: Wohnhaus Martin, Erdgeschoßgrundriß

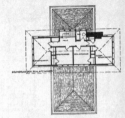

Abb. 117. Frank Lloyd Wright: Wohnhaus Martin, Obergeschoßgrundriß. Nach dem „20. Jahrhundert"

einer anderen Art des Wohnens, die sich von der europäischen durchaus unterscheidet.

Von der gleichen Eigenart wie der Grundriß ist auch der äußere Aufbau, der trotz ausgesprochener Horizontalgliederung durch seine weiten Öffnungen, weit vorspringenden Terrassen und Flachdächer einen leichten, fast schwebenden Charakter bekommt. Die sehr differenzierten Höhenunterschiede des Baukörpers ermöglichen zur Beleuchtung der Räume die Anordnung hohen Seitenlichts, Fenster zu Gruppen oder in ganze Bauteile umlaufende Streifen zu vereinigen. Gleichzeitig akzentuieren die Höhenunterschiede den Baukörper, bringen eine lebhafte kubische Gliederung hervor. Während die amerikanische Architektur wie die deutsche im allgemeinen vertikal baut, bevorzugt Wright die Horizontale. Er überdehnt die Flachdächer seiner Landhäuser, die Loggien und Terrassen zu durchlaufenden horizontalen Teilungen und nutzt die Horizontale zur Verstärkung der Auftreppung seiner stark ter-

rassenartig aufgebauten Häuser. Auch bezieht die Umgebung seiner Bauten in deren Archit tur ein. Die umlaufenden Wege stehen in ein Parallelverhältnis zu den Horizontalen des B körpers. So entstehen aus den Dachvorsprüng Terrassen usw. halbkörperliche Gebilde, die Indifferenziertheit des Luftraums überleiten körperlichen Bestimmtheit des Gebäudes, der Schwere aber gleichzeitig wieder optisch aufhebe Der Einfluß, den Wright ausgeübt hat, läßt kaum ermessen. Fast alle neueren europäischen Ar tekten standen unter seinem Einfluß. Besonders so lebensvolle holländische Architektur ist o Wrights Vorbild nicht denkbar.

Durch die Ausnutzung der konstruktiven Mögl

Abb. 118. Frank Lloyd Wright: Wohnhaus Martin

52

5   These pages are some of the few in the book devoted to single-family houses. Hilberseimer celebrates the work of Frank Lloyd Wright, but illustrates Le Corbusier's Cook House without textual commentary. Hilberseimer applied his own motto "the

Metropolisarchitecture

Abb. 119. Le Corbusier mit Pierre Jeanneret, Paris: Haus Cook, Wohnraum

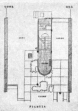

Untergeschoß

Zwischenstock

Hauptgeschoß

Terrassengeschoß

Querschnitt

Hauptfront

Abb. 120—125. Le Corbusier mit Pierre Jeanneret, Paris: Haus Cook. Vgl. die Ansicht S. 54 oben

53

house as commodity" to the single-family house he built at the Weissenhofsiedlung (illustrated elsewhere). One can only imagine what he thought of Le Corbusier's luxurious urban villa.

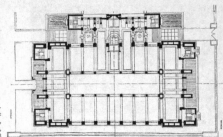

Abb. 143.
Frank Lloyd Wright:
Larkins-Werke, Buffalo,
Verwaltungsgebäude,
Grundriß

wissermaßen symbolhaft umschreibend. Durch seitliches schräges Vorkragen einzelner Geschosse sucht er seine Unabhängigkeit von der stützenden Vertikalen zum Ausdruck zu bringen.

Abb. 148

Mit seltener Konsequenz hat Mies van der Rohe die Gestaltungsmöglichkeit des neuen Konstruktionsgedankens erkannt, mit seinem Entwurf für ein Bürohaus die architektonische Lösung dafür gefunden. Ein zweistieliger Rahmen von acht Meter Spannweite und beiderseitiger Konsolauskragung von vier Meter wurde als das ökonomische Konstruktionssystem ermittelt. Dieses Rahmensystem trägt die Deckenplatte, die am Ende der Kragarme zur senkrecht hochgewinkelten Außenhaut wird und

Abb. 144. Frank Lloyd Wright:
Larkins-Werke, Buffalo,
Verwaltungsgebäude

uildings assem-
demonstrate the
cal scope of
her's book. From
st, it extends

from Frank Lloyd Wright's
Larkin Building in Buffalo,
to Erich Mendelsohn's
Mossehaus in Berlin, to Hans
Poelzig's office building in

Metropolisarchitecture

Abb. 145. Frank Lloyd Wright: Larkins-Werke, Buffalo, Verwaltungsgebäude, Lichthof

Abb. 146. Hans Poelzig: Geschäftshaus in Breslau

Abb. 147. Erich Mendelsohn: Mossehaus, Berlin

s Rückwand der Regale dient, die aus dem Raum-
nern der Übersichtlichkeit wegen an die Außen-
ände verlegt wurden. Über den Regalen liegt ein
s zur Decke reichendes durchlaufendes Fenster-
and, ohne Mauern und Stützen an der Front. Da-
urch wird die horizontale Schichtung des Etagen-
auses aufs energischste betont, zur beherrschen-
en Gestaltungsgrundlage gemacht. Das Gebäude

aus dem Wesen der Aufgabe mit den Mitteln unserer
Zeit gestaltet. Form und Konstruktion sind unmit-
telbar eins geworden.

Abb. 148. M. J. Ginsburg: Verwaltungsgebäude, Moskau

61

Breslau (Wrocław), and
finally to Moisei Ginzburg's
design for a governmen-
tal building, a project completed in Moscow but
intended for the Soviet
Republic of Dagestan.

Abb. 203. Freyssinet: Flugzeughalle in Villacoublay

und durch die Art der Kraftübertragung auf die Auflagerpunkte lassen sich die Brücken auf drei Grundsysteme zurückführen: Balkenbrücken, die den Druck senkrecht übertragen, Bogenbrücken, die den Druck schiefgerichtet übertragen, und Hängebrücken, die zwar den Druck gleichfalls senkrecht übertragen, aber auf einem völlig anderen System der statischen Kraftverteilung beruhen: die Brückenbahn wird nicht mehr von unten her gestützt, sondern von oben her getragen. Alle diese Einzelsysteme können auch zu einem einzigen, dem zusammengesetzten System vereinigt werden.

Die einfachste und primitivste Art der Brücke ist die Vollbalkenbrücke. Sie kann aber nur bei geringen Spannweiten zur Anwendung kommen. Größere Spannweiten machen den gegliederten Balkenträger notwendig: einen Gitterträger mit horizontalen Gurtungen, die unter sich im unverschieblichen Dreiecksverband verstrebt sind.
Eine Abart der Balkenbrücke bilden die Kragbalkenbrücken, gewissermaßen zwei halbe Bogenbrücken im Widerlager zusammengefügt und so die gegenseitigen schräg gerichteten Druckkräfte als Mittelkraft senkrecht übertragend. Selten kommt

Abb. 204. Freyssinet: Luftschiffhalle, Paris

86

e pages illustrate ...ner's appreciation ...mental forms ...rtation structures. ...e does not

comment on Eugène Freyssinet's remarkable buildings, their inclusion prefigures Hilberseimer's later book Hallenbauten

Abb. 205. C. Bernhardt:
Stössenseebrücke
bei Berlin

diese Konstruktionsart wie bei der von Bernhardt erbauten Stössenseebrücke bei Spandau zur Anwendung. Meist bildet sie wie bei der Brücke über den Firth of Forth in Verbindung mit einer Hängekonstruktion die Grundlage der zusammengesetzten Systeme.

Durch die Lage der Fahrbahn wird das Aussehen der Bogenbrücken vielfach variiert. Diese kann oberhalb der Konstruktion liegen: Washington-Brücke in Neuyork; innerhalb der Konstruktion: Treskow-Brücke in Berlin; oder unterhalb der Konstruktion, an diese gewissermaßen aufgehängt: Czerny-Brücke in Heidelberg.

Bogenbrücken Abb. 207

Abb. 208

Bei letzterer Anordnung wird der Horizontalschub infolge der festen Verbindung der Bogenenden mit der Fahrbahn durch die Brücke selbst aufgenommen. Der Druck wird alsdann nicht mehr schiefgerichtet, sondern senkrecht übertragen, wodurch die Bogenbrücke gewissermaßen zur Balkenbrücke wird.

Die schräge Druckübertragung bei den Bogenbrücken bedingt eine starke Ausbildung der Widerlager. Hier können Auflast erzeugende Aufbauten wie

Abb. 206. Czernybrücke, Heidelberg

Abb. 207.
Neuyork,
Washingtonbrücke

87

Visual Documents

8   Here Hilberseimer
illustrates Hugo Häring's
cowshed at the Garkau
farm (1923–26), which he
applauds as a building
designed with specific production processes in mind.
The placement of this image
on the same page as the
title for the book's following
chapter, "Building Trades
and the Building Industry,"
is suggestive: the hand-
crafted materiality of
Häring's building stands in
stark contrast to Hilber-
seimer's call for industrialization. This tacit visual
argument perhaps derives
from the longstanding,
and at times acerbic, dis-
agreement between
Hilberseimer and Häring on
the fundamental premises
of urban planning.

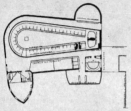

Ignoranz die Herrschaft über die konstruktiven Elemente entglitten. Nur wenn er sie wiedergewinnt und schöpferisch beherrscht, wird er über die Unfruchtbarkeit seines Epigonentums hinaus zu wirklich schöpferischen Leistungen kommen. Künstlerisches Wollen wird zwar stets entscheidend sein. Aber dieses Wollen ist dadurch charakterisiert, daß es keines der die Einheit bestimmenden Elemente außer acht läßt. Errechnete Konstruktion und in-

stinktives Massen- und Formgefühl müssen eins sein, sich Widersprechendes zur Einheit gestaltet werden. Mathematik und Ästhetik schließen sich nicht aus, sie sind gleichberechtigte Hilfsmittel, geradezu die Basis jeder Architektur.

BAUHANDWERK UND BAUINDUSTRIE

Die Großstadtarchitektur unterscheidet sich von der Architektur der Vergangenheit vor allem durch ihre andersartigen soziologischen und ökonomischen Voraussetzungen. Aus den neuen zwecklichen Anforderungen ergaben sich zugleich formale Eigentümlichkeiten, die für die Großstadtarchitektur durchaus bestimmend sind. Wir bedürfen heute keiner Kathedralen, Tempel und Paläste, sondern Wohnbauten, Geschäftshäuser und Fabriken, die allerdings wie Kathedralen, Tempel und Paläste gebaut werden. Das Wohnhaus, das Geschäftshaus, die Fabrik sinnvoll zu gestalten, ist, neben der Gestaltung der Stadt als solcher, die wichtigste Aufgabe der Großstadtarchitektur. Reine Typen dieser Gebäudearten haben sich noch nicht herausgebildet. Diese müssen erst noch geschaffen werden. Bei der Gleichartigkeit des Gebrauchszwecks ermöglicht sich eine umfassende Typisierung und damit eine Industrialisierung des gesamten Bauwesens, eine notwendige Arbeit, zu der heute noch nicht einmal der Anfang gemacht ist. Industrialisierung der Produktion, Normalisierung des Produktionsprozesses, Typisierung der Produktionsprodukte, Verallgemeinerung bis zur Allgemeingültigkeit ist heute die Aufgabe jedes Betriebes.

Das Bauwesen hat sich bisher der Industrialisierung, Normisierung und der damit verbundenen Auswertung, die der gesamten Industrie zugrunde liegt, entzogen. Es beruht noch auf individuellen, handwerklichen Grundlagen, während die gesamte Gegenwart auf kollektiv-industrielle Voraussetzungen gegründet ist. Wirtschaft und Industrie haben die Umwelt wesentlich verändert. Für alle Arbeitsgebiete hat die strenge Methode der Arbeitsteilung einen den neuen Anforderungen angepaßten Produktionsprozeß hervorgerufen. An Stelle des handwerklichen Individualismus ist der industrielle Kollektivismus getreten. Nur das Bauwesen wurde hand-

Visual Documents

9   Although Hilber-
seimer's "Der Wille zur
Architektur" (The Will
to Architecture) is extensively illustrated, his
text does not address the
projects reproduced.
Instead, the images serve
to graphically reinforce
Hilberseimer's assertion that
the visual and spatial arts,
Constructivism in particular,
prepared the ground for
the new architecture. Here,
W. M. Dudok's Dr. H.
Bavinck School in Hilversum
(1921–22) supports Hilberseimer's belief that "simple
cubic bodies" are the basis
of all architecture.

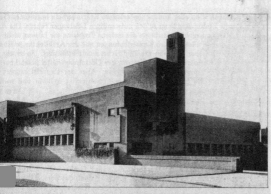

W. M. DUDOK: GEMEINDESCHULE AN DER BOSCHDRIFT. HILVERSUM

DWIG HILBERSHEIMER: Der Wille zur Architektur

e Kunst der letzten Jahrzehnte war eine Flucht vor der Wirklichkeit. Da man
den Tatsachen des gesellschaftlichen Lebens nicht zurechtkam, wandte man
der Mystik zu. Vergaß über metaphysischen Spekulationen die Gegenwart
ihre Aufgaben. Jeglicher Wille zur Lebensgestaltung fehlte. Aus Verantwor-
slosigkeit, aus mangelndem Lebenswillen flüchtete man in eine künstlich idea-
te Vergangenheit. Die Gegenwart aber hat sich wie selten eine Zeit mit den
täten und Erschütterungen dieser Welt auseinanderzusetzen. Erzwang sich
n schöpferischen Rationalismus. Hat eine Revolutionierung der geistigen Mit-
der Politik, der Wissenschaft, der Kunst hervorgerufen. So hat nach vielen
rimentellen Versuchen die Kunst den Weg zur Realität gefunden. Den Illu-
smus, der seit der Renaissance einziges Ziel der Kunst war, ad absurdum ge-
t. Einen neuen Sinn für die Dinge der Umwelt geschaffen. Heute gilt es nicht
r oder weniger gute Bilder zu malen, Statuen zu formen, ästhetische Arrange-
ts anzuordnen, sondern die Wirklichkeit selbst zu gestalten. Nicht Abbilder
aalen, sondern Gebilde zu formen. Die Bildungsgesetze der Kunst auf den
n, auf den Gegenstand als Realität anzuwenden. Es muß versucht werden,
die Kräfte, die heute noch reproduktiv wirksam sind, dem produktiven Ar-
prozeß einzufügen. Planvoll zur Wirksamkeit zu bringen. Denn das Ziel ist:
Welt und die menschlichen Beziehungen zu ordnen. Selbstverantwortliches
deln herbeizuführen. Die wichtigsten und wesentlichsten Lebensbedingungen
egeln.

133

ihm eigentümliche Gesetzmäßigkeit herausbilden. So verschieden diese Objek...
aber auch sein mögen, immer werden sie verbunden sein, durch die Gesetze d...
Klarheit und Ökonomie.

Der experimentelle Charakter der konstruktivistischen Werke schließt v...
vornherein ihre Selbstzwecklichkeit aus. Sie sind nur Werke des Überganges.
utilitarischen architektonischen Konstruktionen. Eine wohldisziplinierte Schulu...
zur Architektur als dem letzten Ziel.

Wie jede Kunst steht auch die Architektur vor der unerläßlichen Notwend...
keit, sich Klarheit über ihre zugrunde liegenden und zu Gebote stehenden Mit...
zu verschaffen. Hier hat ihr die Malerei wertvolle Vorarbeit geleistet. Sie hat
erst auf die geometrisch-kubischen Grundformen aller Kunst aufmerksam
macht. Die einfachen kubischen Körper: Würfel und Kugel, Prisma und Zyl...
der, Pyramide und Kegel, rein bildende Elemente, sind die Grundformen je...
Architektur. Ihre körperliche Bestimmtheit zwingt zu formaler Klarheit. Arc...
tektur entspringt der Geometrik. Wenn geometrische Gebilde zu proportion...
ten Körpern werden, entsteht Architektur. Vielgestaltigkeit bei größter Einh...
Details der zeugenden Hauptlinie untergeordnet. Vor dem entschieden kubisc...
Aufbau treten Einzelheiten völlig zurück. Maßgebend ist die allgemeine Ges...
tung der Massen. Das ihr auferlegte Proportionsgesetz. Die meist heterogen...
Materialmassen verlangen ein für jedes Element gleichermaßen gültiges For...
gesetz. Daher Reduzierung der Bauformen auf das Wesentlichste. Allgemein...
Einfachste. Unzweideutigste. Unterdrückung der Vielerleiheit. Formung n...
einem allgemeinen Formgesetz.

Die Architektur der Gegenwart unterscheidet sich von der der Vergangenh...
vor allem durch ihre soziologischen und ökonomischen Voraussetzungen. Aus e...
neuen zwecklichen Anforderungen ergeben sich zugleich formale Eigentü...
lichkeiten, die für die heutige Architektur durchaus bestimmend sind. Sie s...
das Neue und Belebende. Stellen geformt das heute gültige künstlerische Mom...
dar. Wir bedürfen heute keiner Kathedralen, Tempel und Paläste, sondern Wo...
häuser, Geschäftshäuser und Fabriken, die allerdings wie Kathedralen, Tem...
und Paläste gebaut wurden. Das Wohnhaus, das Geschäftshaus, die Fabrik si...
voll zu gestalten ist eine der wesentlichsten Aufgaben heutiger Architek...
Reine Typen dieser Gebäudearten haben sich bis jetzt noch nicht herausgebild...
Sie müssen erst noch geschaffen werden. Bei der Gleichartigkeit des Gebrauc...
zwecks ermöglicht sich eine umfassende Typisierung. Eine notwendige konst...
tive Arbeit, zu der heute noch nicht einmal der Anfang gemacht ist. Die Ar...
tektur hat sich bisher der Normisierung, die der gesamten Industrie zugru...
liegt, zu entziehen gewußt. Sie beruht noch auf individuellen handwerklic...
Grundlagen, während die gesamte Gegenwart auf kollektiv industrielle Vor...
setzungen gegründet ist. Ignoranz von Notwendigkeiten hat bisher noch im...
zur Erstarrung geführt. Und was ist mehr erstarrt als die Architektur der Geg...
wart. Schöpferkraft offenbart sich aber gerade darin, Gegebenheiten restlos...
verarbeiten. Eine ihnen adequate Form zu finden.

136

se pages, Alfred
nd Martin
Forsterhof office
Halle (1921–
posed with

Hilberseimer's statement that
"today we need not cathe-
drals, temples or palaces, but
rather residential buildings,
commercial buildings, and

A. GELLHORN UND M. KNAUTHE: BÜROHAUS IN HALLE

factories." For the reader, Hilberseimer's reproduction of this early example of the *Neues Bauen* buttresses his opposition to the alleged

"subjective arbitr of Expressionism. alludes to Hilbers solidarity with the left-leaning archi

Ansprüche in technischer und räumlicher Beziehung werden zu neuartiger
wendung der Materialien und zu neuen Formentypen führen. Ihr konstruk
Charakter wird die Eigentümlichkeiten unserer Epoche zum Ausdruck brin
  Die Arbeit des Ingenieurs ist mit der rationalen Leistung vollendet. Die
Architekten beginnt damit. Ihm ist die rationale Lösung Material der Gestalt
Er ordnet sie einer umfassenden Formvorstellung unter. Sie ist ihm lediglich
tel einer Idee Körperlichkeit zu verleihen. Sie im Raume zu verwirklichen.

LUDWIG HILBERSEIMER: ENTWURF ZU EINEM FABRIKBAU

The Will to Architecture

11 Hilberseimer illustrates
his project for a High-rise
Factory (1922) on the final
page of his essay, suggesting that its elementary forms
represent the ultimate aim
of the new architecture: "the
general design of masses."
The spatial tension within this
line drawing recalls the
work of Hilberseimer's friend
László Péri, in whose
"space-constructions" Hilberseimer located the
first signs of a "latent will
to architecture."

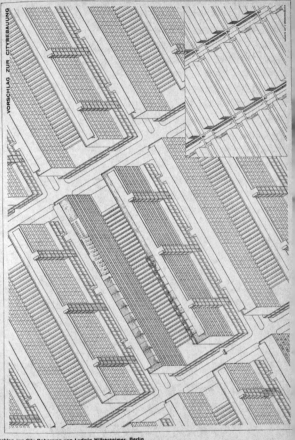

VORSCHLAG ZUR CITYBEBAUUNG

Vorschlag zur City-Bebauung von Ludwig Hilberseimer, Berlin

Projet de construction à effectuer dans la City berlinoise

Proposal for building up a city

Proposal for City-Center Development

12   In this axonometric line
drawing, Hilberseimer's
"Vorschlag zur City-Bebauung" (Proposal for City-Center Development) appears
as a potentially endless field
of repeated blocks. The
smaller, inset image at upper
right presents a variation
of the scheme with elevated
pedestrian paths, recalling
the superimposition of
circulation networks recommended by Harvey Wiley
Corbett and adopted
by Hilberseimer in his High-
rise City.

Visual Documents

13   This plate contains
the most detailed drawings
of Hilberseimer's proposal.
Reading from bottom to top,
we see Hilberseimer's block
structure compared to a
typical Berlin district, plans
and sections of the entire
building, and typical floors
of the office slabs. Their
featureless interiors correspond to what Siegfried
Kracauer called the "spiritual homelessness" of
Germany's emerging class
of white-collar workers,
the "salaried masses" he
profiled in his book
Die Angestellten of 1930.

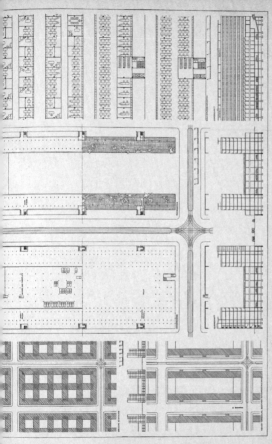

Schnitte der Bürohäuser zum Vorschlag der City-Bebauung von Ludwig Hilberseimer

coupes des bâtiments destinés aux bureaux, se rapportant au projet de constructions à effectuer dans la City

sections of office buildings Proposal for building up a city

Afterword

In Hilberseimer's Footsteps

Afterword by Pier Vittorio Aureli

Ludwig Hilberseimer's oeuvre—both his projects and his writings—has had a strange critical fortune. At first glance, it might seem that his work has been overlooked, almost forgotten in the literature on modern architecture. This is true if we consider that his contribution is almost absent from all the major histories of modern architecture in the twentieth century. Moreover, Hilberseimer's work is known (if it is known at all), only through the two famous perspectives of

Figs.
17–18

his proposal for a High-rise City (1924). These two images have been used so often to represent the horror of the modern metropolis that they have become clichés, especially because they are often considered only as images and not as illustrations of a precise urban proposal. And yet Hilberseimer's oeuvre has inspired the work and the approach of architects and scholars as radically diverse as Manfredo Tafuri, Archizoom, Giorgio Grassi, Rem Koolhaas, K. Michael Hays, Albert Pope, and Charles Waldheim, to name just a few. If Hilberseimer has suffered mainstream neglect, he has surely become an architect's architect, a cult figure whose rigorous theoretical projects paradoxically seem to age much less than the work of many of his contemporaries. This is

due to his radical and uncompromising approach
to architecture and the city. This approach was
sustained not through manifestos or utopian proposals for a different world; on the contrary,
Hilberseimer's radicality consists in his lucid
and realist analysis of the capitalist city. This
realism also informs his design proposals,
which—although executed as theoretical proposals—expressed social, political, and formal
implications that responded to the reality of the
capitalist city. His work was radical because it
lacked all idealism about the reality of the capitalist city, and even if his proposals were drastic
attempts to reform the city within a social-democratic framework, he did not discount the social
and geographical consequences of the new forms
of production brought about by capitalist development. This is particularly evident in the peculiar
style of his drawings. The urban atmosphere
evoked by his drawings for the High-rise City is
neither futuristic, nor dramatic, nor dystopian.
Hilberseimer's images, especially in his early
work, describe an urban atmosphere that is
detached, harsh, precise, and subtly disquieting.
Perhaps the best expression of the attitude con-
veyed by the illustrations of Hilberseimer's
projects is found in the opening lines of Thomas
Mann's *Royal Highness*, which Archizoom used to
introduce its theoretical project No-Stop City
(1969–71), a project that, as we shall see, was
inspired by Hilberseimer's drawings for the
High-rise City:

Figs.
90–91

The time is noon on an ordinary weekday; the season of the year does not matter. The weather is fair to moderate. It is not raining, but the sky is not clear; it is a uniform light gray, uninteresting and somber, and the street lies in a dull and sober light which robs it of all mystery, all individuality.[1]

The sobriety of Hilberseimer's images corresponds to the realism of his analysis of the capitalist city. But despite the clarity of his theories and proposals, his writings and projects have been interpreted in very different, sometimes opposing, ways. Indeed, Hilberseimer's work has inspired radically different approaches to the contemporary city. In the notes that follow, I will outline some of these approaches, in particular those of Aldo Rossi, Giorgio Grassi, Manfredo Tafuri, Archizoom, K. Michael Hays, and Rem Koolhaas.

In 1967 the publishing house Marsilio — founded by Paolo Ceccarelli and Antonio Negri, among others — initiated a book series on architecture and urbanism that was edited by Aldo Rossi and

---

[1] Thomas Mann, *Royal Highness: A Novel of German Court Life*, trans. A. Cecil Curtis (Los Angeles, Berkeley: University of California Press, 1939), v. Quoted in Italian by Archizoom in "Città, catena di montaggio del sociale: ideologia e teoria della metropoli," *Casabella* 350–51 (1970): 22.

called Polis.[2] The previous year, Marsilio had published Rossi's famous book *L'architettura della città* (*The Architecture of the City*), which had a tremendous impact on architectural and urban discourse in Italy. The success of the book was an incentive for Rossi and the editors at Marsilio to publish a series of texts related to architecture and the city. Rossi's ambition for Polis was to publish not only new texts but also old and often forgotten texts, especially texts related to the rise of what Rossi defined as "rationalist architecture." Among the first titles Rossi published was Ludwig Hilberseimer's *Entftaltung einer Planungsidee* (Development of a Planning Concept), 1963, which was translated by Rossi's wife, the stage actress Sonia Gessner, and introduced by Rossi's protégé and early collaborator Giorgio Grassi.[3] It is important to note the similarity between the title of Rossi's book—*L'architettura della città*—and the title of Hilberseimer's most important book—*Großstadt-architektur* (*Metropolisarchitecture*), which is translated into Italian as *L'architettura della grande città*.[4] As has been recently demonstrated, there is no

[2] For a very insightful history of the Polis book series and other editorial projects related to architecture in Italy between the 1950s and 1980s see Fiorella Vanini, *La libreria dell'architetto: Progetti di collane editoriali 1945–1980* (Milan: Franco Angeli, 2011).

[3] Ludwig Hilberseimer, *Entfaltung einer Planungsidee* (Berlin: Ullstein, 1963); Ludwig Hilberseimer, *Un'idea di piano*, trans. Sonia Gessner (Padua: Marsilio, 1967)

[4] Aldo Rossi, *L'architettura della città* (Padua: Marsilio,

doubt that Rossi was inspired by Hilberseimer's book, and although references to the German architect and theorist are rather scarce in Rossi's

Fig. 87 text, his early collaborators confirm his strong interest in Hilberseimer's work, and especially in *Großstadtarchitektur*.[5] It is clear that the affinity Rossi felt for Hilberseimer lay in the idea of rooting architectural form within the reality of the city. Following the example of Hilberseimer's *Großstadtarchitektur*, Rossi sought to elucidate the laws that govern the form of the city as the prerequisite for understanding architecture itself. For both Hilberseimer and Rossi the city comes first: it is the only meaningful context (both physical and conceptual) in which architecture can be understood at a fundamental level. And yet for both Hilberseimer and Rossi, it is precisely through architecture—as a physical artifact—that the city is knowable. This understanding of the relationship between architecture and the city is evident in the organization of Hilberseimer's book. Hilberseimer first puts forward a general

1966); *The Architecture of the City*, trans. Diane Ghirardo and Joan Ockman (Cambridge: The MIT Press, 1982); Ludwig Hilberseimer, *Groszstadt Architektur: L'architettura della grande città*, trans. Bianca Spagnuolo Vigorita (Naples: CLEAN, 1981); a second edition was published in 1998. The Italian edition of *Großstadtarchitektur* was introduced by Gianugo Polesello, an early collaborator of Rossi's.

[5] See Elisabetta Vasumi Roveri, *Aldo Rossi e l'architettura della città: genesi e fortuna di un testo* (Turin: Umberto Allemandi & C., 2010), 34.

understanding of the city as a comprehensive system of relationships, as a plan; only then does he
describe the city through exemplary structures.
Organizing the book in this way, Hilberseimer
stresses the dependence of architecture on the
political and geographical organization of the
city. And yet for Hilberseimer this broader understanding of the city finds its ultimate confirmation
in the interior organization of buildings. Hilberseimer never uses the term "typology," but it is
clear that for him the overall organization of the
city is dependent on the organization of the single
unit: the cell.

These observations can clearly be read in
Rossi's intentional use of specific language,
particularly in the Milanese architect's reintro-
duction of the notion of typology as the
fundamental framework for the study of the
morphology of the city. The similarity between
Hilberseimer's and Rossi's method is striking:
for both architects the form of the city is gener-
ated from the distributive logic urban types. And
both understood types as manifestations of the
ethos of a society in pure architectural terms.
Why, then, did Rossi decide to publish *Entftaltung
einer Planungsidee* instead of the more canonical
Großstadtarchitektur? The answer may be that *Entftaltung einer Planungsidee* was a more recent title
from Hilberseimer's prolific bibliography. But
another reason may be that Rossi felt that
Großstadtarchitektur was too closely related to a
particular moment of the modern metropolis,

while *Entftaltung einer Planungsidee* offered a ret-
rospective analysis of Hilberseimer's career as a
planner. Since the Italian translation was published only a few months before Hilberseimer's
death, we might presume that Hilberseimer himself did not want to republish his old book and
preferred his latest work since it would be a more
up-to-date version of his theory of the city. We
can be sure that Rossi liked the slightly autobio-
graphical tone of *Entftaltung einer Planungsidee*, in
which Hilberseimer presented his theory and
projects as if they unfolded according to a lifelong existential project.

If Rossi's reference to Hilberseimer was
indirect, Giorgio Grassi's relationship to Hilberseimer's writings and projects is clear. One
could say that it was Grassi who rediscovered
Hilberseimer in the 1960s. Apart from his introduction to the Italian edition of *Entftaltung einer
Planungsidee*, Hilberseimer was a central reference in Grassi's book *La costruzione logica
dell'architettura* (The Logical Construction of
Architecture), which was published the same
year as the Italian translation of *Entftaltung einer
Planungsidee*.[6] In this book Grassi focused on the
possibility of producing architecture according
to rigorous and self-evident principles. In order
to find such architecture, Grassi focused in particular on two moments of modern Western

---

[6] Giorgio Grassi, *La costruzione logica dell'architettura*
(Padua: Marsilio, 1967).

architecture: the French *grand siècle*, represented by such figures as Pierre Le Muet, Roland Fréart de Chambray, and Charles-Etienne Briseux, architects and authors of influential treatises and manuals of architecture; and on German architecture of the years of the Weimar Republic, represented by the work of Bruno Taut, Alexander Klein, and Hilberseimer. For Grassi these two moments in the history of architecture, which he identified as Classicism and Rationalism, respectively, advanced an idea of architecture indissolubly linked to an idea of the city. In these two periods, Grassi argued, the project of the city and the project of architecture coincided within the same propositions. These propositions were put forward in a logical way, according to the most basic conventions shared by architects of the time. Think of Le Muet's *architecture d'accompagnement*, in which architecture, freed from the representational role of the classical orders, is reduced to its basic image: the urban dwelling. This approach resulted in an architecture that for Grassi was both autonomous (because it was intelligible in itself, as legible form), but also profoundly rooted within the city for which it was designed. Grassi's interest in Hilberseimer was motivated by the need Hilberseimer shared with Rossi to search for an approach to architecture liberated from the confines of authorship and style. In his introduction to *Entftaltung einer Planungsidee*, Grassi emphasized that even though Hilberseimer's theoretical

Fig. 87 *Arduino Cantàfora, La città analoga, 1973*

Fig. 88 *Giorgio Grassi, Project for the Palazzo della Regione in Trieste, 1974*

Fig. 89 Giorgio Grassi, Project for the Palazzo della Regione in Trieste, 1974; plan detail

projects, including the High-rise City, have precise architectural images, they are nevertheless
characterized by the absence of style. For Grassi
the forms produced by Hilberseimer were not just
types, but archetypes: the slab, the block, the high-
rise building, the row house. Hilberseimer's
method of design was not to seek the invention of
original forms but to assemble unprecedented
combinations and to use them as the basis for the
production of new types. In the High-rise City, for
example, Hilberseimer superimposed two urban
types that were at that time seen as radically antithetical: the block and the slab. In Hilberseimer's
designs, an extreme simplicity of form corresponds to a highly original combination of
different archetypes, the end result of which is an
unprecedented organization of the city and its
functions. Hilberseimer's influence is also evident
in Grassi's design work. Grassi not only adopted
Hilberseimer's terse and precise approach to
architectural rendering; he also quoted projects
like the High-rise City in his competition entry for
the regional administrative offices in Trieste
(1974). And in a lecture delivered in 1978, Grassi
insisted on the validity of Hilberseimer's formu-
lation of the relationship between architecture
and the city.[7] Against the affirmation of Postmod-
ern historicism, which would eventually affect the

Figs.
88–89

---

[7] See Giorgio Grassi, "L'architettura di Hilberseimer"
in Giorgio Grassi, *Scritti scelti, 1965–1999* (Milan: Franco
Angeli, 2000), 183–92.

work of Rossi, Grassi still looked to Hilberseimer as a point of reference for a civic, anonymous architecture completely divorced from concerns for form or expression.

If Grassi and Rossi—early in his career—looked to Hilberseimer as the most important proponent of a rationalist approach to architecture, Manfredo Tafuri and Andrea Branzi understood the German architect in a slightly different way, emphasizing both the political and the iconoclastic dimensions of his work. In 1969, Tafuri published his seminal essay "Per una critica dell'ideologia architettonica" (Toward a Critique of Architectural Ideology) in the Marxist journal *Contropiano* in which he launched an attack on the utopian and reformist aspirations of modern architecture.[8] Tafuri's position was heavily influenced by the theories of the Operaists, a group of radical Marxist militants and scholars gathered around the theories of Mario Tronti. They were very critical, if not entirely against the reformist agenda of the Left, which they saw as a strategic lever for capitalist power over the working class. Tafuri's fundamental argument in this essay was that modern architecture, especially the avant-garde movements, had the ideological role of

[8] Manfredo Tafuri, "Per una critica dell'ideologia architettonica," *Contropiano* 1 (1969): 31–79; trans. Stephen Sartarelli as "Toward a Critique of Architectural Ideology," in K. Michael Hays, ed., *Architecture Theory since 1968* (Cambridge: The MIT Press, 1998), 6–35.

prefiguring models of organization for the city within the incessant development of capitalism. For Tafuri, the allegedly utopian dimension of architecture had the specific role of making emerging cycles of urban restructuring culturally and socially acceptable. For example, Tafuri described the trend of picturesque landscaping as promoting the ideology of an allegedly "natural city" in the face of massive industrial exploitation and land-value speculation. Avant-garde movements such as Cubism, Futurism, Dada, and De Stijl gave this industrial reality its proper aesthetic image, characterized by shock and productive alienation. Once the next cycle of capitalist development was accomplished, these avant-garde projects were left behind as "form without utopia," as useless weapons for both capital and its antagonist: the working class. Tafuri thought the only way to overcome this reality of architecture was to go beyond architecture as the design of objects and to dive into the economic processes that produced architecture itself. For Tafuri the only architect who had adopted this approach was Hilberseimer. Tafuri described Hilberseimer's observation that the architecture of the city is dependent on the solution of two issues, the design of the elementary cell and of the entire urban whole, as the most lucid analysis of the capitalist metropolis. If Rossi and Grassi had interpreted this observation as the foundation of the relationship between typology and morphology, for Tafuri this observation meant

something entirely different. It meant that Hilberseimer had understood the city as a true unity, but
not as a metaphysical or transcendental unity, nor
as a harmonious architectural unity. The unity of
the capitalist city lay, rather, in its identity as an
enormous "social machine," an apparatus in
which the type, not the overall image of the city,
represents the starting point for urban design.
For Tafuri, Hilberseimer had understood that,
reduced in these terms, the city was no longer a
composition of buildings but rather an organization of the economic process. The unity of the city
is thus no longer the city as object, as tangible artifact, but the city as economic cycle that processes
infinitely reproducible types. As Tafuri wrote:

*In the face of modernized production tech-
niques and the expansion and rationalization
of the market, the architect, as producer of
"objects," became an incongruous figure. It
was no longer a question of giving form to single elements of the urban fabric, nor even to
simple prototypes. Once the true unity of the
production cycle has been identified in the city,
the only task the architect can have is to organize the cycle. Taking this proposition to its
extreme conclusion, Hilberseimer insists on the
role of elaborating "organizational models" as
the only one that can fully reflect the need for
Taylorizing building production, as the new
task of the technician, who is now completely
integrated into this process.*

> *On the basis of this position, Hilberseimer was able to avoid involvement in the "crisis of the object" so anxiously articulated by such architects as Loos and Taut. For Hilberseimer, the object was not in crisis because it had already disappeared from his spectrum of considerations. The only emerging imperative was that dictated by the laws of organization, and therein lies what has been correctly seen as Hilberseimer's greatest contribution.*[9]

Tafuri's reading of Hilberseimer as a lucid interpreter of the capitalist city had a profound influence on the Florentine collective Archizoom, especially on the development of Archizoom's most important project: No-Stop City (1969–71). The project was executed for an exhibition of the work by Archizoom in Rotterdam that never took place, and it was intended as an illustration *per absurdum* of the effects of the capitalist city.[10] The basic principle of No-Stop City consisted in imagining the city as the superimposition of

Figs.
90–91

[9]   Tafuri, "Toward a Critique of Architectural Ideology," 22.

[10]   The project No-Stop City was published in several magazines. The most important publications were: Archizoom associati, "Città, catena di montaggio del sociale: ideologia e teoria della metropoli," *Casabella* 350–51 (1970): 22–34; Archizoom associati, "No-Stop City: Residential Parkings. Climatic Universal System," *Domus* 496 (1971): 49–54. See also Roberto Gargiani, *Dall'onda pop alla superficie neutra: Archizoom Associati, 1966–1974* (Milan: Electa, 2008), 169–227.

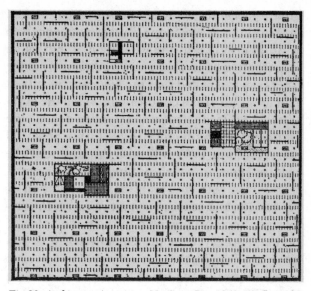

Fig. 90 Archizoom Associates, No-Stop City, 1969–71; floor plan

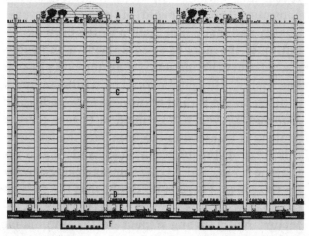

Fig. 91 Archizoom Associates, No-Stop City, 1969–71; section

three spaces: the factory, the supermarket, and the parking lot. No-Stop City was not conceived as an alternative to the existing city, but as an exacerbation of its elements, producing what the Operaists had called the *città fabbrica* (the city as a factory), an urban condition in which the organization of production was extended beyond the perimeter of the factory to all forms of social life. According to Tronti, with the advent of the welfare state, in which production was organically linked with consumption, the evolution of production had reached a stage in which the factory and society coincided in the same "plan of capital." And yet for the Operaists it was precisely at this point that capital would be forced to reveal its ties to the labor force of the working class. With No-Stop City, Archizoom sought to reveal this condition in its most brutal form: a continuous space devoid of any architectural quality and made inhabitable by the even distribution of the most basic equipment: a bathroom placed every fifty meters, for example. As Branzi has stated, the publication of Hilberseimer's projects in the Italian edition of *Entfaltung einer Planungsidee* was a fundamental trigger for the project. It is important to note here the ambiguous relationship between Rossi and Grassi on the one hand, and Archizoom and Superstudio on the other. There is no doubt that the radical rationalism of Rossi's and Grassi's early architecture had a strong impact on the minimalist turn of both collectives around 1968. Branzi observed that Rossi's interest in "extreme" architects such as Etienne-Louis Boullée and Hilberseimer was a fundamental influence that pushed the members of Archizoom to purge their initial interest in pop imagery. And yet Tafuri's more politically oriented and disenchanted reading of Hilberseimer, which took no account of neo-rationalist imagery, was more influential on the development of No-Stop City. Tafuri's Hilberseimer revealed, regardless of the German architect's intentions, the radical dissolution of the city as form within the totalizing space of urbanization. Against the colorful images of Archigram, the rediscovery of Hilberseimer revealed the generic ethos of the modern city. As Branzi has recently recalled:

The idea of an inexpressive, catatonic architecture, the outcome of the expansive forms of logic of the system and its class antagonists, was the only modern architecture of interest to us: a liberating architecture, corresponding to mass democracy, devoid of demos *and of* kratos *(of people and of power), and both centterless and imageless. A society freed from the rhetorical forms of humanitarian socialism and rhetorical progressivism: architecture that gazed fearlessly at the logic of gray, unaesthetic, and de-dramatized industrialism... The colorful visions of Pop architecture were replaced by Ludwig Hilberseimer's pitiless urban images, those of a city without qualities designed for*

people without preordained qualities. Free,
therefore, to express in an autonomous way its
own creative, political, and behavioral energies.
The greatest possible freedom occurred where
integration was strongest... Alienation was a
new artistic condition...[11]

Hilberseimer's projects were thus understood as
an invitation to confront the most radical effects
of the capitalist city. What is more, the High-rise
City was an invitation to go beyond the formal
fetishism through which other avant-garde
groups such as the Japanese Metabolists had
confronted the social and technological trans-
formations of the urban environment. Moreover,
in the High-rise City, Hilberseimer had demonstrated that in an advanced capitalist society, life
and work coincide within the same urban system. He thereby suggested that the desire to zone
the city into different sectors, a desire Le Corbusier clung to, was unnecessary. Even if
Hilberseimer's projects were conceived as solutions to specific problems, his peculiar graphic
presentations, in which patterns replace building forms, inspired Archizoom in its attempt to
define a "nonfigurative architecture" for the
city. Such nonfigurative architecture was meant
to reveal the city's brute objectivity against the
humanist aspirations of modernism.

[11]   Andrea Branzi, "Postface," in *No-Stop City: Archizoom
Associati* (Orleans: HXY, 2006), 148–49.

K. Michael Hays has also sought to counter the humanist interpretation of modern architecture. In *Modernism and the Posthumanist Subject*, published in 1992, Hays interprets Hilberseimer's work as part of a reformulation of the subject-object relationship in architecture.[12] Hays observes that in modern historiography the interpretation of modern architecture has taken the form of two canonical narratives. On the one hand, modern architecture is presented under the rubric of function, in which the objectivity of technological development is seen as overwhelming the human dimension of architectural form. On the other hand, critics and historians who have opposed this view of modern architecture have advocated for a humanist interpretation, in which a sovereign human subject regains full control of his own space. Against both interpretations, Hays proposes that a fundamental category of modern architecture is the specific subjectivity formed by an intense dialectic between subject and object. For Hays, the process of rationalization implied by the process of modernization called the definition of the subject as a "self-creating conscience and will, that is to say, of humanism," into question.[13] Confronted with this reality, in this book Hays seeks to read the legacy of modern architecture in the terms that other disciplines have used

[12] K. Michael Hays, *Modernism and the Posthumanist Subject: The Architecture of Hannes Meyer and Ludwig Hilberseimer* (Cambridge: The MIT Press, 1992).
[13] Ibid., 4.

to interpret modernity: as an act of negation of the most fundamental assumptions of humanism. Like the atonal music of Schoenberg or the non-narrative films of Hans Richter and Viking Eggeling (which Hilberseimer admired greatly), in the most extreme versions of modern architecture, such those advanced by Hannes Meyer and Hilberseimer, architectural form is reconceived according to an aesthetic of renunciation, uncertainty, and incompleteness. For Hays these aesthetic terms are fully developed in Hilberseimer's projects and style of representation. Hays notes how in such a project as Hilberseimer's "Vorschlag zur City-Bebauung" (Proposal for City-Center Development), 1930, axonometric drawing suppresses any sense of depth in the reading of urban space.[14] Urban form is reduced to a pattern in which any idea of origin or composition is suppressed in favor of a serial order. And yet, for Hays such explicit manifestation of the abstract ethos of the metropolis is not simply the accomplishment of the "real" functioning of its architecture. On the contrary, for Hays, it is precisely Hilberseimer's peculiar way of rendering the metropolis that deconstructs any relationship of cause and effect between form and function. In Hilberseimer's drawings, the metropolis appears as an over-determined process in which the two fundamental tenets of the humanist project—causality and origin—are

Fig. 80

[14] On this project see this volume, pp. 290–305.

effaced, yielding an anonymous and nonrepresentational architectural language. In Hays's reading, Hilberseimer's approach to the architecture of the metropolis is neither formalist nor functionalist. Hilberseimer's (and Meyer's) architecture makes visible "that things are just what they are, utterly shorn of any metaphysical illusion of artistic authenticity, unity, or depth."[15]

Similarly, in the work of Rem Koolhaas—particularly in his urban projects and theories of the 1980s—we find an appropriation of Hilberseimer's work in support of an anti-formalist, but also anti-deterministic position. While Hays was writing his book (which originated in his Ph.D. dissertation at MIT), Koolhaas had already started a modernist campaign in favor of the metropolis against the historicist architecture that became very popular in Europe in the 1980s. If for Tafuri and Archizoom Hilberseimer's architecture of the metropolis represented the end of architecture, its final dissolution in the sea of urbanization, for Koolhaas the forces of the metropolis were precisely the last chance for architecture to reclaim its urban role. This position was enthusiastically declared in the very name of Koolhaas and Elia Zenghelis's practice, which in this sense was a clear statement of purpose: Office for Metropolitan Architecture (OMA). As recounted by Zenghelis, Hilberseimer's harsh architectural imagery was also

---

[15] Hays, *Modernism and the Posthumanist Subject*, 171.

Fig. 92 OMA, Project for Welfare Palace Hotel, Welfare Island, New York, 1975–76; detail

present in OMA's early work as a deliberate complement to the hedonism and irony of the practice's metropolitan projects. This is evident in OMA's 1976 proposal for a housing complex with urban facilities on Welfare Island in New York City.[16]

Fig. 92

[16] Elia Zenghelis in conversation with the author, 23 June 2012.

In this project, OMA revisited a classic urban
theme also appropriated by Hilberseimer—the
boarding house, in which the typology of the
hotel is developed as strategy for housing. For
Koolhaas and Zenghelis, as for the Hilberseimer
of the *Großstadtarchitektur* years, a truly metropolitan architecture had to be ruthlessly rooted
within the most adverse conditions of the contemporary city. But while Hilberseimer sought
to tame and reform these conditions, OMA
accepted and accommodated them within a new
urban architecture. OMA's search for a new metropolitan architecture was a radical refusal of
both the historicist nostalgia that, in the early
1980s, affected many European architects, and
of the return to modernism in its critical and
regionalist versions, as was seen in Spanish and
Portuguese architecture. It is precisely within
this attempt that Koolhaas wrote two of his most
important programmatic texts: "Our New Sobriety," published on the occasion of OMA's
provocative contribution to Paolo Portoghesi's
Venice Biennale in 1980, and "Imagining Nothingness," a short text that declared that the
"absence" of architecture can be seen precisely
as the greatest potential for its resurrection.[17]
Both texts clearly resonate with Hilberseimer's

*Figs.
34–35*

[17]   Rem Koolhaas, Elia Zenghelis, "Our New Sobriety,"
OMA, Projects (London: Architectural Association,
1981), 3–9; Rem Koolhaas, "Imagining Nothingness" in
Rem Koolhaas and Bruce Mau, *S, M, L, XL* (New York:
The Monacelli Press, 1995), 198–204.

metropolitan approach to architecture. For Koolhaas, as for the German architect, the complexity
of the contemporary city requires a radical sobriety of form. This is evident in such seminal
projects as the competition entry for the redevelopment of Melun-Senart near Paris (1987) and
the project for the Morgan Bank Headquarters in
Amsterdam (1985), in which architectural intervention is reduced to a minimum in order to fully
accommodate programs that can be hardly pre-
dicted or contained. In the text "Imagining
Nothingness," Hilberseimer's "zero degree"
urbanism is cited—among references to Pompeii
and the Berlin Wall—as an example of urbanism
in which space as "empty space" is more important than form. As already intuited by Archizoom,
and theorized by another admirer of Hilberseimer, the American scholar and theorist Albert
Pope, the post-industrial city is no longer defined
by form; it is defined by space.[18] And yet this empty
space is far from empty. According to Koolhaas
and Pope, the empty space of the post-Fordist
metropolis is congested by all kinds of volatile
programs and activities whose sociological life
reaches far beyond the traditional forms of the
city. Attracted by extreme urban conditions, Koolhaas had already in the early 1970s considered
starting a research institute—in collaboration
with Adolfo Natalini from Superstudio—

[18] See Albert Pope, *Ladders* (New York: Princeton Architectural Press, 1996).

completely devoted to the study of the contemporary city.[19] The idea would be partially realized in
the early 1990s in the Großstadt Foundation, and
it would finally take the form of the Harvard Project on the City, a research program initiated in
1996 completely freed from the necessity of
designing new or alternative cities. Yet, while for
Hilberseimer the chaotic situation of the city was
caused by capitalist exploitation, the word capital
seems to almost disappear in Koolhaas's analysis
of the city. If Koolhaas has moved urban research
far beyond the scope of architectural concerns, he
certainly has not considered what, for the Hilberseimer of *Großstadtarchitektur*, was the cause of
urban chaos: capitalist accumulation. While Hilberseimer, following a Social-Democratic agenda,
believed that the new forms of production brought
about by capitalist development could be tamed
and reformed for a more rational organization of
the city, Koolhaas has not put forward any program for the general reform of the contemporary
city. If Hilberseimer proposed design solutions,
Koolhaas prefers, in his words, to "surf the waves
of the metropolis."

   In these notes I have focused on the legacy
of the European work of Hilberseimer because
of its immediate connection to *Großstadtarchitektur*. However, it is important to mention that
Hilberseimer's American period has also inspired

---

[19] Rem Koolhaas to Adolfo Natalini, 8 February 1973,
Archivio Natalini, Florence.

original interpretations of the contemporary city. In recent years the projects and investigations that Hilberseimer began developing in the 1940s have been revisited by Albert Pope and the theorist of landscape urbanism Charles Waldheim. Though in very different ways, both Pope and Waldheim have found in Hilberseimer's urban projects precursors to an idea of the city that is strongly related to the political and social ethos of the postwar American city.[20] For Waldheim, Hilberseimer's approach to city planning offers a way to structure territory that does not require a differentiation between the city and urbanization. Specifically, Waldheim sees the materialization of a project like Lafayette Park (executed in collaboration with Mies) as the culmination of a lifelong investigation of settlement principles that gives us a far more nuanced view of Hilberseimer as the planner of a potential American city. Pope has offered a provocative reading of Hilberseimer's dissolution of the grid (as evident in Hilberseimer's project for Marquette Park) as an anticipation of the crisis of the American grid caused by the pressures of the splintering forces of the post-Fordist era. Perhaps Pope's attitude toward this crisis exemplifies

---

[20] See Charles Waldheim, "Notes Toward a History of Agrarian Urbanism," *Bracket* 1 (2010): 18–24; "Notes Toward a History of Agrarian Urbanism," *Design Observer*, April 11, 2010, http://places.design observer.com/feature/notes-toward-a-history-of-agrarian-urbanism/15518/.

Hilberseimer's attitude toward the city: accept the present condition and reform it from within.

There is no doubt that in the last twenty years architecture has moved in a direction antithetical to what might be called an approach "à la Hilberseimer." While Hilberseimer advocated an architecture governed by a general law in order to better confront the complexity of the city, today the reality of architectural production could not be further from such a program. While the contradictions and asymmetries of the capitalist city have only intensified, the majority of architects have indulged in a narrowing of their concerns that restricts design to the scale of the architectural object and leaves the city unconsidered. Commercial pressure on offices leaves little space for architects to undertake abstract or theoretical investigations. Practicing architects tend to adjust their rather fragmentary findings into what today is called "research," which very often ends up as nothing more than an unsystematic and compromised collection of flashy images and inconclusive diagrams. Another emerging trend in our time of economic recession is the architect as activist, as a figure who moves beyond a concern for form and directly engages with social problems through much more volatile means: workshops, exhibitions, biennales, events, advocacy. In this case, the immediacy of action risks obfuscating the overall picture of the urban situation, reducing the latter to an "innocent" playground and thus masking structural problems. On the other hand, academic research on the city often succumbs to either unnecessary complexity or imprecision in defining a vision. But the most problematic aspect of research on the contemporary city is the total disconnection between, on the one hand, an understanding of architecture in relationship to urban form and, on the other, an understanding of architecture in relationship to political economy. Those who focus on political economy tend to view the role of architectural form as irrelevant in the development of the city; those who focus on architecture or urban design seem completely uninterested in engaging the political and economic forces that produce the city.

Perhaps it is precisely in confronting this impasse that a new reading of Hilberseimer's *Großstadtarchitektur* is timely. As we have seen, the crux of Hilberseimer's writings and theoretical projects was to root architectural form within a deep analysis of the contemporary city. Hilberseimer proposed neither easy formulas nor a final scenario. He put the problems on the table and identified existing architectural examples that might provide a basis for further research. Gianugo Polesello, an Italian architect close to Rossi and the editor of the Italian edition of *Großstadtarchitektur* published in 1998, observed that Hilberseimer's organization of the book suggests a possible way to update its content.

Hilberseimer both begins and ends *Großstadtar-chitektur* with general remarks, focusing the chapters in between on specific programs and building types contemporaneous with the publication itself. Polesello suggested that if we were to take the introduction and conclusion as they are and change the rest of the book, we could produce a contemporary version of *Großstadt-architektur*. This operation would reflect Hilber-seimer's critical attitude toward research: he never tried to crystallize his theories into definitive principles, and he himself would later criticize his early work.

Of course it is difficult to continue to compare the contemporary city to the metropolis of the euphoric and dramatic early decades of the twentieth century. Yet I still believe that Hilber-seimer's attempt to link architectural form to the reality of the contemporary city remains a fundamental goal today. What is even more important is to consider the city no longer as a self-ruled reality, an unfathomable chaos, or a bricolage of ad hoc actions, but as the end product of conscious decisions: as a project.

Contributors

Ludwig Hilberseimer (1885–1967) was a planner, architect, critic, and educator. Born in Germany, during the 1920s he developed a series of theoretical projects for the city that remain influential today. A prolific writer, he was an art critic for *Sozialistische Monatshefte* from 1920 to 1933, and his books include *Großstadtbauten* (1925), *Großstadtarchitektur* (1927), *The New City* (1944), *The New Regional Pattern* (1949), *Mies van der Rohe* (1956), *Entfaltung einer Planungsidee* (1963), and *Berliner Architektur der 20er Jahre* (1967). He taught at the Bauhaus from 1928, and in 1938 he emigrated to the United States of America and assumed a professorship of city and regional planning at the Illinois Institute of Technology in Chicago.

Richard Anderson (b. 1980) holds a Ph.D. from the Department of Art History and Archaeology at Columbia University, where he is a Core Lecturer for Art Humanities. He is co-author, with Kristin Romberg, of *Architecture in Print: Design and Debate in the Soviet Union, 1919–1935* (2005). His writing has appeared in *Future Anterior*, *Grey Room*, *Log*, and the book *In Search of a Forgotten Architect: Stefan Sebök 1901–1941* (2012).

Pier Vittorio Aureli (b. 1973) is an architect and an educator. He studied at the Istituto Universitario di Architettura di Venezia (IUAV) before obtaining a Ph.D. from the Delft University of Technology. He teaches at the Architectural

Association in London and directs the Ph.D. program "The City as Project" at the TU/Delft-Berlage Institute. The author of many critical essays, his books include *The Project of Autonomy: Politics and Architecture Within and Against Capitalism* (2008) and *The Possibility of an Absolute Architecture* (2011). Together with Martino Tattara, he is a co-founder of DOGMA, an office focused on the project of the city. The office received the Iakov Chernikhov Prize in 2006.